BEANS

BEANS
A History

Ken Albala

Oxford • New York

English edition
First published in 2007 by
Berg
Editorial offices:
First Floor, Angel Court, 81 St Clements Street, Oxford OX4 1AW, UK
175 Fifth Avenue, New York, NY 10010, USA

Berg is the imprint of Oxford International Publishers Ltd.

Library of Congress Cataloging-in-Publication Data

Albala, Ken, 1964-
Beans : a history / Ken Albala. — English ed.
    p. cm.
  Includes bibliographical references and index.
  ISBN-13: 978-1-84520-430-3 (cloth)
  ISBN-10: 1-84520-430-1 (cloth)
 1. Legumes—History. 2. Beans—History. I. Title.

  QK495.L52A567 2007
  641.3'565—dc22

                2007015769

British Library Cataloguing-in-Publication Data

A catalogue record for this book is available from the British Library.

ISBN 978 1 84520 430 3

Typeset by JS Typesetting Ltd, Porthcawl, Mid Glamorgan.
Printed in the United Kingdom by Biddles Ltd, King's Lynn.

www.bergpublishers.com

Contents

List of Recipes

Preface, Acknowledgements and a Note on Recipes

When I first proposed a history of beans, little did I suspect what I was getting myself into. To truly understand beans, to become one with my subject, I resolved to eat beans every single day, ideally a new species or variety with every meal. Soon my cabinets were bulging with heirloom appaloosas, delicate Spanish Tolosanos, football-shaped lablabs, specimens from the far-flung corners of the globe, from tiny teparies to mammoth Greek gigantes. There followed regular visits to ethnic grocery stores, especially Indian for every form of dhal, hours spent hulling and peeling fresh favas, and frenzied Internet bean forays in the middle of the night. I munched pickled lupines for breakfast, snacked on Japanese wasabi peas, frightened the children with sticky natto, and with nearly every supper I pulled out the brimming bean pot. Chickpea flour panisses, South Indian dhosas, African bean fritters followed suit. There was always a bowl or two of beans soaking with zen-like patience on the countertop. I made it about a year before giving up. I still try a new bean every week or so, but I am happy to say, my system is relieved to be done with this prolonged and sometimes grueling experiment. No matter what anyone says, tolerance for the bean and its gaseous effects does not develop over time. You just get used to bloat. At least I can say I am full of beans.

This project also proved to be a challenge in other ways as well. My interest in the topic was initially sparked by the overwhelming prejudice against beans in European dietary literature. This was clearly a class-based antagonism – only rustics and laborers have stomachs powerful enough to digest beans, pundits claimed. I wondered if there were similar prejudices in other times and places. Are beans always considered peasant food, and if not, why? My research, covering every corner of the globe from prehistoric times to the present and traversing a staggering array of disciplines, yielded something fascinating and new nearly every day. Beans are truly an amazing topic. There was a single-subject food book left to be written after all, and for some reason undaunted by the scale and depth of the project, I jumped in.

Readers will notice immediately that I have an inexplicable weakness for botanical Latin. Just the sound of some names thrills me. Even before I studied the language, I would memorize the most bizarre terms – *Lycopersicon esculentum*, the edible wolf peach, alias tomato. I use these Latin terms here not be pedantic, but because names, in whatever language, reveal history and attitudes toward plants. I don't claim to be knowledgeable about botany, and I am a pretty mediocre gardener, but plants do have an irresistible charm, and as I have found, every species in the family Fabaceae has its own unique allure. It was for this reason that I decided to organize this book as a series of bean biographies, with each chapter focusing on an individual or group of related beans.

Although this book is written for a popular audience, I would like to point out that every source I have used is listed in the bibliography and for those of you who have access to primary sources or wish to read the secondary ones, it will be easy to figure out the exact pages from which I have drawn quotes and citations, though space limitations have prevented me from being able to offer footnotes. I would be more than happy to direct any reader to a specific source page or answer any query if you contact me via e-mail at kalbala@pacific.edu. Many of the sources, particularly old cookbooks, are also available online, and can be found easily using any search engine.

This book would also not have been possible to write without all the enormous help I have been given along the way. It never ceases to amaze me how kind and generous people can be, especially with such an odd topic as beans. Jinx Staneic collected stories from West Virginia and scrounged up pinquito beans for me. Linda Berzok sent me teparies from Arizona. Mary Margaret Pack hunted down lyrics. Alice McLean shared with me some black chickpeas from the very last garden tended by Patience Gray. Barbara Wheaton made me a list of old cookbooks with bean recipes among other invaluable favors. Gary Allen, the cannibal, clarified a Hannibal Lecter reference. Janet Chrzan sniffed out zolfino beans in Tuscany before my own trip last summer. Andy Smith answered any question at any time of day or night, in meticulous detail. Darryl Corti pointed out some obscure beans for sale at his store in Sacramento. Robert Merrett gave me a wonderful lentil passage from George Gissing. Some very pleasant farmers were kind enough to chat at the Tracy Dry Bean festival – I still have a few cups left of the many sacks I bought. Mark Brunell enlightened me on the wonders of leghemoglobin. Shawn Chavis lent me her notes on black-eyed peas. Kara Neilsen cooked Scappi's chickpea zeppole. Many people at the Stockton Certified Farmers' Market sold me some magnificent fresh favas, chickpeas and pigeon peas, as did my favorite grocery in town, Podesto's. What I would do without my regular fix of lupines, I cannot guess. Gregg Camfield chortled over Thoreau with me. Rachel Laudan led me down a fascinating path on medieval bean consumption. Jeff Charles sent me a copy of a dreadful lima bean cookbook from the early twentieth century. Mel Thomas, my old Latin pal, from the other end of the continent rescued me from translating blunders in Valeriano's bean poem. Mary Gunderson offered details about Lewis and Clark. Paul B. Thomson after meeting just briefly via e-mail sent me a copy of his book. Adam Balic shared with me the wonders of carlin peas and John Letts let me see some that were left on Baffin Island by Martin Frobisher. And so many other people via e-mail gave me ideas and comments, my thanks especially to friends on the ASFS listserve who for a few steady weeks issued a barrage of bean references.

I must also thank my college, the first chartered institution of higher learning in the state of California, the University of the Pacific, for funding several research and conference trips to Europe, all of which directly contributed to the writing of this book, and all of which proved to be great eating adventures. I am also grateful for a sabbatical to write this book, and to my colleagues in the history department who as usual prove to be great friends. Thanks to the wonderfully helpful people at the Schlesinger Library at Radcliffe, where I began research for this book. Thanks also to the Culinary Trust, philanthropic partner of the International Association of Culinary Professionals, for awarding me the Linda Russo grant to conduct the final stages of research at the Clements Library at the University of Michigan. Special thanks to all the wonderful people I met there – Phil, Barbara, Oxana, Valerie, Laura, Don and especially Jan Longone, who brought me sources from home and literally just dropped them into my lap.

Enormous thanks also to the people at Berg who have proved to be absolutely delightful to work with, in particular Kathryn Earle, Kathleen May, Emily Medcalf, Hannah Shakespeare, Ken Bruce, and all the people I never got to meet as well as Julene Knox who copy-edited the manuscript with remarkable efficiency and aplomb.

As all epics must commence with an invocation of the appropriate muse, I call upon you Aeolus, God of the winds, to blow favorably on my venture.

faba pisumque cano, Asiae qui primus ab oris
Americae fato profugus Terraque veniunt
litora...

I sing of beans and peas, from Asia in the early days,
from America by fate, to all the Earth's shores they came...

A Note on Recipes

Although this is a history, it does contain many historic bean recipes, which have been left in the original wording and format. They have not been updated, partly because they serve as historic documents but also because bean cookery is inherently unamenable to precise measurements and instructions. There is no accurate way to gauge how long a bean will take to cook. Every rule must be flouted for a tired old bean and recently harvested dried beans will cook up without soaking and in half the time recommended in cookbooks. Larger beans usually take longer than smaller ones, sometimes up to an hour and a half, but not always. Therefore, let your senses be your guide, taste as you go along. Soaking overnight is a matter of preference. What one loses a little in flavor and depth of color, one supposedly gains in abdominal comfort. The quick soak method in boiling water is an option and takes about an hour, but seems to demand a little more energy than just soaking the night before. Soaked beans, gently cooked, tend to retain their shape better if this is something you desire. In general I have found the longer and slower you can cook dried beans, the better they taste. Baked beans, the apotheosis of the humble legume, need at least six hours. The only general rule is not to add salt or acidic ingredients to the cooking water until after the beans become soft, though this too is ignored in some recipes. Some people add baking soda when cooking beans, as the alkali softens the skins making them more digestible. This is a very old practice, in fact. It also apparently destroys some nutrients too, so in the interest of health, it is perhaps best omitted. Apparently those with very hard water may need to "soften" it with alkali, though.

Some recipes also instruct you to sift through your beans first for debris or rocks, but I have never seen either in a batch of beans. They sometimes suggest skimming the foam from the top of the pot in the first few minutes of boiling. I'm not sure what this is supposed to do apart from keep the cooking liquid clear, as is done with making stock. Do it if you like, but I haven't found it necessary with beans. Some authors suggest not adding cold water to a pot of simmering beans, as this supposedly toughens the skins, and I have experienced this a few times. I think it is a myth that putting a cork into a pot of beans will make them tender. Another odd trick, if you're disinclined to taste your beans for tenderness, is to remove one from the pot and blow on it; the skin will separate from the flesh in a strangely magical way. Try this, if only for kicks. The one thing I can unequivocally agree with is that if you happen to scorch beans at the bottom of the pot, they might as well be tossed, but fascinatingly enough there are medieval tricks for removing the burned taste.

Most cultures that cook beans also recommended a special seasoning to mitigate their gaseous effects. In Mexico it is epazote, similar to oregano but with an alluring funky aroma. In India they use a highly aromatic and rank-smelling resin called asafetida (stinking hay), which although it does mellow significantly in cooking, nonetheless perfumes the whole kitchen when stored. Germans use bohnenkraut (savory) as a carminative. In the Middle East, the spice of choice is cumin, which although very pleasant, to me is vaguely redolent of armpits. Garlic with beans is of course a typical combination in European cultures. In Japan they use kombu, a giant seaweed, which has its own intriguing ocean scent. Why have so many different cultures struck upon the idea of smelly seasonings for beans? The only scientifically verified flatulence remedy is a chemical trademarked and sold as "Beano" in little plastic droppers. All the others I would say have a greater historical cachet; so do try them. Whether they work chemically, psychosomatically or not at all, I won't venture to guess.

As mentioned, the historic recipes in this book have been left in their original form without tinkering. The historian in me cannot abide by such malfeasance, especially if the point is to learn about the past. Unless otherwise specified, the translations from the original languages are my own and are as literal as possible. (All unattributed recipes are my own too.) Canned or frozen beans have not been offered as options in these recipes for the simple reason that the results will usually be quite different. But of course if you want an authentic twentieth-century flavor, by all means feel free to use them. I do.

You will also notice that my own recipes do not follow standard modern format with a list of ingredients, precise measurements or cooking times. They are written the way people in the past actually cooked beans. They harbored no pretense that cooking is a science and I see no reason to either. I admit that my results in testing these recipes were not absolutely consistent, but neither would they be if I dictated exact measurements. Everyone's pots and appetites are different. Our modern recipe format dates only to the early twentieth century. Before that and stretching back to the sixteenth century measurements were given, but not consistently. The first cookbook author I know of who insists on exacting measurements is Alexander Hunter, a physician, whose *Culina Famulatrix Medicinae or Receipts in Modern Cookery* of 1810 complains about most recipes that fail to give measurements, which he believes "may prove the source of much doubt in the mind of some future Culinary Historian." Doubt notwithstanding, most people in the kitchen did not measure or time their cooking, nor do they need to today.

If you want a full pot of beans and leftovers, make three cups of dried beans. Unlike most foods, they only improve the more they are reheated. If you want one or two servings, cook only a cup of beans, which will roughly triple in volume when cooked, depending on the bean. If you prefer a lot of seasonings, add more; if you like mushy beans, cook them full throttle. This goes against conventional culinary wisdom, which insists that people can only learn to cook when they are given exacting rigorous commands. I see it otherwise. The fewer the instructions the more the readers must make conscious decisions based on their own preferences, and the better they learn what works and what doesn't. The recipes here demand some familiarity with basic cooking procedures but are for the most part very simple and the results have all very obligingly gone down my gullet.

Now, as Jay Bush, front man for one of the US's best-selling brands of baked beans, says in the commercial – "Roll that beautiful bean footage."

1

Introduction

The world is but a hill of beans. Nearly every place on earth has its own native species and nearly every culture has depended on beans. For many people, they have made the difference between life and death. Beans are practically indestructible if thoroughly dried and well stored and thus have provided critical insurance against times of famine and dearth. They are also one of the simplest plants to grow. The cultivation of beans has been crucial to the development of civilization: as a source of protein, as cattle fodder and as a means of replenishing nitrogen in the soil. Though all great agricultural societies have their own staple starch – wheat in the Middle East and Europe, rice in Asia, corn in the Americas – beans are perhaps the one food common and indispensable to all. Because of their ubiquity, beans are one of the few foods that serve as a unit of analysis and comparison across time and space. They are also among the few foods so avidly traded and transplanted across the continents throughout history that today few people apart from botanists can keep all the species straight. Sorting out the bean genealogy is a major goal of this book.

The family Fabaceae is also wildly disparate in form and function. Although they all have pods, their distinguishing feature in the plant kingdom, some are dried and boiled, others are eaten fresh and immature; some are ground into flour; some are processed into foods only vaguely reminiscent of beans such as soy milk, tofu or vegetable oil. Some are even used as spices or condiments. Family members include some delicate sweet species, some hulking giants and even a few nefarious poisonous relatives. In all, this family includes some of the most fascinating and economically important plants on earth.

Beans are not enthusiastically embraced by everyone though, and they are often deeply charged with social and ethnic bias. More than any other food, beans have been associated with poverty. There are simple economic reasons why this is so. In any culture where a proportion of people can obtain protein from animal sources, beans will be reviled as food fit only for peasants. Beans are indeed a cheap and economically efficient way to meet nutritional requirements, and for this reason, regions with a high population density or sparse grazing land came to depend on beans. In many places, China and India in particular, beans retain a central role in the diet to this day. But in Europe and the so-called developed nations, only those people who could not afford meat depended on beans. Thus beans became a marker of class, the quintessential peasant food or "poor man's meat." Thomas Wyatt in the mid-sixteenth century masterfully evoked the image of rustic poverty as he described the country mouse who lives in a damp cave.

> She must lie cold and wet in sorry plight;
> And worse than that, bare meat there did remain
> To comfort her when she her house had dight –
> Sometime a barley corn, sometime a bean,
> For which she labored hard both day and night

Beans have also been firmly associated with particular ethnic groups, especially in the course of mass migrations. Foreign peoples and their foodways have been stigmatized by dominant cultures as dangerous and threatening, and it is not surprising that bean eating has often been featured as the most visible symbol of this difference. Just as Frenchmen were called frogs, Germans krauts, and British *rostbifs*, ethnic antipathies have also been projected on Mexicans as bean-eaters or simply beaners. But the stigma against beans can also backfire. That is, once the group itself identifies with beans as an indelible characteristic of their identity, the bean is re-valorized. Eating beans, especially prepared in traditional ways, can become a way to reconnect with one's ethnic roots, a way to express communal solidarity and pride. In much the same way, black-eyed peas are centrally featured in Soul Food, once disdained as cheap food for slaves, but later something reclaimed as uniquely and proudly part of the African-American culinary heritage.

Whole nations too consciously promote certain dishes as emblematic of national identity and these often include beans. Think of ful medames in Egypt or the feijoada in Brazil; both are not only typical foods, but are also populist – foods that have been historically consumed by the masses. Constructing such symbols of national identity is not only a way to promote national coherence, but also to exclude others. The battle over who may rightfully claim falafel as their own – Palestinians or Israelis – shows that something as simple as a fried ball of mashed chickpeas can be invested with deep political sentiments. These are no longer just a lowly peasant food, but a matter of national pride.

The social connotations of beans can also be reversed under certain historical circumstances. When people want to claim solidarity with the poor or working class, eating beans can be construed as a literal and physical way of overcoming one's inborn prejudice. This may partly explain the strange obsession with baked beans in Boston, even among the wealthy Brahmin class. To eat lowly food is to gain empathy for the lower classes; simple hearty fare like beans seems to efface the economic boundaries that otherwise separate people. If you can partake in a person's food, you must truly understand him, or at least not harbor fear of contamination by sharing a common diet. Thus attitudes toward bean eating are a sure index of attitudes toward the impoverished or at least what one construes to be their plight. A romantic appropriation of peasant fare may actually be a disguised form of elitism too. That Tuscans call themselves *mangiafagioli* or bean-eaters appears to evoke their simple tastes and peasant roots, but how can one make sense of the heirloom bean varieties, such as zolfino, that now sell for astronomical prices and are hunted down by enthusiastic tourists in search of authentic culinary experiences? What modern food writers call "shabby-chic" is an aesthetic that may actually serve to help people ignore the social realities of poverty.

The bean in one context may be the object of reverent nostalgia, and a reminder of one's roots and homeland in another. It can also be a way to appropriate the exotic and "other" in a post-colonial world, something quite often capitalized upon by enterprising retailers searching for new products. The rapid rise and popularity of edamame, lightly salted and boiled green soybeans, is just one example of this, as was the sudden popularity of hummus a few decades ago. We can fully expect more bean novelties to appear on our shelves given the pace of globalization.

Apart from the social, ethnic and nationalistic associations of beans, this book will also explore the many fascinating philosophical and religious reasons why people have eschewed or embraced the lowly bean. Obviously for any group that rejects meat, whether ancient Hindu or twentieth-century Counter Culture, the bean has been a necessary part of the diet. But some groups, most infamously the Pythagoreans, reputedly avoided beans. As a source of protein and, in the case of soy, oil, it is ironic that beans have also become one of the most important industrially grown and now genetically modified crops. That tofu, as a heavily processed food, could become part of a back-to-nature health food movement is itself fundamentally baffling. Of course all foods can be worked in one way or another into complex food ideologies, but beans are truly protean. A slow-cooked dish of baked beans was used as a way to identify crypto-Jews in early modern Spain and a similar product in a can became an icon of British working-class identity, served by employers in a celebratory feast or "beano."

Beans have also been consciously cultivated and eaten as an emblem of rustic simplicity, or as part of a diet of austerity among ascetics, and perhaps the food most frequently considered a base vehicle for self-abjection. Wild vetches and lupines are the lowest of legumes and serve this purpose best, but so too are any inexpensive beans for those who seek a simple penitent diet. On the other hand, they are the first food one rejects when meat is abundant, or when austerity and self-punishment is considered foolish. John Milton expresses this best in his mask *Comus*. In a call to accept nature's bounty and eat freely of all her gifts, he wonders how anyone could live on beans alone.

> ...If all the world
> Should in a pet of temp'rance feed on pulse,
> Drink the clear stream and nothing wear but frieze,
> Th'all-giver would be unthank'd, would be unpraise'd,
> Not half his riches known, and yet despis'd;...

Further complicating the story of beans, and hopefully adding some levity to the topic, is the persistent association of beans with flatulence. Any speaker of English knows at least one version of the ditty: *Beans, beans, they're good for your heart – the more you eat the more you fart...* Despite expert opinion, this is not something one overcomes with extended soaking, special cooking methods or regular consumption. And there are those unwilling to even chance it. Attitudes toward beans therefore offer unique insights into the history of etiquette and manners. Apart from any social or ethnic stigma, fear of farting in public adds to the rich bean associations. Speaking of gas, it is not your body that produces the gas, but bacteria in your gut that break down the indigestible compounds found in dried beans. The culprits in question are a series of complex sugars or oligosaccharides with sinister sounding names such as raffinose and stachyose and verbascose (the noisy, talkative one). It is the metabolic activity of these bacteria that produce hydrogen and methane gas, which of course eventually finds its way out of your body.

Interestingly, these gas-producing properties are not found in fresh beans or in sprouts. It is not by chance that fresh beans, string beans in particular, have never had the same negative associations as their dried forms. In fact, they are often enthusiastically adopted by elite cuisines, precisely because they are seasonal and fairly difficult to obtain fresh. Botanically, string beans are merely immature pods of the same *Phaseolus* species eaten dried, but ideologically they are an entirely different food.

This book will cover every major species of legume eaten by humans around the world, including some species we accidentally don't think of as beans, such as lentils and chickpeas. The largest chapters focus on the most common beans and those that have the richest historical legacy: favas, kidney beans and soy, but also more obscure beans as well as those disguised members of the family, such as tamarind and fenugreek. Not included are those extremely important legumes used as cattle fodder such as alfalfa, which although fascinating in their own right, are never eaten by humans.

Absolutely complete coverage of all legumes would have been both impossible and tiresome. The US Department of Agriculture lists 236 genera in the Fabaceae family found just in the US. Around the world there are many more, so many that the family is often divided into three groups. Forty are categorized as mimosa-like and are mostly tropical or subtropical trees such as the acacia. One hundred and fifty are called caesalpinoid (named after the sixteenth-century Italian botanist Andrea Cesalpino), which are also mostly trees like carob, tamarind and the Kentucky coffee tree. A further 429 are in the faboid or fava-like group (*Papilionoideae*), which gives us 619 genera in total. Among these there are some 18,815 species, and no doubt new ones being named by botanists every day. A good number of these legumes serve as food. Guar and locust beans, mesquite, not to mention peanuts, are all legumes. So is licorice and even jicama – basically any plant that produces seed pods.

Of the genera in the Fabaceae family, those used principally for food include *Phaseolus*, which now refers to the New World beans – basic kidney beans, pinto, navy and so forth; *Vicia* or the Old World vetches including fava beans; *Vigna*, which includes black-eyed peas and many mung bean types; and lastly *Glycine* or soybeans. These basic divisions nicely correspond to the origins of beans covered here – America, Eurasia, Africa and India, and East Asia. Within these there are also countless species. Plus, many other completely unrelated bean genera will be discussed: *Cajanus, Lathyrus, Psophocarpus, Canavalia* and a host of others with equally enticing names. This book proceeds roughly chronologically: it begins with the first domesticated species, lentils, and continues to the beans most used in modern industry, though there is also significant chronological overlap since many chapters focus on a single geographical region.

The common English word bean is of solid Germanic stock, in its proto-Germanic form *baunō* and Old Saxon *bōna*. It is cognate with modern German *Bohne*, Dutch *boon* and similar words in Danish and Norwegian *bønne* and the Swedish *böna*. The origin of the word is unknown. The word legume, on the other hand, has Latin roots and derives from the verb *legere* meaning to gather, which makes perfect sense. One can easily picture the ancients coining the term – these are vegetables "gathered." In a turn of phrase the root also gives us other words denoting gathering of sorts. To gather information is *lego*, I read, and to do so publicly is to lecture. The meaning of the word *legume* in French, denoting any vegetable, is, however, a more recent usage. The word pulse, an old synonym for legume, has an equally interesting origin, coming from the ancient Roman dish of cooked bean meal: puls or porridge.

The term *Phaseolus* today refers to New World beans but originally meant a black-eyed pea, which is now in the *Vigna* genus. The word comes from the ancient Greek *phaselus* (*fasóli* in modern Greek), which refers to a canoe-like boat reminiscent of a bean pod. The association makes perfect sense for this sea-faring people. The Italian *fagiuolo*, Portuguese *feijão* and Romanian *fasole*, and French *fayot* all descend from this word as does the Arabic *fasoulia*. Confusingly in all these languages, the word referred to one bean before 1492 and both Old and New World beans thereafter. This is why, for example, the Indian mung bean was not very long ago called *Phaseolus aureus* but is now *Vigna radiata*. Only in recent decades have these two groups been given their own taxonomically distinct names, but it has left all New World beans in the muddle of a huge genus *Phaseolus*. In coming decades botanists may very well divide them up for the sake of clarity. As with all nomenclature used in this book, it is the most current available at the time of writing. The "authority" or person who first named the species is not included here, as it mostly interests botanists.

Beans also have a unique and fascinating flower structure. Apart from the delicate range of hues and subtle fragrance, each flower has two little wings, hence the archaic family name *Papilonaceae* – or butterfly-like. Beneath these wings is a little keel which swoops under the other petals. When an insect lands on the flower, the keel pops up and rubs the bee's belly with pollen, which is then transferred to the flower's ovary, or to the next flower on which the creature alights. Coleridge captures the sensory beauty of the interchange in "This Lime Tree Bower My Prison":

> Yet still the solitary humble-bee
> Sings in the Bean-flower! Henceforth I shall know
> That nature ne'er deserts the wise and pure;
> No plot so narrow, but be Nature there
> No waste so vacant, but may well employ
> Each faculty of sense, and keep the heart
> Awake to Love and Beauty!

Most bean plants are also hermaphrodites in the true botanical sense of that word; they are described as perfect flowers. That is, the flower has both male and female parts and can actually fertilize itself. This means that the species are stable over many years and do not depend on accidental fertilization by another plant as say apples and other fruits do. Thus spontaneous hybridization is unusual. Some genetic variation does occur randomly, but breeding lines can still be kept distinct. That is, you can select exactly the characteristics you are looking for and keep them intact over many generations. This means that the bean plants unearthed by archaeologists from millennia ago are genetically close to those still grown today, although domestication has altered their forms significantly. All this has made the reconstruction of bean history pretty straightforward, in a way that say the genetic history of corn or wheat is much harder to discern.

We begin this biography of the bean family with the oldest of beans, or at least the first domesticated by humans – the tiny ancient lentil.

2

Lentils: Fertile Crescent

The lentil is an ancient sentinel among beans, weathered, time-worn and tolerant of the harshest conditions. Without this lowly legume, the course of human history might have been entirely different. The lentil was among the very first plants ever domesticated some 10,000 years ago along with grains such as einkorn wheat, emmer and barley. Somewhere in the Fertile Crescent, what is today eastern Turkey, northern Iraq and Syria, some unsuspecting nomad decided to gather tiny wild lentils and plant them next to the caravan tents. There they sprouted and grew untended. Returning several months later, she would have harvested her crop, saved and replanted seeds from the largest and sturdiest of plants. In successive years the plants improved through what is unsystematic but nonetheless selective breeding. Improvements would have also been stable since lentils are self-pollinating, and could have remained separate from their wild cousins.

After many generations the little lentils had changed. They no longer shattered spontaneously to spread their seeds as wild species do, and this made them easier to harvest. Their seeds grew larger and the plants sturdier – more suitable for growing in open fields than the leggy wild plants that like to climb up trees. The seed coats of lentils also accidentally became thinner, thickness of the coats which delays germination no longer being a naturally selected and advantageous property, as in the wild. Stored seeds germinate whenever you plant them, and with thinner coats they are also easier to cook and digest. Of course the lentils' human caretaker had changed too. Increasingly dependent on her crop and more willing to protect it from predators and marauders, she decided to settle down. Like the lentils, she too became domesticated – or housebound. Thus a few simple plants gave rise to what we now call civilization, for better and worse.

In fact, no one knows for sure how or why plants were first domesticated. It may have been an accident, stored seeds perhaps getting wet and sprouting. No one is even sure whether permanent settled dwellings or agriculture came first, and there is ample evidence that the process of "discovery" and abandoning the gatherer-hunter life took many generations. There was probably a mixed economy for thousands of years. Evidence also suggests that a long spell of colder and drier weather around 9000 to 8000 BCE may have gradually forced people to abandon their nomadic lifestyle and adopt agriculture and permanent shelter. Planting food is generally more dependable than gathering and hunting, and lentils are ideally suited for marginal land. As a winter crop in the Middle East, they also provide food in the spring when there is little else to eat. The other incalculable benefit of legumes and grains is that when grown in surplus they can be dried and stored, rather efficiently once pottery was invented. This in turn provides, if not better, then at least more consistent and dependable, nutritional intake. In the long run this increased the fertility rate, which in turn caused the population to grow, which in turn created a greater demand for food. And since grains, legumes and a small amount of dairy and meat provide fewer calories per unit of energy expended than the varied gatherer-hunters' diet, these agricultural settlements grew ever more dependent on their limited range of foods. They were thus forced to continue farming or move somewhere else.

The story of what is called the Neolithic Revolution has been told many times. The crucial role of wheat, goats and sheep is always emphasized. Legumes, not just lentils but chickpeas, vetches and later peas, somehow get short shrift.

But it is likely that they play as great or even a greater role than meat and dairy in supplying protein to the growing population. This is a simple matter of efficiency. Per acre lentils provide more calories than grazing cattle. Just as important, rhizobium bacteria, which thrive on the root nodules of legumes draw nitrogen from the atmosphere and fix it in the soil. They provide a kind of natural fertilizer, which would have in turn made the wheat grow better. Furthermore, the stems and husks of the plant can be fed to cattle, which of course in turn provides more fertilizer. As in many early agricultural societies the combination of plants works synergistically in the soil and so does the combination of starches and legumes in the human diet. The amino acids lacking in lentils are supplied by grains, and the lysine missing from the grains is supplied by legumes. That is, a person can subsist mainly on this vegetable-based diet and it will support a large population in a way that gathering and hunting cannot. Without the beans it is certainly less likely that these early civilizations would ever have arisen.

Keep in mind also, that this was probably never a conscious process. No one woke up one morning and said, "honey let's settle down and plant some lentils." Some scholars speculate that it was population pressure in the first place that forced people to change their way of life. Or perhaps it was the dispersal of wild herds following the last great ice age when animals could roam across the expanses of the Eurasian continent. This meant that hunting populations perished while larger and increasingly organized societies survived, especially those with armies and efficient weapons. All this is speculation, but the archaeological evidence shows that at some point the wild ancestor of *Lens culinaris*, which grew from Greece all the way east to Uzbekistan, was domesticated.

Lentils were naturally eaten before domestication. The earliest charred remains of wild lentils, an indication of cooking, date from about 11000 BCE and are found at the Franchthi Cave in Greece. A few thousand years later a Syrian site, Tell Mureybit, contains similar specimens dated between 9000 and 8000 BCE, but it is uncertain whether these are small domesticated lentils or large wild ones. Somewhere around 7000 BCE or earlier the lentil began to be domesticated, the modern species of *Lens culinaris* most likely deriving from a wild progenitor *Lens orientalis*. The fact that large stores of lentils have been discovered in Fertile Crescent sites also suggests that they were harvested. By around 5500 BCE there is archaeological evidence that the species had changed, and around the same time lentils are found in agricultural settlements in Europe. Candolle, the father of plant evolution, noted that domesticated lentils were found in Bronze Age sites of the so-called Swiss Lake dwellings. Thereafter they were grown as far away as Britain, southward in Ethiopia, and eastward in the direction of India, where they were probably taken by Indo-European invaders, speakers of Sanskrit. Apparently, forms of the word lentil are found across the Indo-European languages, supporting the idea that they were carried with the invaders, though there are also lentil remains in the earlier Indus River Valley civilization sites.

The ancient Sumerians, the first civilization in historical times to leave written records, developed just south of the probable site of lentil domestication, in lower Mesopotamia between the banks of the Tigris and Euphrates. The Sumerians grew and stored their lentils along with other domesticated plants such as wheat and barley, millet and chickpeas. These were the staples of the diet. Sumerians were also what we might call the first stratified society, with well-delineated classes. The majority of people were farmers, but the massive irrigation projects demanded organization and government on a large scale. Professional bureaucrats and priests kept written records on cuneiform tablets – at first merely counts of heads of cattle and bushels of grain, but later tax records and even literature like the great Epic of Gilgamesh.

The separation of social classes also meant that the basic diet of the masses came to be distinguished from that of the rulers, priests and warriors. Whereas most people, farmers, ate grains in the form of bread or beer supplemented by pulses and vegetables, the wealthier ate more meat and could afford the luxury of wild hunted game. For the average family, cattle were far too valuable as a source of dairy products for them to be slaughtered for meat. This basic pattern would persist through Western Civilization and has particular importance for lentils and other legumes. When one can afford meat, beans are the first food excised from the diet, and naturally the first food associated with the poor. We have no direct evidence that this happened in ancient Sumer, but the oldest written recipes from this same area give some hints.

The earliest culinary texts to have survived are in the form of three cuneiform tablets dated to about 1600 BCE. They are not exactly Sumerian, but rather Akkadian – a people from the north who conquered the older cities. The recipes are mostly for meat and fowl, which makes sense if they were composed for wealthy households. This may just be an accident of the historical record, but if these are any indication, the wealthy were most interested in meat. But tucked away among a series of porridges there is one recipe for husked lentils "which are milled for me" – perhaps into a kind of lentil flour which is subsequently sieved. This is then cooked with beer in which aromatic wood has been steeped, and served with meat. The translator, Jean Bottéro, was not able to make out every detail, but in any case it is the very oldest explicit legume recipe on earth. That there is only one among all the recipes, when we know lentils and beans were a staple, provides at least a little evidence that the diet was divided along class lines. It has also been suggested that these recipes may have been intended for sacrifice to the god Marduk, and as gods rarely consume solid food in anything but a spiritual sense, the leftovers went to the king and his court. If this is the case, it still supports the idea that the diet was distinguished by class.

The Egyptians also used lentils as funerary offerings and in meals to feed the dead in the underworld. Large stores were found beneath Zoser's pyramid and even pre-dynastic tombs contain lentils. Lentils appear to have been associated with the god Horus. Like other plants, such as barley, which die and are reborn in the spring, they may have served as a symbol of resurrection, and been particularly fitting for repasts in the afterlife. Clearly there was no stigma against eating lentils. In fact in the classical world Egyptians were often credited with growing the best lentils and there are aficionados who still make this claim today for the delicate split red lentil. Paraphrasing the second-century Greek/Egyptian food writer Athenaeus, Alexis Soyer, nineteenth-century food writer, said "The Egyptians, whose ideas were sometimes most eccentric, imagined it was sufficient to feed children with lentils to enlighten their minds, open their hearts, and render them cheerful." Athenaeus himself, who would have known, believed that Alexandria was the real center of lentil culture. You "have been brought up on lentil food and your entire city is full of lentil dishes."

Perhaps nowhere was the success of the lentil greater than in ancient India. Not only do they grow very well in an arid environment and in marginal soils, but they are also easily cultivated in small plots, and so lentils or dhal became one the major cornerstones of the Indian diet, and remain so to this day. Vegetarianism certainly played a major role in this too, a topic that will be discussed below with India's native bean species. For the moment, the Hindu proverb says it all: "Rice is god, but lentils are my life."

The importance of lentils in the ancient Middle East is also well illustrated by the Bible. Everyone knows the story of Esau, who sold his birthright to his brother Jacob for a bowl of lentil soup (see below). But few recognize that food always plays a central role in the Old Testament and the Hebrews typically defined their relationship to God in dietary terms. That is, there is a deeper meaning to this story than might be suspected. To begin with, Adam and Eve lived in the Garden of Eden in a state of perfect innocence and killed nothing for their food – subsisting on fruits and seeds which sprang spontaneously from the earth. Today we would call them fruitarians or you might say that they were pure gatherers. This was of course ruined by the transgression of eating from the tree of knowledge, the punishment for which was exile from the garden and having to earn their bread by the sweat of their brow. In other words, they become settled agriculturalists. In both this version and in real life, greater labor was involved, but this was the only way to support a growing population. The professions of their offspring, Cain and Abel, also reflect something like historical reality. One was a farmer, the other a shepherd. For reasons that are not explained, the offering of Abel was accepted by God, while Cain's was rejected. Cain kills his brother and is forced to wander – returning in a sense to the life of the nomad.

The relationship of these two figures is replicated in the story of Isaac's sons, the scions of two separate nations. Red and hairy Esau was born first and was skilled in hunting, a man of the open plains. His younger brother Jacob led a settled life and stayed among the tents. At least in mytho-poetic form, this society had not yet made the complete transition to agriculture, and in fact Isaac still preferred to eat venison, which is why he favored his elder son, the hunter. But hunting being the less reliable way to earn a living, one day Esau comes back empty-handed and near starving. His brother the farmer is happily sipping some red lentil broth, and as rival brothers are inclined to do, Jacob refuses to share it with him, unless Esau sells him his birthright. A dirty trick, but the message to the Hebrews is clear enough: pick a safe and profitable profession like farming or you may get into trouble. Jacob sows his seed, reaps a hundredfold and hosts feasts. In the end he even tricks his blind father into giving him his blessing, by serving a savory dish of kid prepared by his mother Rebecca instead of the venison he expected from Esau. As all uncouth and uncivilized men do, Esau plots to kill his brother – but in the end, Jacob escapes and goes on to father the twelve tribes of Israel. Again, it is a simple moral but one that affirms the agricultural and settled life of the Hebrews, which of course includes lentils.

Lentils are mentioned throughout the Old Testament, but one of the odder references is found in the directions given by God to the prophet Ezekiel. He is sent among the Israelites who have rebelled against God and his laws, to warn them of their impending doom. Among his instructions is the command to lie on one side and eat bread made of wheat, barley, beans and lentils, millet and spelt, scantily measured out for 190 days. And this mess is supposed to be baked with human dung as fuel, though after protest God softens up and lets Ezekiel use cow dung. This is supposed to show the Israelites the kind of unclean bread they will eat after God punishes and exiles them and they are forced to measure out their meager stores. It is also clearly meant to be symbolic, not just a bad-tasting bean bread, but something defiled by being composed of various grains and legumes. (One suspects the modern company which sells a multi-grain loaf called Ezekiel's Bread has missed the point of the story.)

The message would have been clear to the Israelites; one of the chief tenets of the Levitical laws governing clean and unclean food was never mingling two species unnaturally. This even extended to two different fibers in one's clothes. This was a form of adultery – our word itself means to add the "other" (*ad ulter*) and we still speak of adultery of foodstuffs. Symbolically this was precisely how the Israelites had broken God's commands, not in sexual escapades or baking strange breads, but in mixing themselves with other peoples, by losing their identity. By adopting "vile and abominable rites" they had ceased to be Israelites and God punished them with pestilence, famine and war.

In these prophecies it is not beans and lentils per se that are denigrated, but only mixing them unnaturally with other grains. It is only among the ancient Greeks that the pulses themselves begin to get a bad rap. Lentils specifically first are seen as a dangerously unhealthy food. Combined with a social stigma against them as food of the poor, it is here that the deeply negative associations with lentils in Western Civilization begin.

Galen, the first-century Greek physician working in Rome, goes on at length in his *Alimentorum facultatibus* about whether lentils bind or loosen the belly, and in various forms he employs them as medicine to these ends. But as a regular food they are downright dangerous: "people who are excessive in the use of these foods have what is called elephantiasis and ulcerating growths, for it is usual for thick, dry food to generate black bile." Being excessively drying they are especially harmful to those with dry constitutions and they damage the eyesight. Lentils, he suggests, can be cooked with savory and pennyroyal, which makes them more easily digested, but the worst is what cooks make for the wealthy: lentils with reduced grape must, which causes obstructions of the liver and inflammation of the spleen. Equally as bad is cooking lentils with pickled meats, which causes the blood to thicken. Inadvertently Galen offers some rudimentary recipes, which in terms of cuisine are entirely successful combinations, but obviously his concerns were of a medical nature. Dietary authority was one source of the stigma against lentils.

There was also a firm association with lentil eating and the poor. A common saying was "he became a rich man and suddenly he no longer likes lentils." The proverb suggests that it is particularly those who fear being mistaken for a member of the common rabble that would try to cast off the most obvious signs of their origins. Change of dress, manner of speech and especially diet are the dead giveaways. To play the part of the wealthy, who of course would not feel this social pressure as strongly as the nouveaux riches, one must forgo peasant foods like lentils. It would be much like someone today giving up cheap beer and junk food. It might be for health concerns, but these items also have strong class-associations. Because few people in the contemporary developed world are forced to live on lentils, naturally this explicit association has been lost, but that was not the case even a century ago. In the 1911 edition of the *Encyclopedia Britannica* we are told "Lentils are more properly the food of the poor in all countries where they are grown, and have often been spurned when better food could be obtained, hence the proverb Dives factus jam desiit gaudere lente." This is merely the Latin version of the proverb cited above. That is, the social stigma against lentils, as we shall see with most beans, remains firmly in place from the time of the ancient Greeks up to the twentieth century.

Many Greeks, the majority perhaps, nevertheless, ate lentils all the time. The philosopher Zeno reputedly said "A wise man acts always with reason and prepares his lentils himself." What exactly this means is anyone's guess, though there is another story that he was made to carry a pot of lentils through the streets of Athens to humble himself. Lentils were usually cooked in the form of a porridge or phake, from the word *phakos* for lentil. Though no explicit recipes survive from the classical period, the Greek physician Anthimus, visitor to the court of Theuderic king of the Franks in the early 500s, may give an approximation of how it was served. The lentils are first washed and boiled in fresh water, which is later poured off, a precaution that shows some trepidation at eating them, befitting a physician. More water is added and they are slowly cooked on the hearth with a little vinegar and sumach, which is said to add flavor, as do a spoonful of fresh olive oil and some sprigs of fresh coriander (cilantro) whole with the roots attached and a bit of salt. This recipe works marvelously.

The sumach is a hard red berry common in Middle Eastern cuisine, which is finely ground and adds a nice fruity sourness to the dish. The addition of sour and cleansing condiments may also have been intended to help cut through the tough and indigestible lentils. The coriander can be removed after cooking, although one can chop the leaves finely and add them at the end, contrary to Anthimus' directions.

Our word lentil comes from a late Latin word *lenticula*, the diminutive form of lens or lentil. The botanical nomenclature *Lens culinaris* means cooking lens. Remarkably, our word for the optical instrument comes from the bean rather than the other way around. The convex sides of both lenses were apparent enough for Edmund Halley (of comet fame) to name one after the other, or at least he was the first to use the term in print in 1693. The lens of the human eye, in turn, takes its name from the glass lens and was used in this sense first in 1719. But what does lens itself mean? There is a lovely folk, or rather fake, etymology that goes back to the sixth-century theologian Isidore of Seville. Because lentils were reputed among the Romans to cause heaviness in the limbs and general sluggishness given that they were so hard to digest, Isidore imagined that the word came from *lentus* – meaning slow, sticking and clogging in the system. The Romans did have a definite prejudice against lentils.

But in their early history the Romans were not terribly fussy about their food. In fact, farmer-warriors they valued simplicity and self-sufficiency. No one exemplifies the stern character of the early Roman Republic better than Cato the Elder, who lived in the second century BCE. Apart from his life as a statesman he also wrote a farming manual, which describes lentils not only as a crop but also as medicine in poultices. Cato was also a very pious man and gives instructions on how to make proper offerings to the gods, and he even provides recipes for various sacrificial cakes. Before planting, for example, an offering should be made to Jupiter, in this case of wine. "When you make the offering, say as follows: 'Jupiter Dapalis, since it is due and proper that a cup of wine be offered you, in my home among my family, for your sacred feast; for that reason, be honored by this feast that is offered you.'" Only then is it safe to plant millet, panic, garlic and lentils. It is interesting that these are precisely the plants that would be associated with poverty in later centuries, but Cato has no reservations about growing them.

By the time of Imperial Rome, however, lentils came to be associated with the diet of the poor. For the wealthy they were merely a good packing material. The most famous lentil anecdote from ancient Rome concerns the giant obelisk brought from Egypt during the reign of Caligula, which Pliny says was packed in 120 bushels (about 2.8 million pounds) of lentils on its journey across the Mediterranean to Rome. It stands today in front of the Vatican. Whether these ever made it onto people's plates, we shall never know.

Despite the social prejudice against lentils in the Imperial period, the cookbook attributed to Apicius, which was largely intended for wealthier patrons and even perhaps for those nouveaux riches trying hard to impress with wildly exotic ingredients, nonetheless has a few fairly simple lentil recipes. One is for lentils with chestnuts. The lentils are first cleaned and put in a new pot with water and a pinch of nitrum (or baking soda, which some cooks still use when cooking beans). To this are added crushed pepper, cumin, coriander, mint, rue, silphium root and pennyroyal. Silphium is a plant now extinct which grew in northern Africa and which scholars think may have been like asafetida – very strongly aromatic and to some vile-smelling. Then follow the standard flavor trio of the ancient Romans: a dab of vinegar, honey and garum, a kind of fish sauce. Then this is added to the cooked chestnuts with a bit of oil, and everything is pounded in a mortar, tasted and a drizzle of fresh oil is added. This might be considered a kind of lentil dip, a cousin of hummus. Now whether after this complex procedure it can still be considered a humble dish is a matter for debate, but it is certain that people were eating lentil dishes when this was written, probably at some point in late antiquity. Another recipe is even a little simpler, made with leeks and green coriander leaves and flavorings similar to the first recipe.

Medieval Europe inherited the ancients' prejudice against lentils, especially after the year 1000 when the population began to grow again and social divisions became more pronounced. At the same time they began to rediscover ancient medical texts which further emphasized the dangers of this tiny bean. The first authorities they encountered were not the Greeks themselves but rather Arabic writers who had translated and interpreted them. It was these Arabic authors translated into Latin that Europeans read first. As in phone tag, the message gets a bit muddled in transmission. For example, when discussing lentils the Italian physician Antonius Gazius first cites the Arab Averroës, who claims that lentils cause melancholic blood, obscure vision, constrict the stomach and impede sexual activity. That would be enough to keep most people away. Some of this information seems to have come from Galen, but he also claims that lentils are hot and dry, which makes little sense if it is a melancholic food. Haliabbas, another Arab, claimed lentils are cold in the second degree of intensity and dry in the third, which is why lentils cause melancholy as well as elephantiasis, mania, cancer, bad dreams and so forth. In any case, even though the information is often derived from medieval Arab authorities, the Europeans had very little positive to say about lentils. Gazius also claims that eating lentils with salted meat, a very common custom, was the worst: much better to soak them, skinning them and adding vinegar, oregano, mint, pepper, cumin and almond or sesame oil. That doesn't sound so bad, and maybe that's why Gazius must remind us not to eat lentils unless there's absolutely nothing else better to eat.

Gazius' comments suggest that people were eating lentils, but surprisingly there is an almost complete dearth of lentil recipes in medieval cookbooks. The *Viandier* attributed to Taillevent uses no lentils, nor does *The Forme of Cury* or other English cookbooks. It seems unlikely that cookbook authors took physicians' warnings seriously; they paid little attention to other recommendations. It may merely be that cookbooks were written mostly for wealthy audiences and if there was a stigma against lentil eating, then surely they would not bother with recipes. On the other hand, there are fava bean recipes despite the social prejudice. Perhaps all beans were considered more or less interchangeable and there was no reason to specify favas, lentils or chickpeas.

There also remains the distinct possibility that lentils were not commonly grown. They don't do well in wet and cold northern Europe, and this may account for their absence from English and French cookbooks, though one does frequently find peas, which do thrive there. The medical authors may merely have been repeating the opinions of the authorities without reference to common practice. For example, the combination of lentils and salted meat comes from Galen – maybe it was not yet a common dish in medieval Europe. It is equally interesting that even the Italian and Spanish cookbook authors neglect lentils. Neither the Catalan *Libre de Sent Sovi* of the fourteenth century nor the *Libre del Coch* by Rupert of Nola mentions lentils. The Italian cookbooks of the Middle Ages such as that by Martino of Como make no mention of lentils either. Interestingly Martino's cookbook was published in 1470 crammed into Platina's health-oriented *De honesta voluptate*. Platina as a good classical scholar has an entry on lentils, drawn largely from the ancient Roman Pliny. Lentils like thin dry soil, there are two varieties, they are difficult to digest, cause leprosy and flatulence, and suppress the amorous urge. This, and the advice on tempering lentils with barley to correct their faults, comes right from Galen. There is really nothing here about contemporary practice, and nowhere in the recipes taken from Martino are lentils even mentioned.

Lentils really do not appear to be a common food in medieval Europe. It is only in the sixteenth century that lentils begin to appear in cookbooks, most notably six recipes in the *Opera* of Bartolomeo Scappi published in 1570. This is not surprising though, because Scappi went out of his way to at least mention every single food that could possibly be used in a recipe. Still, in five of these six recipes, lentils are only suggested briefly as an alternative to peas, beans or other legumes (II:191, 192; III:261; V:91, 224). In a book containing thousands of recipes there is only one specifically designed for lentils. It is worth translating in full, partly for the author's trepidation:

To Make a Thick Soup of Dried Lentils (Book III:254)
Clean the lentils of all impurities, and place in a vessel of tepid water, and remove those that float, and boil the rest in the same water, and while it

boils take the lentils that rise up above the bubbles with a big perforated
spoon and put them in a separate vessel. You do this so that the sand which
is sometimes in the little nodule comes out and falls to the bottom of the
vessel. Put the good lentils in a vessel with garlic, salt and a little pepper
and saffron and water and a sprig of beaten herbs and let it finish cooking,
and to be good make the broth thick. You can also cook it with garlic cloves
or big pieces of tench or pike.

Apart from the fact that it is highly unlikely that sand could wedge anywhere
on a lentil, the directions to remove those that rise above the bubbles is quite
odd, which may support the idea that lentils were not a common food in Europe
– or perhaps something only eaten by the poor. Giacomo Castelvetro, an Italian
exile living in England in the next century, put it nicely if a little bluntly in his
book about vegetables: "Like many other countries we also have lentils, one of
the most, if not the most, unhealthy vegetables one can eat, except for the broth
which they say, is a miraculous drink for children with smallpox." (That's an
idea he got from the French surgeon Ambrose Paré.) "In general lentils are only
eaten by the lowest of the low."

That pretty much sums up the prejudice toward lentils in Western Civilization for the next four centuries. There might be an odd lentil dish such as
lentilles a la reine supposedly named for Louis XV's wife Maria Leszczynska,
eaten probably only as an ethnic curiosity. Otherwise they are avoided if at all
possible and cookbooks are almost completely silent on the topic. Even in the
early twentieth century we find statements like Ella Kellogg's. She believed that
the skins are tough and indigestible and lentils "are of little value except for
soups, purees, toasts and other dishes as require the ejection of the skin. Lentils
have a stronger flavor than any of the other legumes, and their taste is not so
generally liked until one has become accustomed to it."

This prejudice is nowhere better expressed than by British novelist George
Gissing, a working-class writer who defended the poor. Nonetheless he could
not bear the vegetarian diets promoted at the turn of the century and had a
particular loathing for lentils. This is from his novel *The Private Papers of Henry
Ryecroft*, published at the end of his life in 1903.

There is to me an odd pathos in the literature of vegetarianism. I remember the day when I read these periodicals and pamphlets with all the rest of hunger and poverty, vigorously trying to persuade myself that flesh was an altogether superfluous, even a repulsive food. If ever such things fall under my eyes nowadays, I am touched with a half-humorous compassion for the people whose necessity, not their will, consents to this chemical view of diet. There comes before me a vision of certain vegetarian restaurants, where at a minimum outlay, I have often enough made believe to satisfy my craving stomach; where I have swallowed "savory cutlet," "vegetable steak," and I know not what windy insufficiencies tricked up under specious names. One place do I recall where you had a complete dinner for sixpence – I dare not try to remember the items. But well indeed do I see the faces of the guests – poor clerks and shopboys, bloodless girls and women of many sorts – all endeavoring to find relish in lentil soup and haricot something-or-another. It was a grotesquely heart-breaking sight. I hate with a bitter hatred the names of lentils and haricots – those pretentious cheats of the appetite, those tabulated humbugs, those certified aridities calling themselves human food!

Lentils would only gain grudging acceptance, oddly enough among gourmets. In a perverse reversal of fate, the tiny elite De Puy lentil has become a cherished and quite expensive luxury food. So too has the miniscule black "beluga" lentil, which when tasted one can almost imagine popping on the palate like real caviar. As we shall see in subsequent biographies, the tiniest of beans sometimes elude their humble origins entirely and find their way onto restaurant menus and into the pots of those seeking novelty in the unlikeliest of places.

3

Lupines: Europe and Andes

The lupine is the oddest rebel among beans. For those who have never encountered them, they break every rule known about bean cookery. To start with, they are poisonous. Their bitter alkaloids can affect the central nervous system, causing depression, convulsions and respiratory failure. The alkaloids also render them resolutely unpalatable unless they are boiled and then washed, not merely soaked, for about a week or so with frequent changes of water. Apparently leaving them in the bathtub with the faucet running is an old trick. And then, they never become soft. Who knows how many adventurous cooks have waited impatiently at the stove for the taciturn lupines to submit? The only way to deal with lupines is to let them be themselves, accept the fact that they are supposed to be crunchy and that they are meant to be a snack, like olives, rather than cooked as a proper bean. They also have to be salted, or rather soaked in brine. Even then, the outer seed coat is usually tough and best removed. Like olives, which are also painfully bitter when raw, one wonders how anyone ever figured out these could be used as food.

But here's the biggest surprise: lupines have just about the highest protein content of any bean, about 40 percent, which means they compare favorably to meat. A six-ounce hamburger (170 grams), for example, contains 48.6 grams of protein. That's less than 30 percent protein. Actually that's about all the protein your body needs in a day, but comparing the rate of efficiency is staggering if you consider how many lupines it takes to feed a steer to make a hamburger. It makes more sense to just eat lupines. *Lupinus mutabilis*, just one of several species, contains about 25 percent fat – the good unsaturated kind – and thus they have potential as an oil crop, again not unlike olives. The others range from about 5 to 10 percent. Importantly, lupines do not contain the trypsin inhibitors commonly found in soybeans, which is an anti-nutritional factor, preventing the absorption of nutrients. Once you've soaked away the alkaloids, they are an ideal food, and much work has been done developing sweeter varieties.

Also unlike other beans, there are native species of lupines on both sides of the Atlantic. *Lupinus albus* and *luteus* (aka white and yellow lupine) as well as *angustifolius* (narrow-leaf or blue) come from southern Europe and *Lupinus mutabilis* or tarwi comes from the Andes and is uniquely adapted to growing at high altitudes. In Peru and Bolivia it is roasted and ground into flour, which is to this day used in breads, noodles, sauces and soups. Although difficult to process, some report that this flour contains up to 50 percent protein.

Most people in the West recognize lupines not as a bean but as a flower, one of the showiest and most colorful of garden plants. There is a hilarious Monty Python episode in which Dennis Moore, the legendary eighteenth-century vagabond who steals from the rich and gives to the poor, brings one destitute family lupines – not the bean but flowers. They grow sick of them and ask for money and jewels – but Moore steals so efficiently that the poor have everything, and he is forced to steal from them to give back to the rich. The whole skit is launched by misunderstanding what part of the plant is eaten.

Lupines have an ancient but not very distinguished past in the Mediterranean region. This probably stems from their principal use as cattle fodder and as so-called green manure, which means that the plant is sown merely so it can be turned back into the soil to provide nutrients for another crop. The Greeks and Romans were consistent in labeling lupines as food for animals or only the poorest of people. Pliny defined them as food "shared by humans and hoofed quadrupeds." According to Athenaeus, a playwright named Lycophron wrote a satire of philosophers' dinners and rather than the usual fare, there were lupines: "And there danced forth the plebeian lupine in lavish abundance, that companion of the paupers' triclinium." Triclinia were the couches on which Greeks reclined while dining. More than any other food, lupines were derided as food of desperation, for when else do you eat cattle feed? You don't unless you're a crabby old cynic, as rebellious as the bean itself. The Cynics were a school of philosophy in ancient Greece founded by Diogenes, who hated people so much he lived in a barrel. Apparently to prove a point that food really doesn't matter he tried raw beef – unthinkable to the Greeks. He was even said to have died after downing a raw octopus. (Sushi was apparently equally unthinkable.) The Cynics were also known to eat lupines, just to show their disdain for decent food and perhaps so they could generate enough wind to offend people in public places. The point is: what is condemned as food of the poor can also be adopted for precisely that reason, in the case of Diogenes he was trying to be shameless, trying to break society's conventions by doing outrageously filthy things like masturbating in public. Eating lupines was his way of thumbing his nose at the rest of humanity and creating a stink about his contempt.

Many people thought the Cynics were mad, but madness could take on a perversely holy twist. Ascetics among the early Christians were also known to break society's conventions, eat disgusting foods and in doing so they became more abject and even Christ-like for their suffering. In the seventh century Leontius of Neapolis wrote a *Life of Simeon the Fool,* clearly getting his clue from Diogenes. The protagonist eats raw meat, consumes vast quantities of lupines and defecates in public. From our vantage point it is difficult to see how such acts could be construed as holy, but it was precisely in turning away from society's norms – even to the point of madness – that one could achieve a greater spirit. Among the more conventional ascetics – those who merely gave up sex and starved themselves – the viler the food and the more punished the body, the stronger the soul. There are stories among the sayings of the church fathers in which monks try to outdo each other with their austerity and even conscious self-punishment. One tries to go the whole day without water in hot weather so he can "crucify himself," another leaves a bottle of oil on the shelf for three years just so he can suffer in its presence. Another, about to get angry when a brother coughs up phlegm on his robe, decides instead to eat it. Freud would have a field day with these guys. It does seem that this kind of heroic self-mastery springs precisely from the resentment felt toward the rest of the world who can happily enjoy life's physical pleasures – food, sex and regular sleep. What does this have to do with lupines? As the most reviled and base of foods, they make the ideal diet for those who turn away from the world and even their own bodies. Bitter beans are perfect for masochistic monks whose reward for eating them will be eternal life.

Mad philosophers and ascetics aside, medical opinion about lupines was divided, but normally focused on their ability to produce flatulence. The Pseudo-Hippocratic appendix to *Regimen in Acute Diseases* makes this sweeping claim:

> All pulses produce flatulence, whether they are raw, boiled or roasted, but least when steeped in water, or green. They are not to be employed except with other foods. Also each of them has its own particular dangers. The chickpea, both raw and when roasted, produces flatulence and pain; the lentil contracts and is laxative, if it has its hull. The lupin is the least injurious of the pulses.

So maybe Diogenes should have eaten chickpeas if he wanted gas. Actually this author was not terribly observant. Among all the pulses lupines have one of the highest percentages of stachyose, one of the offending gas-producing oligosaccharides.

The real Hippocrates, or whoever wrote the *Regimen*, was a little more cryptic. "Lupins are in their nature strengthening and heating, but by preparation they become more light and cooling than they are naturally, and pass by stool." The strengthening part may have something to do with the high protein content, the heating and cooling effects refers to the ability to generate humors which regulate bodily health.

Fears among physicians may have stemmed from observing cattle which were poisoned after feeding on lupines. Certainly the same thing could happen to humans. Yet, they definitely understood the long process of soaking to leach out the toxins. The philosopher Zeno of Citium, normally a tight-lipped and nasty Stoic, one day was found very pleasant after drinking copious amounts of wine. When asked what happened "he answered that he underwent the same process as the lupine; for they too are very bitter before they are soaked, but when steeped they become sweet and mild."

The connection between philosophers and beans is truly perplexing, as we shall see further with Pythagoras and his ban on fava beans. This must have struck people as funny, because the satirist Lucian mocks it. In "A True Story" Lucian has a sojourn on the Isle of the Blessed where he gets to meet his Homeric idols. For various misdeeds he is banished, but would be allowed to return someday as long as he kept these precepts: "neither to stir the fire with a sword blade nor to eat lupines nor to make love to anyone over eighteen." These are parodies of real Pythagorean injunctions, the lupines looking fairly ridiculous in this context, because who in their right mind would want to eat them, and what Greek would find hardship in the last command?

The Western tradition clearly had little use for lupines except as fodder for cattle or poor people. But what of the Inca who had their own lupine or as it is called in Quechua tarwi? Unlike the Mediterranean species, which were a relative latecomer to domestication, the pre-Inca population domesticated theirs as early as 2000 BCE. Even more marvelous was the development of varieties that would grow at thousands of feet above sea level in thin dry soil and survive the extreme cold. Along with potatoes, quinoa and corn, tarwi was one of the staples of the Andean diet, and it was often sown in rotation with potatoes to improve the soil. Tarwi can contain up to 50 percent protein and is also very high in lysine, and thus in combination with corn and quinoa makes for a highly nutritious diet.

After the Spanish conquest of Pizarro, Old World crops, including beans, were introduced and many native plants were eaten only by the indigenous population or in remote areas. Thus here too a stigma developed against lupines as food of the poor indigenous population, although obviously for very different reasons than in the West. In Cuzco, the ancient Inca capital, tarwi is still widely consumed, but it is almost completely unknown outside the region. The seed is used in a variety of surprising contexts. It is made into a creamy soup, thrown into stews, and there is even an orange custard made with tarwi and the flour is mixed with papaya juice. The flour is also used in a nutritional supplement given to schoolchildren, and it increases the shelf life and protein content of bread.

It is ironic that in the Western tradition using various inferior beans such as vetches and lupines as extenders for bread was considered such a harmful practice and something that only the most famished poverty-ridden peasant would think of doing. In seventeenth-century Alsace, Melchior Sebizius noted that he had heard of lupines being used as medicine, but never as food. "But there is no doubt that in times of famine the devouring force of hunger can compel people to think about far more bitter, harmful and unhealthy" food. Platina a few centuries before thought lupines a good medicine against worms in children and good for obstructions, but "it is digested with difficulty and generates raw and bad humors."

With statements such as these, lupines were completely effaced from the culinary record in the West. That is not to say ordinary people avoided them. They continued to be eaten commonly as a snack, especially at popular fairs in Italy. This, in fact, is the origin of the current lupine fashion. Lupines or lupini beans can be found in jars on the shelves of Italian grocery stores in the US, and in Provençal olive mixes. One would not exactly call them gourmet foods, though they can be a little pricey. Rather they are traditional foods eaten by people as a reminder of their homeland and by adventurous eaters hoping to experience simple and authentic peasant fare. Lupines are thus eaten today for exactly the same reason they were avoided in the past – because they are a traditional food of rustics.

Nostalgia aside, lupines have enormous potential as a new crop and might even rival soybeans someday. This is especially true since so-called sweet varieties with low levels of alkaloids were developed in the 1930s by German botanist R. von Sengbusch. As a fodder crop they are still grown in Eastern Europe, the US and particularly in Western Australia and South Africa, but clearly the potential of this plant has not yet been realized and awaits further development of completely alkaloid-free strains. Someday the world will rediscover lupines.

4

Fava Beans: Europe

Fabas indulcet fames – hunger sweetens the beans

The fava or broad bean is the biggest and brashest of beans. Because it has no tendrils to grip onto other plants, it's a loner, supporting itself with a stout and hearty stem. Uniquely, its seed scar (hilum) or belly button is on the top narrow end rather than the side. It's also stubborn. When eaten fresh, the big fuzzy pods and tough seed coats of fava beans make it one of the most labor-intensive beans to process and it is perhaps no wonder that it was often fed to horses. When dried it can be one of the most recalcitrant of beans to cook. But favas are also eminently adaptable and one of the few that will tolerate a frost, so they can be grown in northern Europe. This adaptability to a wide range of climates allowed favas to proliferate not only in the arid Middle East and Africa but practically anywhere as either a winter or spring crop. Surprisingly, China grows most of the fava beans on earth, but in most places cultivation is scaling back in favor of soy, corn and other grain crops.

Although the plant was included among the early Fertile Crescent domesticates, the origin of *Vicia faba* is unknown and its wild ancestor is probably extinct. Its closest wild relatives *Vicia narbonensis* and *Vicia galilea* have a different number of chromosomes and cannot be crossed with fava beans which suggests that neither of these is an ancestor. Like corn, the fava has been so thoroughly altered in domestication that the seed has no means of dispersing itself and depends on humans for propagation. That is, without cultivation the fava bean would cease to exist.

The oldest archaeological remains of favas were found in a site near Nazareth dated between 6500 and 6000 BCE, which contains a cache of some 2,600 well-preserved beans, evidence that they were being gathered and stored, but these are probably wild. Oddly, the archaeological record is otherwise silent and the next findings date from several thousand years later. Exactly when and where favas were domesticated remains a complete mystery, and they quite suddenly appear in Bronze Age sites in the third millennium BCE in places as far flung as Spain and Portugal, northern Italy and Switzerland, Greece and the Middle East. It has been suggested that favas may have been independently domesticated in Spain and around Israel, but most likely they spread from the Fertile Crescent in every direction, becoming the premier bean of the ancient world. When the word bean is used in European texts prior to 1492, it is almost always the fava.

Opinion is divided about the status of fava beans in ancient Egypt. Classical authors, most notably Herodotus, claimed that the Egyptians would not grow beans, nor could even look upon them. But this probably refers only to priests, who were said to avoid beans either because they were used in sacrifices (Rameses III offered 11,998 jars of shelled beans to the Nile God), or because this was seen as a means of conscious self-denial for priests. Pliny claimed that priests abstained from beans because they dull the senses and cause sleeplessness. There is no doubt though that ordinary people ate fava beans, and they are even found in some tombs, said to be as old as the 12th dynasty.

The fava bean remained a staple in Egypt through successive ruling dynasties, Persian, Greek, Roman and Muslim. The medieval *Kitab wasf al-At'ima al-Mu'tada* (Book of the Description of Familiar Food), compiled in Cairo in 1373, has many interesting recipes, some of which are specifically intended for the sick, monks or for Christians during Lent. That is, they contain no meat. The maghmuma, for example, is a pot layered with onions, carrots, favas, eggplants all sprinkled with coriander and caraway and soaked with vinegar and murri (a kind of salty fermented barley-based sauce). This is then boiled, flavored with olive oil and sesame oil and eaten with flat bread. There are also simpler recipes, such as Tharida, beans with crumbled bread, spices, lemon, walnuts and yoghurt.

Egypt has remained steadfastly addicted to the fava bean and it is said that they still supply the principal source of protein for the poor. Ful medames is also considered the national dish of Egypt and it is claimed that it is recorded in ancient hieroglyphs. The word 'ful' apparently derives directly from the ancient language, and medames means 'buried' in Coptic, probably referring to the original method of cooking, slowly over hot embers under ground. Coptic is the language spoken by early Christians in Egypt and the only surviving link to the ancient language. Ful medames is eaten for breakfast with flat bread; it is essentially just slowly cooked fava beans with garlic, olive oil, lemon and cumin and sometimes parsley. The beans can be whole or mashed or served with chopped hard-boiled eggs. Eating this dish is not only very traditional, stretching back literally thousands of years, but it also seems to be a conscious act of nationalism. Ful medames is an expression of identity for modern Egyptians who choose to resist the onslaught of contemporary breakfast foods; it is a way to remember who they are.

A dish cooked like this, slowly in a pit, is also mentioned in the Jerusalem Talmud. It is usually called hamin or, by modern-day Ashkenazi Jews, cholent. It is specifically designed to be food for the Sabbath. Since no work is to be done on the day of rest, nor fires lit, something had to be devised that could cook slowly for hours before sunset on Friday. The next day the pot could be opened and a meal served without labor. Today cholent is made with New World phaseolus beans, meat and barley, and must certainly vie for one of the most filling and satisfying of dishes ever created. Heinrich Heine, the nineteenth-century German poet, called it divine: "This Cholent is the very Food of heaven, which on Sinai, God Himself instructed Moses In the secret of preparing."

The original would of course have been made with favas and was probably something closer to ful medames. The dish traveled everywhere the Jews did, to Iraq in the east, northern Africa and westward to Spain where it was called adafina and made with chickpeas. This Hebrew word means "to press to the wall," apparently referring to how the oven is sealed with wet clay to keep in the heat. We will return to this topic in the context of medieval Spain and how cooking chickpeas was a sure way to identify secret Jewish observance, but for the moment, the Talmud or mishna mentions hamin a few times particularly in the context of what kinds of fuel are allowed. For some reason, perhaps the obvious, dung and peat are not allowed. But wool and feathers are, though it is hard to imagine that these smelled any better smoldering. Inclusion of eggs is also something discussed in the Talmud; whole eggs in the shell would be thrown in and left to cook for hours until brown and indescribably fragrant. There is still a dish among Sephardic Jews called huevos haminados, which involves cooking the eggs alone for hours, sometimes with onion skins, until brown and smoky.

Returning to ancient times, we should not forget the central importance of beans to the Israelites. When David is in the wilderness during the rebellion of his brother Absalom, the foods brought to him were wheat and barley, meal and parched grain, beans and lentils, honey and curds, sheep and fat cattle (II Samuel 17: 28). These were precisely the staples of Fertile Crescent agriculture.

These were also by this time the staples in ancient Greece. Homer is usually more forthcoming about roasted oxen and food appropriate for warrior heroes, but he does let a bean slip in, naturally in describing warfare: "On a threshing floor one sees how dark-skinned beans or chickpeas leap from a broad shovel under a sharp wind at the toss of the winnower: just so from shining Meneláos' cuirass now the bitter arrow bounced up and away." Homer would certainly not have used this simile unless every reader, or listener, understood precisely the process of winnowing beans.

Perhaps more ink has been spilled over the question of the Pythagorean ban on beans than any other ancient food question. This is partly because no writings by Pythagoras survive, his famous theorem notwithstanding, and it was left to followers and detractors to figure out his motives. The interest in his diet also stems from his alleged vegetarianism, in fact the word Pythagorean meant vegetarian; the latter term was not coined until the nineteenth century. The typical explanation for his avoiding meat, recounted by Diogenes of Laertius, Porphyry, Iamblicus (authors writing about 800 years after Pythagoras) and also Plutarch, was the idea of metempsychosis, or the transmigrations of souls, an idea he picked up either in his sojourn in Egypt, Persia or even, some claim, in India – the other ancient culture espousing reincarnation. Pythagoras and Buddha were near contemporaries. So the logic goes – if one can be reincarnated as a cow, for example, you might just be eating Aunt Tillie when you chomp down on that steak. One account even has Pythagoras recognize an old friend reincarnated as a puppy.

Pythagoras, who hailed from the Greek island of Samos, was born about 570 BCE, and dissatisfied with the tyrannical rule of Polycrates he left on his travels through the ancient world, eventually settling to found a kind of counter-culture commune in Croton, part of Magna Graeca, modern southern Italy. Reputedly about 300 men flocked to his side. There they practiced their mysteries, speculated on the universal truth of numbers (hence the connection to geometry), strummed their guitars (the octave divisions of a string reflect the cosmic music of the spheres) and ate vegetables, honey, bread and, if Porphyry is to be believed, fish (once in a blue moon). This vegetarianism stemmed not so much from concern for animal welfare, but from the rejection of violence in general, especially of the sort officially sanctioned by the Greek state – public animal sacrifices (more or less state-sponsored barbecues) and of course warfare. The comparison to twentieth-century hippie communes is not too far-fetched.

But whence the cryptic injunction to abstain from beans? Normally, as in India, beans are a mainstay of the vegetarian diet. Among the Pythagoreans the ban was so strict that even crossing through a bean field in flower was forbidden, and in one account this is how Pythagoras met his death when pursued by enemies – he refused to escape through a bean field and was captured. In Iamblicus' version it is his followers who are chased to the edge of the field and slain, down to the last, a pregnant woman, Timycha, who bites off her tongue and spits it out rather than reveal the secret of the prohibition. The simplest, and perhaps most plausible explanation is that beans are part of the whole cycle of reincarnation and they house human souls. To eat a bean is thus a form of murder. This was Varro's explanation. An Orphic fragment puts it like this: eating beans and gnawing on the heads of one's parents are one and the same.

Other explanations range from the equally sublime to the ridiculous. One often reads that Pythagoras really meant that his followers should stay away from politics, since beans were used to cast votes. A white bean meant yea, a black bean, nay. Thus he wasn't really saying anything about eating beans. Actually the comment, so some modern scholars claim, was a little more directly a rejection of democracy. Since the Pythagoreans favored oligarchy – the rule of the few and "best" put in office by appointment – they were rejecting the system of democratic elections.

A more down to earth, if simple, solution is that Pythagoras was concerned with pure mystical thought and as everyone knows grumblings of the belly and flatulence are incompatible with philosophizing. Among Aristotle's list of reasons, from a now lost tract, is "because they are injurious" perhaps meaning damaging to health and clear rational thoughts. In ancient medical theory a sound mind could only exist in a healthy body, free of physical perturbations like gas. Others contend that this was an injunction against gluttony and gourmandizing, beans being so delicious that they tempted the followers to over-indulge. We will not take issue with this supposition, but then Pythagoras might just as well have banned any number of other delicious foods.

Equally plausible is the notion that beans somehow resemble the female sexual apparatus, when viewed from the side, with just a little imagination. When roasted (a common way of preparing favas to this day in Greece) they not only become crunchy, but also split open and the similarity to vaginal lips becomes a little less ridiculous. Thus they were seen as a symbol of creation, perhaps again a bearer of souls, a portal for life. There are references to a magical trick performed by Pythagoras, as told by Porphyry, that he planted some beans in a pot and after ninety days they looked like a vagina. In another version they turn into a human head – presumably a soul caught in transit and only partially reincarnated.

Aristotle also picks up this thread when he explains that beans are like testicles, but adds that they are like the gates of Hades in being the only plant that has no joints. That is, bean stems are hollow and have no nodes and thus serve as a kind of elevator shaft from the underworld, the means of exchange for souls. Actually they are specifically compared to a "ladder" and this makes sense if one has ever seen fava bean pods protruding horizontally from the plant; they do resemble a ladder. This would explain the reluctance to run through a bean field and trample the stems, as well as the ban on picking the pods or rungs of the ladder. In short order Aristotle also claimed that the beans were avoided because they are like the form of the universe – perhaps again a veiled reference to their regenerative power. Even odder is the idea that a nibbled bean left in the sun will smell like semen or the blood of a murdered person – which must smell different from ordinary blood. In any case, all these notions point to the idea that beans are some transitional form of human in the great transmigration of souls.

There is a certain logic to all these assertions. The very word for bean in Greek is *kyamos*, which may be related to the verb *kyein* meaning to swell out. That would make sense if referring to flatulence, but the bean pod itself also swells out much like a pregnant woman's belly. The Germanic word *Bohne* (related to our bean) may derive from *bhouna* – "that which swells out." The word fava too may descend from *bhabha* – again meaning swelling rotundity. It seems as if in most Indo-European languages the bean is connected with the idea of pregnancy and regeneration. The bean was thus a potent symbol of fertility and there was even worship of a bean god in Attica called Cyamites, who had some connection to the Eleusinian and Orphic mysteries. His shrine was found on the road from Athens to Eleusis.

If the bean was a living symbol of regenerative power, it would also explain why ancient authors claim that they serve as an aphrodisiac, and it would also explain why priests would abstain from beans, not wanting to be distracted by sexual potency. Strangely, this too is connected to flatulence. *Pneuma*, meaning air, breath or soul, or in Latin *anima* (as in animal, animate), was the basic principle of life and it is generated in the stomach in the form of gas just as it is transferred in the act of reproduction. This also explains the bizarre association among authors like Pliny of flatulence with the libido. In other words, eating beans not only makes you fart, it helps you conceive. The bean actually contains the regenerative force. So depending on your lifestyle, you might want to absorb the power of the souls in transit, or like the Pythagoreans, avoid them so as to live a non-violent life.

There is yet another, quite recent explanation provided by modern science and anthropology. There is an inherited deficiency among some people of Mediterranean origin called favism. These people are lacking the enzyme glucose-6-phosphate dehydrogenase (G6PD) in their red blood cells. Eating a fresh raw fava bean causes sudden destruction of red blood cells or acute hemolytic anemia, and so can breathing in the pollen – which again explains not running through a bean field. In either case it can cause weakness, fatigue, jaundice and can even be fatal. The disease is extremely rare, and mostly affects young boys, but nonetheless is not unheard of in southern Italy, precisely where Pythagoras set up his commune. Unfortunately there are sparse contemporary descriptions of this disease among ancient physicians. The disorder is also so rare that it seems highly unlikely that an odd case, even if Pythagoras had witnessed it himself, could have led to this overarching prohibition. By this logic Pythagoras would have made a list of many potentially poisonous foods, and clearly that's not what the ban on meat attempts to accomplish.

The Pythagorean concept of beans as the means of transit for souls may have yet another simple explanation. Ancient commentators do not mention this, but something very strange and wonderful takes place in the nodules that form on legume roots. When infected by rhizobium bacteria (*rhizo* means root, *bio*, life), little anaerobic chambers are formed on the roots. Here the bacteria thrive in a symbiotic relationship with the plant. The plant gets ammonium nitrate from the bacteria, which it alone can wrest from the atmosphere, and a protein created by both scavenges oxygen from the node so that the bacteria can survive. This protein is called leghemoglobin and functions much the same way hemoglobin does in our blood, binding oxygen with iron for our bodies to use in cellular respiration. Moreover, when cut, the nodes are red, exactly like blood. Observation of this might very easily have led Pythagoras to conclude that the same life force was at work in beans and humans, and he would be quite right. In another sense, the nitrogen which supports life is reincarnated, if we consider the soul something chemical rather than mystical and immaterial. That is, the nitrogen does get recycled from the bacteria and the bean to the creature that eats them to the person that eats the animal, and so on and so forth. Though why Pythagoras would have wanted to break this chain of causation remains a mystery, but it does indeed resemble Buddhist ideas, where some claimed Pythagoras got them.

We will probably never know exactly why Pythagoras banned beans, but the prohibition is found elsewhere in the ancient world and the idea that beans contain souls seems the most plausible explanation. This is not to discount, however, the overwhelming social prejudice against fava beans in the ancient world. As a food of the poor, all cosmic considerations aside, to eat fava beans was to become like the poor. Anyone who could afford to do otherwise ate meat. Athenaeus cites a dialogue by one Alexis in which a woman complains about her poverty and her three children. "Sounds of wailing untuneful we utter when we have nothing, and our complexions grow pale with lack of food." Dinner, when they can get it, consists of a bean, a lupine, greens, a turnip, pulse, vetch and handful of other oddments including cicada.

Other Greeks also spurned beans, which were sometimes eaten as an after-dinner snack. Archestratus, the gourmet from Gela in Greek Sicily writing about 330 BCE, whose works survive in fragments in Athenaeus, offers vivid suggestions about various topics such as where to find the best fish and various breads, for which he recommended sources across the Mediterranean. Normally he prefers food simply seasoned and fresh, but in one fragment discussing these after-dinner desserts he approves of boiled sow's womb in cumin, sharp vinegar and silphium sauce, and roasted birds. But "All those other tragemata are a sign of wretched poverty, boiled chickpeas, broad beans, apples and dried figs." These lowly foods are comparable to living beneath the earth and the bottomless pit of Tartarus.

Among the Romans, beans were also considered lowly fare, though this was not always a negative association. Columella, the agricultural expert, mentions that artisans eat beans. Pliny and Horace claimed that peasant farmers live on beans and Martial mentioned that builders eat them. In his epigram V, 78 in which he invites a friend to a meager repast, he admits that he can't afford fine luxuries or gyrating flute girls, but he can offer leeks, some boiled eggs, cabbage and pale favas with pink lardo (a kind of cured pork fat). Thus even in this self-deprecating poem, the food that most clearly expresses his noble poverty is beans, not just favas, but hot chickpeas and tepid lupins – "it's a paltry meal, who can deny?" One can live nobly on such wretched foods, and better than with luxuries when you have to suck up to some wealthy patron.

In very much the same vein Juvenal's Satire XI contrasts the wildly extravagant and expensive feasts common in Imperial Rome with a simple homegrown repast. He exclaims "You will find out today, my good friend Persicus, whether I live up, in my life, to all my beautiful maxims; Whether I recommend beans, but live on *paté de foie gras*, Whether I mean *petit fours* when I send my boy out for polenta." The meal he proposes is simple but good honest food: tender young kid, mountain asparagus, fresh eggs and local fruits. Again, beans are associated with rustic simplicity, but here seen as authentic food that tastes good to unjaded palates. Rich men, he thought, have no real pleasure in dining when all they eat is pheasants and flamingoes flavored with a perverse array of seasonings. In days gone by Romans were satisfied with hearty simple foods like beans.

Thus rather than completely negative associations with poverty, beans were seen as a traditional and simple food. Fava beans also played a part in

Roman religious festivals. The bean harvest in central Italy was normally at the end of May so June 1 was celebrated as Calendae Fabariae and the new beans were used in sacred rites. Bean meal or lomentum was also baked into cakes and used as an offering. There was also a ritual of bean tossing to placate wandering spirits called the Feast of the Lemures or Lemuria in mid May. In it the father of the household goes out barefoot at midnight and tosses beans over his shoulder saying nine times "shades of my ancestors, depart" while banging on pots. The beans and the souls they contain are meant to substitute for the family members whom the ghosts might snatch, or the ghosts consume the spirits contained in the beans and are sated. Remarkably this festival was later converted to All Saint's Day in the seventh century, originally May 13 and only later moved to coincide with the Celtic holiday, which we celebrate as Halloween (All Hallows Evening), a pale shadow of its original role as an exorcism of angry ghosts.

Faba beans also lent their name to one of the most respected patrician clans of ancient Rome, the Fabius family. When you hear the modern name Fabio, as in the male supermodel on the cover of romance novels, consider that his name means bean. The Fabii served as consuls, and were war heroes – Fabius Maximus fighting against Hannibal. But why would an ancient noble family take the name of the lowly bean? They were certainly not friends of the common rabble. The association seems to be more with the ancient staple crops and Roman piety. Romans liked to think of themselves as tough farmers, despite their wealth and power. In other words, this name was a kind of marketing ploy, such as might be used by the descendent of a founding father, to recall the original roots of Roman society. There was also a pea family and a chickpea family whose most famous member was the lawyer and statesman Cicero.

That wealthy Romans ate fava beans is also strongly suggested by the few recipes that have survived in the manuscript attributed to Apicius. Although the preparations are hardly simple, they show that even in the most extravagant of cookbooks, beans had their place. What is strange is that two pea/bean recipes are named for Vitellius, who was notorious as one of the greatest gluttons of the ancient world, right up there with Heliogabalus and of course Apicius himself. Vitellius was known to snatch offerings off the altar during services. It may be that the compiler of the cookbook merely attached names of famous gourmands to the recipes. In any case this gives some idea of how beans were eaten by the rich, a strange twist on mushy peas or bean dip.

Peas or Fava Beans Vitellius

Cook peas and mash. Crush pepper, lovage, ginger and over the condiments hard boiled egg yolks, three ounces of honey, garum, wine and vinegar. All this put into a pot and with the crushed condiments, add in oil and boil. Season the peas and mash so they are smooth, add honey and serve.

There is also a version that uses unmashed beans or peas, leeks, coriander, herbs and spices. Although the main ingredient is fairly simple, the treatment and in particular the contrast of flavors, the interplay of spice and sweetness, herbs, fish sauce and sour vinegar makes this a good example of elite taste in ancient Rome.

The Roman association of beans with rustic simplicity and piety disappeared with the fall of their empire. In general, agriculture and the neat, controlled rows of grain, vineyards and olive groves – the Mediterranean diet – gave way to a wilder means of subsistence. The Germanic tribes, Visigoths and Ostrogoths, Vandals who came armed with spray-paint cans, and eventually the Franks, neglected the rigorously ordered latifundia, or huge slave-operated estates, and drew more heavily from the forests and from cattle. They let pigs run wild in the woods, and ate meat and dairy products from their herds and above all hunted game and wildfowl. This is an oversimplified picture of the dietary changes, but it is true that cultivated land shrank in the early Middle Ages, just as the population had. The great Roman trade networks also collapsed, forcing the population to consume locally grown produce. It is for this reason that Charlemagne in his famous Capitularies had to order farmers throughout his empire to plant various crops (including chickpeas and beans) so that his armies could have food ready and waiting when they passed through.

During these years the meaning of beans in Europe also changed, primarily under the influence of Christianity. Although in the early years there was no consistent rule about when people should fast, by the time of the Council of Nicea in 325, a period of forty days or Quadragesima, preceding Easter, was set aside for prayer and self-denial. The Anglo-Saxon word for this period, Lent, merely means springtime. Although there were various interpretations of what exactly constituted a fast, it came to mean complete abstinence from all meat and related products such as eggs and dairy. Fridays were also designated fast days, and hence the persistence of the custom of eating fish on Fridays among Catholics. Fish, in particular stockfish – a virtually indestructible form of dried cod – along with pickled herring became the quintessential food for Lent, especially for those far from the coast. Wealthy Christians could afford more expensive fresh fish, extravagant species such as sturgeon and salmon, and even sea-mammals like whale and dolphin, and, after papal approval, other forms of sea-creature such as puffin, beaver's tail and barnacle geese, which were said to be hatched from actual barnacles. All these foods made Lent less than a hardship for the less-than-devout and affluent medieval diner and individuals, and even whole towns could purchase dispensations from these rules.

For the impoverished, Lent was a more difficult time. The fall harvest's bounty had been consumed through the winter, and spring's crops were barely pushing through the soil. Then suddenly any remaining meat in the household, usually preserved in the form of hams and sausages, had to be consumed, in a festival which came to be called carnival. The word seems to have some connection to *carne* or meat. It was a holiday in which the world was turned upside down, villagers got to mock their superiors while masked, mock weddings and trials were held and everyone for this one Tuesday – Fat Tuesday or Mardi Gras – ran amuck. This mayhem was tolerated only because the regular order of society was restored and indeed strengthened for the rest of the year, carnival serving as a kind of safety valve.

Immediately after the feast, the austere period of Lent began. What was left to eat, especially for the poor peasant and townsmen? There was stockfish if you could afford it, but more than any other food there were beans – cheap, filling and nutritious. Through the Middle Ages and into the early modern era, the most persistent association with beans was not only Lenten austerity, but poverty. One need only recall the story of Jack and the Bean Stalk. The destitute family, once surviving, is under duress forced to sell the family cow. Simple-minded Jack trades it for "magic" beans, which everyone knew was a really bad deal. The cow would have provided milk as long as it was fed, the beans only one measly meal – unless they were planted. But they turn out to really be magical after all: the prodigious bean stalk soars into the clouds and Jack climbs up to find the giant, riches, a goose that lays golden eggs, a singing harp and so forth. The end of the story is a peasant's dream come true: the family becomes wealthy, small triumphs over big, poor over rich. One can easily imagine why this story would have appealed to your average peasant. Such things never happened in real life. But the story also has a hidden moral that has been lost over time and with the watering down of the fable into a children's story. Beans, although seemingly of little worth, are indeed magical. They contain the regenerative force of life, and can maintain human life, but only if they are carefully saved and planted. You may not get a bean stalk like Jack's, but with hard work beans can save the poor.

The association of beans with poverty might be considered negative, but not if your whole aim in life was consciously dedicated to personal poverty, as it was among ascetics. Among the early monastic groups meat was regarded as an unnecessary luxury, a food that would distract the devout from their contemplation because it heats the body, creating an excess or plethora of blood and flesh, and the remaining nutrients are converted to sperm, which activates the libido, something to be avoided at all cost among the celibate. St. Benedict of Nursia in his Rule, the founding document of Western monasticism, details a kind of measured moderation, which nonetheless specifies that except for the very weak, no one should be given meat at any time. Among later groups, the Carthusians in particular were strict vegetarians. Beans necessarily became a staple in such diets. That is not to say that all monks actually practiced austerity, in fact quite the opposite, and it appears that since many of them were drawn from the aristocratic class, they grew rich with pious benefactions, owned extensive land and ate extremely well, which is precisely why new monastic orders were continually founded, reemphasizing their poverty. St. Francis of Assisi is perhaps the best example of someone in conscious imitation of Jesus, who gave up all his personal possessions, traveled around begging, and lived without any worry about tomorrow. It is even said that for this reason, taking the biblical text literally, his followers would not soak their beans the night before as was customary, but only on the day they were to be consumed. Nor would they accept more alms than could support them for a day.

Fava beans, despite the association with poverty, became one of the mainstays of the medieval diet along with various other legumes such as vetches, peas and what was called phaseolus, which at the time referred obviously not to the New World species but to something in the Vicia family, probably black-eyed peas from Africa. There are some very simple reasons why this was the case. After about the year 1000 the European population began to grow dramatically. In 300 years it nearly doubled from 38 to 74 million. This caused the expansion of agriculture, moving onto less fertile lands, up hillsides and even reclaiming land from swamps and from the sea as in the Netherlands. The impetus was quite simply warmer weather. We are understandably concerned about global warming today, but severe fluctuations in climate have occurred throughout the history of our planet – though now admittedly we are causing it. In the Middle Ages warmer weather meant greater productivity of the soil and a longer growing season. Apparently, wine grapes were grown by Cistercian monks in northern England, as they are, frighteningly, again today. The surplus in food meant greater security and less frequent famine despite regular crop failures. A more consistent diet also meant greater human fertility, or to put it another way, as a general rule more food always equals more people. Compounded with agricultural innovations such as the mold-board plough which could cut through heavy soils, the horse collar which allowed horses to be harnessed to ploughs without strangling them, as well as iron horseshoes, Europe witnessed a kind of agricultural revolution.

The development of crop rotation systems is also central to this story. Normally soil is depleted of nutrients if the same crop, say wheat, is grown year after year. In order to restore fertility the soil must be allowed to rest or go fallow for a season. In any given year, perhaps a third of the arable land would be left out of cultivation. Step in the legume. Rather than left fallow, legumes could be grown, whose roots host the aforementioned rhizobia which draw nitrogen from the atmosphere and "fix" it in the soil. The soil thus becomes ready for another crop immediately thereafter. The legumes, normally something like alfalfa, could be fed to cattle, which in turn provide manure which further enriches the soil; or beans can be grown and fed directly to humans. Apparently the ancient Romans understood this system, but it was only with the recovery of classical agronomic texts that the system was explained to medieval Europeans in books like Pier de' Crescenzi's book on agriculture. Renowned author Umberto Eco goes so far as to speculate that it was beans that "saved civilization." "When in the 10th century, the cultivation of beans began to spread, it had a profound effect on Europe. Working people were able to eat more protein; as a result, they became more robust, lived longer, created more children and repopulated a continent." That is, the greatness of medieval civilization, magnificent gothic churches, universities, thriving commerce and industry all depended on the lowly bean.

This may be stretching it a little, but agricultural historians do agree that there was a shift from land-intensive agriculture of grains combined with cattle rearing, to more labor-intensive farming, specifically of legumes. This makes perfect sense if the growing population puts a pressure on land and there is a greater demand for food. Although grains were still the staple and were grown on large estates, and hence show up more regularly in account books, legumes would have been found in small gardens for private use, feeding the poor who could no longer afford meat. Meat was reserved for those enjoying the fruits of medieval civilization.

Not surprisingly, included in this efflorescence of culture and the arts were cookbooks, intended of course mostly for wealthier households since they incorporate spices and other expensive ingredients. One may infer from the relative paucity of bean recipes that they were not considered among the more elegant dishes that might be served. The oldest surviving medieval cookbook, the *Libellus de arte coquinaria* of the thirteenth century, contains no recipes featuring beans, but then neither does it include any vegetable dishes, not because these were never eaten, but because they were normally prepared simply and required no recipe. The only reference to beans here is in a recipe for chicken with bacon which in one version instructs that the bacon be diced the size of fava beans. Clearly, cooks were familiar with them, but it seems unlikely that elegant diners would have been impressed with a fava bean recipe. The *Viandier* attributed to Taillevent, the nickname of Guillaume Tirel, chef to King Charles V of France, is comparably silent, though it does mention a series of "*menuz potaiges*" or little pottages – not meaning small in size but in estimation. These include soups of beet greens, cabbage, turnips, leeks, all familiar to poor households, as well as "*feves frasees*" or favas mashed, sieved or whole in the shell. No recipe for these is offered because "women are experts with these and anyone knows how to do them." That is, these are common lowly foods such as would be prepared by women in modest households, while for aristocratic kitchens run by men, these are beneath their dignity.

We do have a record of the kinds of foods that would be served in ordinary households though, principally the *Ménagier de Paris*, which is an advice book written by an elderly professional for his 15-year-old bride. It seems that this man wanted to make sure that after his death his young widow would be competent enough to cook and run a house so she could attract a suitable man to remarry. Here are fava recipes of precisely the kind Taillevent denigrated. The author is instructing his wife with the absolute basics. For example, he says that old favas must be soaked the night before, then the water thrown away. The favas are cooked in fresh water and then pureed. All this is to remove the strong flavor. To this is added either broth of meat and bacon or during Lent plain water and oil or onion broth. He also includes the fèves frasées made of whole favas for Easter, the same mentioned by Taillevent. These are cooked in the pod, scraped out with a spoon and then recooked until they split and then served in meat or fish broth, fried onions and garnished with fresh bean leaves wilted in hot water. There are also directions for dealing with fresh beans, all quite simple and homely. Here is some evidence of beans being eaten in urban households.

Another fascinating record of some of the class and ethnic associations of food is found in the fifteenth-century *Registrum de coquina* of Jean of Bockenheim. For each recipe, the author, a German cleric in Rome, lists to whom the recipe should be served. We find recipes for nobles and peasants, Germans and Englishmen, priests and whores. His recipe for fava bean soup is worth quoting in full:

> *Thus make minestra of favas. Take and clean these well in warm water and let them soak for a night. Then boil in fresh water and chop them well and add white wine, and add above them onions with olive oil or butter, with a little saffron. And it will be good for Lollards and pilgrims.*

Here the association is not specifically with poverty, though pilgrims en route to a holy site could be poor, but rather with religious austerity and for some odd reason with heresy. The Lollards were followers of John Wyclif, a medieval precursor to Martin Luther who advocated a vernacular liturgy and Bible and doctrines that would later be espoused by Protestants, such as the emphasis on faith rather than works. They were vigorously persecuted in the early fifteenth century, though not necessarily poor. Some of their leaders were nobles. Why Bockenheim thinks fava bean soup would be good for religious fanatics may have something to do with religious purity – eating simple common foods for cleansing of the soul through suffering. This is one of the simplest and cheapest of recipes; the others like it, turnips for example, are offered to rustics.

The English cookbooks of this era also contain bean recipes. Some are similar to the purees mentioned above, but they are also souped-up, so to speak, with expensive ingredients, more fitting for noble households. For example, the *Curye on Inglysch* (Cooking in English) has a pottage of "wite benes" seethed in water, pounded finely in a mortar, boiled with almond milk, wine and honey, and then garnished with raisins soaked in wine. The lowly bean is thus ennobled with expensive imported ingredients. Even more interesting is this recipe from the *Forme of Cury* for fried beans, here left in its original language. The symbol þ is a thorn standing for *th*. To seethe means to boil and the powder douce is a spice and sugar mixture.

> *Benes yfryed. Take benes and seeþ hem almost til þey bersten. Take and wryng out þe water clene. Do þereto oynouns ysode and ymynced, and garlic þerwith; frye hem in oile oþer in grece, & do þereto powdour douce, & serue it forth.*

The Catalan *Libre de Sent Sovi* of the early fourteenth century includes a similar recipe: tender favas with almond milk. The beans are cooked first in water and then steeped in almond milk, a favorite ingredient in medieval cookery, especially for Lent. It was made by grinding and soaking almonds and then straining off the thick milky liquid. To this is added parsley, alfàbegua (basil), moradux (marjoram) and other good spices, ginger and verjuice, the juice squeezed from green unripe grapes.

Roughly contemporaneous is the Latin *Tractatus de modo preparandi et condiendi omnia cibaria* (Tract on the way to prepare and cook every food), probably written in France. In the introduction to ingredients the author states that the book will include food for nobles and the wealthy, such as partridge and pheasant, chicken capon and so forth, but also "whatever is truly fitting for robust men who live by laboring, such as beef and mutton, salted pork, deer, peas, fava beans, and bread made of barley mixed with wheat." The logic is that lighter and whiter foods are more appropriate for those with delicate digestive systems and only robust workers have enough digestive heat to break down tough or crass foods like mutton or beans. This idea is standard in the medical literature. But it is also a scarcely veiled class-based prejudice. The cheaper forms of protein are for the lower classes, and delicate and expensive fowl only for the rich.

Nonetheless true to his word, there are fava bean recipes, both for fresh and green beans, cooked with almond milk, pepper, ginger, saffron, cumin and cinnamon as well as for "hard and old" beans. These get a quick boil, a soaking over night, and are cooked in fresh water until they split. Then they are pounded and seasoned either with butter, meat broth or bacon. There is also a recipe for skinned favas, dried without the seed coat. These too are cooked and pounded into a smooth paste and flavored with fried onions, finely chopped bacon or saffron. We should perhaps take the author on his word, that these are typical dishes of the working classes.

Also of the fourteenth century is the *Liber de coquina*, most likely of Italian origin since the author specifies all the countries where his recipes come from, except Italy. Here there are seven distinct fava recipes plus others for chickpeas, lentils and "fasseolis." Most interesting are fava flowers, simmered with fresh pork, and thickened with beaten eggs and spices into which the pounded meat is then returned. Or they can be cooked with bread and almond milk, presumably a version for Lent, during which one might easily find beans in flower. The other fava recipes are similar to those mentioned above, though there is one option that includes fatty fish served with a dried bean pottage.

As might be expected, southern European cookbooks offer more recipes for favas and with a greater variety of preparations. Here the social stigma against beans may not have been as strong as in the north, but there may also be socio-economic reasons for the proliferation of bean recipes. Strangely the willingness to eat beans may have had something to do with the plague. In 1348 the bubonic plague hit Europe with a terrible ferocity. The bacillus *Yersinia pestis* arrived in the bodies of fleas from the steppes of Central Asia. There it survived by being transferred from fleas to rats. Apparently the infected flea chokes up and goes on a kind of feeding frenzy and is willing to bite anyone, including humans. The humans in question were Mongols who had recently conquered Baghdad, which in turn was also connected to Europe via revitalized trade routes for spices and other luxuries. It's a stiff price to pay for spices, but the rats followed the caravan routes, and the fleas and the bacteria hitched a ride all the way to Europe. Once infected with the bubonic form (there were probably also worse pneumonic and septicemic versions), grotesque black swellings appear in the armpits and groin with a red "ring around the rosy" – the so-called boo-boos. The victim usually died within a few days. Estimates for the death toll state that about one-third of the entire population of Europe perished. That's around 35 million people.

Obviously at first this wrought havoc on the European economy, totally dislocating business and agriculture. But perversely enough, if you were lucky enough to survive, it usually meant that you inherited your relatives' wealth, and in general there were more opportunities to thrive. With a greater demand for labor, wages rose, the price of land plummeted and life for the average peasant vastly improved. Landlords were desperate to keep their tenants so they often offered excellent bargains – low fixed rents. What has this to do with beans? With this added wealth, a greater proportion of the average household income could be spent on meat. Food historians often call the latter fourteenth and fifteenth centuries the golden age of meat. The diets of the rich and poor became less differentiated. The average person might even be able to afford some pepper and other spices. No longer relying heavily on beans as a source of protein – as the rule goes, once you can afford not to eat beans, you don't – they are less associated with poverty. There is no longer the powerful stigma against bean eating because fewer people are forced to do so to survive. Therefore, there is less danger of being considered a peasant by eating beans. That is, one can do so for the sake of pleasure without risk of social degradation. One might also add that this fear of debasement could never have been so strong among the very wealthy; there was no possible way one could be confused with a peasant. But among the middling sorts this danger was very real, until of course the peasants were eating meat regularly.

This is mere conjecture, but this period witnesses a real plethora of bean recipes, mostly quite inventive. The fifteenth-century Venetian anonymous cookbook known, appropriately, as Anonimo Veneziano, not only includes beans but also distinguishes between favas and faxolli (again probably black-eyed peas). A Fresh Fava Tart of King Manfred is particularly interesting.

Take the favas and clean, then cook in good milk, then drain. Take cooked pork belly and pound it with a knife, and then put the favas and the meat together. Take sweet and strong spices and saffron and place in a basin and add in good fresh cheese and make the dough. Then make the tart and add in this mixture into the crust and put in the middle and above slices of sweet rich cheese.

Another novel recipe from this period is found in the Anonimo Toscano cookbook which instructs to take dried fava beans boiled quickly and then drained, then boiled again in fresh water, being careful not to let them burn. This appears to be the quick method without overnight soaking. These are made into a thick soup with oil and fried onions, or with pepper, saffron, honey and sugar. Furthermore, "With these favas you can serve tench or other fish. And know that with the aforementioned, you can make mortadella." The author is suggesting a kind of bean- and fish-based sausage, probably as a meat substitute for Lent. This is one of the most fascinating culinary inventions of this era.

As with this anonymous author, Rupert of Nola, writing in Catalan for the Aragonese court ruling in Naples, also has a dish entitled Royal Fava Beans. They are essentially boiled in almond milk or goat's milk and flavored with sugar, cinnamon and rosewater – a typical flavor combination. The recipe is really a vehicle for explaining how to get the acrid flavor out of a pot that has accidentally burned – something that must have occurred often enough in busy kitchens for Rupert to give precise instructions. Anyway, all these are ample evidence that noble and wealthy households were interested in bean recipes in the fifteenth century. Rather than being served simply, they posed a challenge to the cook who sought to discover new and exciting ways to serve them.

There is no other way to explain the remarkable and labor-intensive recipe offered by Martino of Como in the mid-fifteenth century for Stuffed Fava Beans. The dried beans are soaked and then the skin on each is carefully removed without breaking. Then almonds are crushed with rosewater and sugar and the marzipan-like mixture is stuffed back into the skins and heated gently. These mock-beans are then served in meat broth with chopped parsley and fried onions. One can easily imagine Martino's patron being offered what seems to be a fairly common dish only to be surprised and delighted by the trick. Although not really a bean dish, it gives a good impression of the kinds of marvels enjoyed in late medieval Italy. There are actual bean recipes here as well. One mixes the crushed beans with onions, sage and finely chopped figs or apples. This mixture can also be fried in oil into a kind of frittata or bean cake, covered with fine spices.

What is perhaps strangest about these recipes is that they first appeared in print around 1470, translated into Latin in *De honesta voluptate* by Bartolomeo Sacchi, known as Platina. Strange because Platina borrowed these recipes from Martino, whom he claims as a friend, and yet juxtaposes them with his own odd mixture of classical references and medical advice. So just a few pages before these recipes we are told that, "The power of favas is cold. When fresh they tend to moistness and so harm the stomach; dried are even worse. In whatever manner eaten, they cause bad insomnia. It is believed that sprinkled with aromatics they harm less." This was not schizophrenia on the part of Platina, but reflects the contrary advice that would have been given to any diner when faced with a plate of beans. Yes, they are a lowly food, but prepared in elegant ways they can be quite interesting, says the gourmand. The physician on the other hand warns about the dangers of flatulence, disturbed digestion and bad dreams. Like today, people were assailed with a barrage of conflicting ideas about food, and beans in particular are prone to mixed messages, partly because of their social connotations but also because of the medical tradition which denounced beans.

This tradition goes all the way back to the ancient Greek and Arab medical authorities. A few key passages in Galen were picked up and amplified by later authors. First, gladiators eat fava beans, but it makes them flabby with spongy flesh rather than solid. Beans cause flatulence, even if cooked for a long time – and that this flatulence occurs in the whole body, particularly when one isn't accustomed to eating beans or if they're badly cooked. This idea is not quite as silly as it sounds, considering that the ancients believed that any default in concoction in the stomach (the first stage of digestion) was later passed on through the liver into the bloodstream and then incorporated into the flesh, and even brain, hence the bad dreams. This is also why it makes the flesh spongy and soft, we literally inflate a little. Bean soup causes gas, but whole cooked beans are even worse. Roasting mitigates this, but then they become indigestible. All Galen can counsel is that hot foods and those that tend to thin, meaning those that speed digestion by cutting through the crass substance of the bean, serve as correctives. This would in part explain the combination with onions and spices.

These ideas persisted through the centuries, obviously supported by people's own experience of eating beans. Benedict of Nursia, a physician contemporary with Platina, for example, contends that fava beans are cold and dry. This means that they increase the cold and dry humors in the body, namely melancholy. Because they are difficult to digest they also generate vapors – just as happens in a pot of boiling beans, because digestion in the stomach is a kind of cooking. These vapors rise up to the head and thicken the spirits. The spirits are the super-refined form of nutrition which in a sense nourishes our brains. With proper digestion these spirits are light and vigorous and so too are our thoughts. But when clouded by gross, thick and unrefined gases from the stomach, our ideas become muddled, we become depressed and, especially after an evening meal, our sleep is disturbed. John White also notes "It's said, that if a Woman with Child eats Quinces and Coriander seed much it makes the child ingenious; & on the contrary, if on the contrary, if they eat much Onions, or Beans, or such vaporous Food, they will be Lunatic, or Foolish." Again, it is the idea that gases disturb thoughts, even in the womb. Prosper Calanius, citing Byzantine author Michael Psellus, claims that even staying too long in a bean field sends pestilent fumes into the head, which renders our thoughts slow and weak. Eating fava beans was not merely a matter of slight discomfort and possible embarrassment, but a complete disruption of the whole physiological mechanism. Again, hot herbs and aromatics offer some correction, but beans are inherently dangerous and best left to common folk with stronger stomachs and those less concerned with clear and rational thought.

As we pass into the early modern era these ideas remained firmly in place and are just as starkly juxtaposed against gastronomic concerns. As before, the wealthy could afford to eat expensive fish during Lent and beans perhaps as a novelty, but down the social scale people were forced to eat beans and thus the social stigma remained firmly in place. It was perhaps even strengthened anew once the population began to rise again, when inflation hit hard in the sixteenth century, and once again the disparity of wealth made social distinctions greater. Fewer people could afford meat regularly and beans became ever more firmly associated with poverty. This meant that the middling ranks of society were once again faced with possible debasement for eating beans. Bean recipes still appeared in elite cookbooks, but increasingly they focused on fresh fava beans and "green beans" eaten pod and all, brought in from the New World. Because these were necessarily seasonal and supplied by market gardeners, they stood apart from ordinary peasant fare. The negative social and medical connotations against beans thereafter focused more heavily on dried beans, which only the poorest were forced to consume.

For example, Girolamo Cardano, the sixteenth-century physician and mathematician, writes about the same fried bean cake mentioned in Martino a century earlier. He explains how during Lent it is diligently cooked and mashed, seasoned with oil, pepper and onions or leeks and then is eaten by plebeians. Though he admits it tastes good, it is nonetheless too dangerous for studious people to eat, and especially harmful for boys. What had earlier been merely a patent medical warning now became a specifically class-based ban. In a similar vein Baldassare Pisanelli claims favas "generate much wind, and make the senses stupid, and cause dreams full of travails and perturbation ... they are good in cold weather, for rustic folks." The author of a little treatise on salad, Costanzo Felici, although he likes favas, still reveals the prejudice of many people: "... finally it is a food very common for men and gives a great deal of nourishment, and even if it is vulgarly said you give favas to gross men [i.e. bulky], nonetheless they give pleasure to many." This was the best defense he could muster.

Similar opinions can be found throughout Europe. Ludovicus Nonnius, a Spaniard writing in what is today Belgium, recounts the various dangers of fava beans, and that those boiled whole in the pod are "often served up among rustics and plebes." In England Tobias Venner contends that utterly ripe beans (i.e. dried) are worst of all and should be considered "meat only for ploughmen." By meat he merely means food, but for ploughmen they did serve as meat in our modern sense of the term.

One of the strangest opinions about favas is that they are an aphrodisiac. Thomas Moffett writing in late sixteenth-century England says that fava beans are a very hurtful meat unless eaten young at the beginning or middle of a meal with butter, pepper and salt. But they are best avoided because they "too much encreaseth the seed to lusty wantons." So much for celibate monks eating them, though this may be the reason that St. Jerome forbad beans for nuns – because "they tickle the genitals." The logic of such statements partly stems from agreement among ancient authorities that beans are highly nutritious. This was probably based on empirical observation of people actually living off them, without of course any knowledge of proteins. According to theory any food which is nutritious, after having replaced the blood, flesh and spirits, is then converted into sperm, both the male and female variety. As merely an excess of nutritional matter, if not stored in fat, it is converted to sperm, which then signals the urge to procreate. There may also have been a vague intuition that the physical consistency of cooked beans, although usually chickpeas in the ancient authorities, is similar to and thus easily converted into sperm. Yet more surprising, beans inflate not just the stomach but the whole body. This creates a kind of artificial aid to sex, an early modern Viagra, if you will.

In a discussion of truffles and oysters as aphrodisiacs, Laurent Joubert also considers how vulgar people think that gassy foods aid sex, which would then mean peas and legumes would do the trick. In fact, he claims, neither do. The gross vapors might "render people salacious" but hardly fecund, which is the real purpose of foods that "render men more gallant in the venereal act." Though the association with sex may just be a springtime thing – there is a saying in French

"*Quand les fèves sont en fleur, les fous sont en vigeur*" meaning that people go a little silly and twitterpated.

Despite these medical warnings and sexual associations, fava beans might still have been served in noble households. As Melchior Sebizius writes in the seventeenth century "the use of legumes is greatest, but not only among the lower sort of men; truly they frequent even magnates' meals, especially in times of fasting, usually prepared as porridge." The cookbooks of the early modern period scarcely bear out this impression though. Normally the recipes either use fresh favas or they are cooked in ways elaborate enough to disguise their humble origins.

In the 1540s Christoforo di Messisbugo includes not a single recipe for fava beans, and only one recipe for tiny fasoletti, eaten fresh and lightly fried. The English *Proper Newe Booke of Cokerye* of about the same time includes a tart of pounded beans, made with eggs and curds, but these are disguised. The contemporaneous *Livre fort excellent* offers something a bit more homely, and one is tempted to think this reflects a broader readership, other than the wealthy. It reads:

> *Boil favas in water and when they are well cooked take onions very small fried in salt, butter or oil and let them cool a little, and when they are cooled place these things in a pot and let them boil again on the fire in the sauce, stirring often. A little saffron. One serves them with herrings, salted porpoise and other sauce.*

The optional inclusions are difficult to interpret; the herrings are probably for modest households and the salted porpoise was most likely much more expensive. In either case, the interest in bean dishes seems to wane in the sixteenth century.

It is surprising that the largest and most comprehensive cookbook of the sixteenth century makes only passing reference to fava beans. Bartolomeo Scappi's huge *Opera* with thousands of recipes mentions them in two places as an alternative to peas or chickpeas when cooked in a tart. There is also one brief recipe (II.252) that says to cook dried favas or chickling vetch (a bean even lower than favas) by soaking in lye, washing in several changes of water, after which they are cooked in oil, water and salt and garnished with fried onions, herbs and saffron. Interestingly, there are several recipes that call for fagioli, which by this point may be New World species, and others that include various legumes. But fava beans, unlike any other food in this book, are merely an afterthought. Either the papal court, for which Scappi cooked, was uninterested in favas, or there was indeed a stigma against consuming them. Putting them in the same recipe with vetches is a good indication of this.

On the other hand, Scappi may just be indicating that any legume dish will work with peas, which are preferred, or something else similar, and thus there is no reason to specify favas. To give an idea of where favas might appear, here is a generic legume tart. There are different versions with fresh and dried legumes, this is the latter. Provatura is merely fresh cheese, something like farmer cheese. Mostaccioli are perfumed biscuits. The combination of sweet and savory flavors with spices is very typical of this century.

To Make a Tart of Peas, Fagioli or Other Dried Legumes

The peas being cooked in a good meat broth, pound them in a mortar and pass through a sieve, and for every pound of the paste add six ounces of grated Parmigiano cheese and six ounces of fresh ricotta, or fresh provatura pounded in a mortar, and six ounces of goat's milk, or cow's or not having milk, take cold rich broth, and a pound of sugar, six beaten egg yolks, or three with the whites, half an ounce of cinnamon, an ounce of powdered Neapolitan mostaccioli, half an ounce of pepper, three ounces of fresh butter. Place this composition in a tart with pastry dough beneath, and let it cook in the oven and serve hot with sugar and cinnamon on top. In this way you can make fagioli, having first been parboiled and then cooked again in meat broth. Split chickpeas can be boiled just in good broth, as can red chickpeas and lentils. Split favas when they are well cooked, you can mix with little onions beaten and fried added to the above mixture, adding fewer eggs than is in the other.

There can be little doubt that the relative paucity of bean recipes in early modern cookbooks reveals a reluctance to eat them on the part not only of the wealthy, but also of the ever-expanding audience for these printed books, the growing middle class. There can be no doubt, however, that fava beans were grown. The agricultural manuals of the period all discuss them, specifically as human food. For example, Gervase Markham in his *A Way to Get Wealth* explains not only when and how to plant them, but also how they should be dried. When one is compelled to harvest early, beans must be kiln-dried, after which they will remain sound for "the space of many years, without turning or rolling; nor need you to respect how thick the heap lie, since beans after they are once dried in the Kilne, or in the Sun, never after will thaw, give again, or relent, but remain in their first soundness." Those you intend to feed to servants can just be kept in barrels, up to twenty years, he claims, and he has even heard of beans lasting 120 years this way. His comments about servants are revealing, but so too is the idea that this is the one food that can withstand time and ostensibly feed people in time of want.

Common experience with beans is also revealed in the *Maison Rustique* by Charles Etienne and Jean Liebault, translated into English as *The Country Farm*. The authors specify that beans should be soaked overnight in nitre dissolved in water – much the same effect as baking powder used by some today – or they recommend boiling with mustard seed. Also observant, they note that "beanes will keep long if you water them with sea water, notwithstanding that they will not boile any thing at all in salt or sea water." That is, they never soften if you salt the boiling water. Comments such as these suggest that people were still growing and cooking beans despite the fact that they were neglected in elite cookbooks.

There is other indirect evidence that points to the negative association of beans with the poor, namely art. The most startling and sudden appearance of poor people and lowly subjects in paintings in the sixteenth and through the seventeenth century is difficult to explain. It seems unlikely that people were empathizing with their plight. Nor are such subjects to be seen through the modern lens, as charming rustic folk living out their humble daily lives. When Pieter Breughel was painting his chunky rustics dancing and swilling wine, this was meant as a social satire. The patrons of these works were most likely middle- or upper-class buyers who held these paintings up as examples of how not to behave. The same can be said of literary depictions of the sweaty masses, including the Grobianus books and Rabelais, in whose *Gargantua and Pantagruel* giants greedily chomp their way through unimaginable heaps of lowly peasant fare: sausages, tripe and, yes, beans. The same spirit pervades Dutch art of the seventeenth century as well, although the peasants are now a little more clearly the laughing stock.

Although not specifically about beans, there is a subset of genre paintings entitled *The Bean King*. These depict the Feast of the Epiphany when a bean would be baked into a cake and whoever found it would be made king for the day. This actually took place and survives, for some reason, in Mardi Gras celebrations in New Orleans, which would not be complete without a king cake. There are a series of works with this title from the mid-seventeenth century by Jacob Jordaens. (These can be found easily online in a moment with a simple search.) In them, carousing drunks in a world-turned-upside-down scenario toast the Bean King. In all versions the elderly king is clearly past his limit and is being egged on to drink more. The crowd crammed in the canvas are not lowly peasants though, the surroundings are opulent and the clothes resplendent if untidy. So perhaps this is a kind of heavy-handed warning not to go over board, as the one vomiting man down left has done as well as other hideously sloshed figures.

The most interesting work in the Bean King genre, sometimes also called *Twelfth Night* or the *Lord of Misrule*, is by Gabriel Metsu. It does depict a more modest household, simply furnished and with homely clothes. It is also the most subtle and perceptive. Apart from the possible religious symbolism and the patently comic elements like the baby in the toilet or the grimacing figure cooking over the fire, there is a fascinating family dynamic at play. The king must be the elderly grandfather, carefully trying to down the last of his drink. The children look on in amazement, as does a fool pointing derisively and looking directly at the spectator to make sure we notice. There is also someone we might construe to be his wife, who looks on lovingly and is ready with the pitcher for a refill, ready to humor his binge. The dominant figure, and one whom we might consider his grown daughter, whose children litter the room, offers the most engaging look of tired amazement, disgust, apathy and renouncement. One can almost hear her say "Dad, I can't believe you're still at it!" This is far more incisive as a social satire, very clearly pointing out to the viewer exactly how not to behave. Again, the painting is not about beans per se, although their presence here in a peasant household makes more sense than in the Jordaens versions, where the message is clearly just mayhem. In Metsu, tellingly, there is a lone slab of prime rib, this being perhaps the rare occasion when this family did not actually have to eat beans but got to celebrate them in cake.

In another genre entirely, and somewhat older than these, is a painting by Annibale Carracci painted in Rome in the late sixteenth century, entitled *The Bean Eater*. Perhaps never before was an ordinary peasant depicted with the intention of showing real life. There is no moral message or satire, merely a man caught in the act of shoveling a bowl of beans down his hungry throat. He almost seems a little contemptuous for being interrupted, as he glares directly at the spectator or perhaps the artist as he bursts onto the scene with his sketchbook. Carracci's motives can only be guessed at, but it may be a real desire to capture ordinary life, and what better way to express the experience of peasants than to show one eating beans? Incidentally, it is hard to identify the species. They could be stewed fava beans, or maybe black-eyed peas, though by this time they could be *Phaseolus* from the New World.

The most persuasive evidence that beans had truly become exclusively the "poor man's meat" after the sixteenth century comes directly from cookbooks. Domingo Hernàndez de Maceras, cook for a college refectory in Salamanca, makes absolutely no mention of favas, only chickpeas and lentils in his *Libro del arte de Cozina* of 1607. In Francisco Martínez Montiño's *Arte de cocina* of 1611 there are a few recipes. The author was chef to King Philip III of Spain, so it is a good indication of what nobles would or would not eat. One soup of favas for Lent is made from tender young beans and lettuce, water, spices, cilantro and a bit of vinegar and raw eggs broken into the pot. You can add fennel as well, though some señores don't like it. A similar version for meat days includes fried salt pork and can be served under a plate of meat. Importantly, these are fresh young green favas; nowhere are dried beans mentioned.

In the same century, the English Robert May in his *The Accomplisht Cook* mentions beans nowhere, except for a bean bread, which, as it turns out, contains no beans whatsoever. His contemporary William Rabisha in the *The Whole Body of Cookery Dissected* does not seem to even mention the word bean once anywhere. The same is true of the Dutch *De Verstandige Kock* (The Sensible Cook) whose translator points out quite rightly that the book was intended for affluent households and thus dried beans and peas, eaten by the poor, are nowhere mentioned.

With the advent of classical French haute cuisine following the publication of La Varenne's *Cuisiner François* in the middle of the seventeenth century, dried fava beans are completely banished from elite cookery. Green peas are still to be found and even enjoy a vogue at the court of Louis XIV. There is French saying, "*s'il me donne des pois, je lui donnerais des fèves*" meaning you do something to me, I'll give you back the same or "tit for tat," but given the falling estimation of beans, it seems to imply you get back worse. Green beans also make a dramatic appearance, but the ancient staple fava is left for the poor and horses.

L'Art de bien traiter by L.S.R. describes many recipes for peas, but for favas there is but one. These are very young, just when they begin to form, and are served with their skins intact, seasoned just like peas with chopped marrow, savory and bouillon. Only when a little older is the skin removed and they are cooked longer. Mature dried beans are not mentioned at all. In *Le cuisinier* of Pierre de Lune there are actually four fava recipes, again all for fresh young beans, blanched and peeled. The first is served with crème, egg yolk and nutmeg. The second *au lard* can be served with mutton broth. Favas in the Italian fashion are fried and served with fried parsley and the last, a faufracho à l'espagnole, is as follows:

When tender favas have been peeled, pound them in a mortar, season with
salt, pepper, three raw eggs, and cook them in a tart pan with melted lard,
like a tart without a crust, and serve it whole or cut up.

The absence of fava beans in eighteenth-century cooking is even more startling, perhaps because these books consciously target bourgeois households and
country farms. Again, it may be that among these middling ranks of society the
stigma against fava beans would have been the strongest. A fairly prosperous
family would have no reason to eat beans, unless they are fresh and tender.
It is also at this point that New World species began to definitively displace
fava beans, a part of the story that will be picked up later. For the moment, it
will suffice to show that through the eighteenth and well into the nineteenth
century, fava beans and usually dried beans of any sort have no place even in the
most comprehensive of cookbooks.

In eighteenth-century England, Mary Kettilby's *A Collection of Above Three
Hundred Receipts*, which went through many editions after 1714, makes some
very revealing comments in the preface about the status of beans. Her point is
basically that most cookbooks give "strangely odd and fantastical" rules that
spoil many a good dinner. It is not only the great chefs who contrive "relishes
a thousand time more Distasteful to the Palate" but also "a Poor Woman must
be laugh'd at, for only Sugaring a Mess of Beans." The association with poverty
is clear enough, and not surprisingly, there is not a single mention of beans
elsewhere in the book.

In Mrs. Fisher's *The Prudent Housewife* of 1750 one would naturally expect
something thrifty such as beans. An illustrated table setting does indeed show a
plate of Beans and Bacon along with other elegant dishes such as stewed carp,
chine of veal and fricassee. But there is no recipe, perhaps because she assumed
any housewife would know how to cook it. On the other hand, judging from
her menus, beans appear only once in August. Susannah Carter's *The Frugal
Colonial Housewife*, which was reprinted in Boston on the eve of the Revolution,
never mentions dried beans. Only fresh broad beans are boiled and it is "best
not to shell them till just before they are ready to go into the pot." Mrs. Raffald,

much of which was taken from Fisher, does include a recipe. To make Windsor Beans, "Boil them in a good quantity of salt and water, boil and chop some parsley, put in good melted butter; serve them up with bacon in the middle, if you choose it." Apart from not being much of a recipe, these must be fresh beans or the salt would probably prevent them from ever cooking properly. Charlotte Mason's *The Lady's Assistant*, by any account a thorough cookbook, lists beans in the menus, but nowhere mentions dried beans. Judging from the corpus of eighteenth-century English cookbooks, it seems as if dried fava beans were not eaten, except by the poor.

An illustration of this is found in *Shrove Tuesday: a satiric rhapsody* by Anthony Pasquin published in London in 1791. In it a bunch of pedantic scholars are wrangling about the botanical classification of beans. An F.R.S. is a brother of the Royal Society, the leading scientific institution of the day.

> *When Joe Soho was in the massy chair,*
> *All-gorgeous carv'd, and rais'd above his peers,*
> *He ask'd a question, made his brethren stare,*
> *Pulling his side curls down to hide – his ears!*
> *"As we've complete arrang'd both grubs and greens,*
> *Pray in what genus do ye class your beans?"*
> *"How class our beans! Cried Fungus, let me see,*
> *"How class our beans! Roar'd Horace, (vis à vis)*
> *"How class our beans!" went individual round,*
> *And all seem'd lost in reveries profound!*
> *Silence assum'd the absolute command,*
> *Each head lean'd pond'rous on its kindred hand;*
> *No band of nincumpoops were e'er so pos'd,*
> *And some o'er-wrung by study, dreamt and doz'd;*
> *Chagrin'd, discomfited, perplex'd and pang'd*
> *Each sober judgment by its fancy nag'd:*
> *Some look'd toward the ceiling some-the floor,*
> *The wisest doubted, and the wicked swore!*
> *D.D.'s, Lords, M.D.'s seem'd in deep distress,*
> *And ignorance hoodwink'd every F.R.S.*

'Till and old woman (who at their desire
Was wont to empt the pot and stir the fire)
Ended the matter, as Bystanders ought,
And sav'd their brains from being pierc'd by thought,
"Your Honor sure (quo' she) can't be mistaken,
"I always class my beans with bacon!"

The satire only really makes sense when you consider that the learned know nothing about beans; it's only the old woman servant who understands what to do with them.

Why beans disappear from genteel tables appears to be partly due to growing affluence among average cookbook readers and a desire to showcase meat at the center of every meal. But it may also have something to do with yet another Agricultural Revolution which made fava beans one of the premier fodder crops for horses; in fact the term horse bean – although a slightly different variety – becomes the more common usage, while Windsor beans, eaten fresh, remain as human food. That is, why would anyone serve a bean so universally recognized as fodder, unless under duress?

In a nutshell, this revolution, which spanned a few centuries only culminating in the eighteenth century, transformed agriculture from a local subsistence activity to a more market-oriented business. Growing population was once again central to this process, particularly in the Netherlands where land was scarce and urban populations were densely packed. With good prices and growing demand for food, especially in cities, there was an incentive for landowners to convert peasant holdings into capital-intensive enterprises. Why allow backward peasants to farm the land in traditional ways when you could directly exploit the land yourself, perhaps kick the tenants out, a process called enclosure, and then apply new methods of irrigation, fertilizers and improved breeds? Land could be amassed into larger parcels and the former tenants even employed as a rural labor force, and paid wages. Crop rotation systems thereafter became more complex, the most celebrated being that of Charles "Turnips" Townsend who introduced this vegetable in a four-field system as a winter fodder crop along with clover so that cattle could be kept year round rather than slaughtered in the fall. More cattle of course meant more fertilizer. New machines were also introduced such as Jethro Tull's seed drill, the Rotherham plough and new threshing machines. With the push to increase productivity both of cattle and crops, a major effort was made to find a fodder which could both fatten cattle quickly and serve to replenish the soil.

Although this simple picture of a sudden "revolution" has been qualified and called into question in recent decades, there is no doubt that business-oriented farmers were increasingly interested in legumes, including fava beans. This is not the place to debate the extent and significance of overall productivity, and for this story the central fodder crop involved, clover, is irrelevant because it cannot be used as human food. But use of fava beans as fodder appears to have had a direct impact on their slow disappearance from English and northern European cuisines.

This interest in growing beans is evidenced in a wide diversity of agricultural texts in eighteenth-century England. For example Joseph Randall's *The Farmer's New Guide for Raising Excellent Crops of Peas, Beans, Turnips or Rape* was published in 1764 with the intent of introducing these crops to entrepreneurial farmers. Thomas Hale's *A Compleat Body of Husbandry* makes a distinction between horse beans, which are sowed in fields, and so-called great garden beans, which are cultivated more intensely in gardens around London for human consumption. He believes that the larger fields could also be cultivated with the same industry, manure and care, but evidently they were not – most beans were merely grown for fodder and planted by broadcasting haphazardly. An anonymous book *An Enumeration of the Principal Vegetables* of 1796 was designed to introduce new crops to substitute for wheat in times of scarcity. The author is unequivocal: "The green, unripe seeds of this well-known vegetable, are a favorite summer-food in this and other countries. But the meal obtained from the ripe and dried seeds is seldom made use of." He cites some experiments of the Board of Agriculture to add bean meal to extend bread, but these do not appear to have had any effect. Such beans are, after all, for horses. Antoine

Parmentier, though admittedly trying to promote potatoes, says of legumes such as peas, favas and haricots when worked into bread, "this compact aliment, disagreeable and viscous, often costs more than the best wheat bread."

Likewise in France, dried fava beans carried a social stigma. In the *Dictionaire oeconomique*, Noel Chomel under the entry for poverty offers a fava bean recipe in which eight pints are dried in an oven and then milled for quick and easy use in soups. This cuts down the cooking time and fuel use. He comments that the same can be done with rice, "but this is not a food for the poor. It's too delicate and expensive." In a remarkable encyclopedic *Dictionnaire des plantes alimentaires* of 1803, Pierre-Joseph Buc'hoz describes how fresh young favas are eaten with aromatics. But older dried beans are only eaten "in some provinces and at sea"; "The people love best fèves de marais when they are biggest … they're cooked first in a bit of water, then browned lightly in butter, with salt and pepper and a pinch of savory, to lift up the flavor, because these are a bit bland." By distancing his own taste from common practice, he ultimately denigrates the bean, further commenting that during the revolution people used favas to make bread, but it was far too tough and astringent. These, at least, he does not completely disregard as he does vetches, which are only for the most robust of stomachs and peasants.

Not all writers in France expressed their disdain for beans though, and there might even be a lesson learned by growing them. There is a remarkable episode in Jean-Jacques Rousseau's *Emile*, a revolutionary educational tract, which features growing beans. Rousseau was in large part rejecting the effete and superficial culture of eighteenth-century France, which is why he proposes how to raise young Emile in a natural way, without being confined or ordered about. The young boy is let loose to run in the fields and discover nature and real human nature on his own rather than try to learn it from books. The particular lesson he hopes to impart to Emile in this episode is about the origin of property. Living in the country, he will know about labor in the fields, but Rousseau thinks doing it himself with his own hands will really help him understand, something most spoiled children it seems could not grasp.

Rousseau has his young student plant beans. He helps him with the harder work, but the beans themselves are put in the earth by Emile. After the earth is plowed, "He takes possession of it by planting a bean in it. And surely this possession is more sacred and more respectable than that taken of South America when Núñez Balboa in the name of the King of Spain planted his standard on the shore of the South Sea." Every day they water and tend the beans and Rousseau reminds him that "there is in this earth something of himself that he can claim against anyone whomsoever…" Then one day the beans are gone (according to Rousseau's plan) and they discover that the gardener has torn them out. He then learns that there had been melon seeds planted there before by the gardener, now ruined. In the end they come to an arrangement whereby Emile will be lent a little plot as long as he shares his produce with the gardener. The lesson is not only that labor makes something yours but that property is the right of the first occupant and that to live with others we must respect their rights, entering into a social contract of sorts. Conflict has been avoided and both walk away happy. The entire mode of living in a free society has been taught to Emile, no, rather experienced firsthand, through the act of growing beans.

Interestingly, and in direct contrast to the north, fava beans do remain steadfast in southern European cookbooks and culinary practices. They were still being extensively grown there as human food and of course the diet in general was more vegetable-based than in the more affluent north. But it also reflects the very different economy of the south. Here there was no comparable agricultural revolution. The majority of people subsisted on the same basic foods they had for centuries and with the exception of the very wealthy, most people still did survive on grains, legumes and minimal amounts of meat. Rather than large capital-intensive farms, there were still small peasant holdings, and the mezzadria or share-cropping system in Italy. The absence of a significantly large middle class hoping to distance themselves from the diet of their ancestors, mainly by eating more meat, seems to explain in part why favas are still featured prominently in culinary texts. Climate alone cannot account for this, because, as we have seen, they were grown in the north, just not for human consumption.

Two examples here should suffice: Juan de Altamiras' *Nuevo Arte de Cocina* consciously attempts to address the culinary interests of both rich and poor alike. Not surprisingly, there are several recipes for dried beans, which scarcely differ from those of several hundred years before. For example, his *Potage de Judias Secas* is seasoned with fried onions and garlic, pepper, saffron, mint, grated bread and a bit of cheese, and it would be good with a little rice as well, he adds. Apart from the fact that these might have been made with New World beans, the recipe is extremely conservative. Altamiras' readers did not have such a clear social stigma against beans because everyone was still eating them. It may also explain the survival, as opposed to revival, of traditional dishes like the fabada asturiana, similar to the above recipe though now considerably richer with chorizo and morcilla (blood sausages) and various other more expensive ingredients.

In Italy fava beans also remained a staple ingredient. Vincenzo Corrado's *Del cibo pittagorico* (Pythagorean Life – meaning vegetarian), rather ironically, offers a remarkable range of recipes. Though he does mention that in the Salento the *minuto populo* – or little people – make great use of favas; there is no stigma at all towards them. There are twelve recipes, including soups, fried favas, with cream, and in a "sauce of the rich," which directs to "fry the favas in oil, garlic, thyme, tarragon, salt and pepper and moisten with fish broth, and when they're cooked, serve with this rich sauce moistened with the same broth and lemon juice." The interest in maintaining Lenten fasts partially explains dishes such as these, but there is really no social stigma against eating them, precisely because there is not a large class of people forced to eat them, from which another (middling) class hopes to maintain a distinction. Corrado also offers bean fritters, in a frittata, and this recipe for fave alla bianca involves slowly cooking the beans, seasoning with salt oil and parsley, celery and bay leaf, and then mashing them into a fine cream and serving them on fried toast points. This dish can easily be found today in many Italian restaurants, what was originally called pan unto, or today fettunta or bruschetta.

Nineteenth-century sources are also revealing, especially since they directly address concerns of the poorer classes. In England in the early part of the century, the high prices of grain before the legislation of the Anti-Corn Law League led several cookbook authors to comment on the poor state of the common diet. Bell Plumptre's *Domestic Management* of 1810 is very interesting in this regard. Apart from mentioning that people should live according to their means and not try to imitate others, she complains that the "prevailing error in the diet of this country is the too great use of animal food" and attributes many diseases to it. Furthermore the artificial scarcity of corn (meaning grain) undermines "the health of society at large, and dwindle(s) it down to a race of invalid dwarfs." The English also ruin their vegetables by overcooking. "The English use vegetables with a cold distrust, as if they were natural enemies." And "From being little used at our tables, vegetables have been little noticed in our cookery books." Not surprisingly, it is here that many vegetable dishes appear, including the beans and bacon, which presumably had been eaten all along by lower classes. These are her directions:

> *When you dress beans and bacon, boil them separate, for the bacon will spoil the color of the beans. Always throw some salt in the water, and some parsley nicely picked. When the beans are enough, which you will know by their being tender, throw them in a cullender to drain. Take up the bacon, and skin it, throw some raspings of bread over the top; and if you have an iron, make it red hot, and hold it over to brown the top of the bacon; if you have not one, set it before the fire to brown. Lay the beans in a dish. And the bacon in the middle on the top, and send them to the table, with parsley and butter in a bason.*

The same attitude is struck later in the century by Charles Elmé Francatelli, renowned as a chef to the royal court, but he was also concerned enough to compose *A Plain Cookery Book for the Working Classes*. It presents simple straightforward instructions to help a poor family make ends meet. Although there is a brief recipe for broad beans, he specifically promotes white haricot beans, that is, the American variety, over favas, claiming that "In France haricot beans form a principal part in the staple articles of food for the working classes, and indeed for the entire population; it is much to be desired that some effectual means should be had recourse to for the purpose of introducing and encouraging the use of this most excellent vegetable among the people as a general article of their daily food, more especially in the winter season." They might even reduce dependence on the potato crop, which had just failed. At present he thinks they are only an expensive luxury, but could be imported in greater number and would "become cheap enough to come within the reach of the poorest." This is exactly what will happen later in the century, but it is equally fascinating that he does not suggest the favas might serve the same purpose.

Most interestingly, quietly through the course of the centuries, fava beans are replaced with New World species, even in traditional dishes which retain the name of fava, like the fabada asturiana. In others, like the cassoulet, the new beans at some unrecorded point in time become traditional, and the original dish is entirely forgotten. These will be discussed in subsequent chapters, but for the moment, favas do retain a significant place in modern cookery, especially when green and fresh as harbingers of spring. For some inexplicable reason fresh favas were rediscovered in the last decade or so and can be found in most grocery stores, farmers' markets and on the menus of even posh restaurants.

Dried favas have enjoyed a fleeting revival too, though nowhere near the enthusiasm afforded to heirloom *Phaseolus* varieties. As an English writer put it (W. Teignmouth Shore) fresh favas are lovely while young. "But alas, he quickly grows old, and as an 'old bean' is not so pleasant." They remain one of the few beans eaten only in traditional contexts, as in the festival of San Guiseppe. This is celebrated fervently by devout Sicilians and recalls a drought during which the populace prayed to Saint Joseph for succor. He answered their prayers by making sure the crop of fava beans was spared, thus saving the people. Because the festival is celebrated on March 19, it falls during Lent so no meats are served. Rather it features a special bread given away to the poor, vegetables, sweets and other treats like zeppole, a fried horn of light airy dough. But the star is a soup of fava beans, broad noodles and other vegetables sprinkled with breadcrumbs to recall the sawdust of St. Joseph's workshop. A stepped altar is also erected to hold offerings to the saint, which include all the aforementioned foods, and as it is celebrated by Sicilian-Americans, a huge variety of sweet pastries formed into various symbolic shapes, like carpenter's tools and such. Sicily has remained devoted to the fava bean, Pythagoras and favism notwithstanding. A fritedda is a traditional springtime dish of chopped and lightly boiled artichokes and fava beans dressed simply with olive oil, which can also be used as a sauce. There is also maccu, a crushed fava bean soup (*maccare* means to crush) made with wild fennel. Why are such dishes still eaten today, especially by expatriates? They are a way to remember one's roots and homeland, and especially to recall hardship in a life of relative affluence.

When you mention fava beans to modern Americans inevitably someone thinks of the scene from *Silence of the Lambs* in which Hannibal Lecter discusses how he ate the delivery boy – his liver in particular with fava beans and a "nice chee-aunt-ee." Actually in the original book it wasn't chianti, but an amarone, a much darker and richer wine that would go much better with liver, as this gourmet would know.

Lastly, fava beans have a single if totally obscure use in modern medicine. They are the primary source of L-DOPA, used to increase dopamine levels in Parkinson's patients, and thus they take central stage (indirectly) in Oliver Sacks' *Awakenings*, which recounts the drug's use for briefly curing neurological disorders.

5

Peas, Chickpeas and Pigeon Peas

It is a linguistic accident that we distinguish peas from other beans. They have a shared history, if not a common fate. Somehow the social stigma that has traditionally been attached to beans never quite stuck to peas, probably because they are often consumed fresh and green. But they can be dried. Dried peas have been especially important in colder climates, as in Scandinavia, or yellow split peas in Quebec. Another accident has led us to call *Cicer* chick "peas" as well as other peas like the *Cajanus* species or pigeon peas. These are all really beans, but their sweet delicate disposition and alluringly round form have set them apart as taxonomically above beans. Peas are the relative who did well, rose above her rank and now only visits the Bean family on occasion. The pea fancies herself a princess.

By another accident we have confounded the plurality of peas in English. Peases (from the Latin *Pisum*, and an older related form in Sanskrit) denotes many individuals and pease originally meant one single pea. She even managed to hide her identity by changing her name, and thus the word pea was born, posing as single. But if we look back into her ancestry, the pea was there at the dawn of agriculture, side by side with the lowly lentil in the complex of Fertile Crescent crops. Peas are also far more adaptable than one might imagine and they have the broadest range geographically and climactically than any other legume. That is, they have gotten around – from the subtropics to cold and arid climes.

We also owe an enormous debt of gratitude to the pea. The pea expresses its genes very consistently, and of all the crops Augustinian monk Gregor Mendel could have used in his groundbreaking work on genetics in the mid-nineteenth century, he chose to work with peas. Mendel's discovery of the laws of inheritance was not appreciated until the early twentieth century, but he is recognized as the father of genetics, peas serving as his subject.

As mentioned, peas were probably one of the earliest domesticated plants along with wheat and barley, archaeological remains of which date back as far as 8000 BCE. Its wild progenitor was probably the tall *humile* type distributed throughout the Levant, eastern Turkey, Syria and northern Iraq. A related shorter *elatius* type overlaps this distribution and spreads into the Balkans. There is also a distinct wild species of *Pisum fulvum* which has yellow-brownish flowers. But all the cultivated varieties used today are *Pisum sativum*. This domesticated pea spread rapidly, reaching Western Europe by 4000 BCE and thereafter south to Egypt, north into the Caucasus and Eastern Europe and east eventually reaching India by about 2000 BCE.

In the ancient world peas were usually dried for storage like other beans since the edible fresh whole pods now known as snap peas, mange-tout and snow peas were much later developments. Even eating fresh green peas or "garden peas" is fairly novel, them having been specifically bred in sixteenth- and seventeenth-century Europe. They enjoyed a vogue among elite gardeners and at the court of Louis XIV, but only after this transformation from a lowly legume to a sweet seasonal green vegetable. For most of the pea's history it was dried "white" or yellow, whole or split, and most commonly cooked until it disintegrates into a smooth soup. Dried peas are quite difficult to cook without disintegrating, and this is probably another reason for their culinary distinction from beans.

Pea soup was the standard way to serve peas in the ancient world. The Greeks made their *pisinon etnos* or *konkhos*, which was considered pretty lowly fare. In Aristophanes' comedy *The Knights*, in which a sausage seller is set up as leader of Athens, he serves this very soup: "This is pea-soup, as exquisite as it is fine; Pallas the victorious goddess at Pylos is the one who crushed the peas herself." The humor here is that like lentil soup, pea soup was considered simple and inelegant, not something a goddess would concern herself with. In this same vein the now lost satire by Timon (as recorded by Athenaeus) mentions the soup "conch." Here it is preferred to the fine barley cake of Teos and spiced gravy of the Lydians, rather "in the vulgar and squalid conch my Greek poverty finds all its over-flowing luxury." This was funny to the Greeks because no one in their right mind could prefer pea soup to fine dainties.

The Romans also made a kind of puls or porridge from peas. Like other legumes, peas also lent their name to a Roman family, the powerful Piso clan. Julius Caesar's wife Calpurnia was a Piso and her father Lucius Calpurnius Piso Caesoninus, known for his epicurean tastes, quarreled with that other bean-named statesman Cicero, who perhaps had the last word by accusing him of extortion and corrupt administration of Macedonia in the orations *De provinciis consularibus* and *In Pisonem*.

Apicius as usual takes the homely pea and seasons it with a variety of gastro-nomic enticements, no doubt making it much more appealing to his audience. He has a recipe for the concicla (conch) mentioned above, though laden with slices of sausages, meatballs and pork shoulder as well as the usual medley of Roman herbs and spices: pepper, lovage, oregano, dill, dried onion and coriander leaves, plus some garum and wine. Another version named for Commodus includes eggs and is baked so it sets solid. With this elegant treatment, peas can no longer be considered such a common dish.

The same can be said of medieval pea soup recipes: they are adorned with expensive ingredients. In common households, if the rhyme is to be believed, a huge pot with little more than peas would be left in the hearth indefinitely or at least nine days, being reheated at every meal. "Peas porridge hot, peas porridge cold, peas porridge in the pot, nine days old." Peas were also sold fresh and cooked in the pod, the peas inside being scraped out between the teeth. The *Ménagier de Paris* has a recipe for these called *pois en cosse*. But cookbooks of the era, intended for noble households, embellish dried "white" peas into various complex creations, adding almond milk, spices and other ingredients. Pea broth or puree was even used in place of meat broth for Lent in various extravagant recipes. Chiquart d'Amiczo cooking for the House of Savoy in the fifteenth century describes how this puree should be prepared in quantity for use in a variety of fish dishes for Lenten banquets. *The Forme of Cury* of the previous century gives a good idea of a typical medieval pea dish. Judging from the title, it originated in Germany.

Pesoun of Almayne

Take white pesoun; waisshe hem. Seep hem a grete while. Take hem up and cole hem thurgh a cloth; waisshe hem in colde water till the hulles go off. Cast hem in a pot and couere hem pat no breth go out, and boile hem right wel, and cast perinne gode mylke of almaundes and a pertye of flour of rys wip powdour ginger, safroun, & salt.

Pea soups like these, though without the medieval flavorings and often abetted with smoked pork in some form since they were no longer designed for Lent after the Reformation, have survived especially in Scandinavia. There is still ärtsoppa in Sweden, gule aerter in Denmark, Finnish hernekeitto, Dutch erwtensoep. Pea soup had been such a common food and so beloved and trusted that it is said Eric XIV, deposed and imprisoned king of Sweden, was poisoned by his brother John in 1577 with a bowl of arsenic-laced pea soup. The recipes survive to this day and are eaten avidly by Americans of Scandinavian descent, dried whole peas now being available only through specialty suppliers.

Pea soup is found in one form or another in most early modern cookbooks. The affection for peas among the English (even when "mushy") is revealed in a startling episode in *Robinson Crusoe* when the hero finds a stash of gold and silver, useless of course on a deserted island, and for which "I would have given it all for sixpenny-worth of turnip and carrot seed out of England, or for a handful of pease and beans and a botle of ink." E. Smith's recipe for Peas Pottage in *The Compleat Housewife,* written just a little later than Defoe, is complicated but still quite homey and gives a good sense of eighteenth-century taste preferences, just the sort of dish Crusoe would have dreamed about. Colewarts means cabbage, as in our term coleslaw. The forc'd meat is merely chopped meat, formed into tiny meatballs.

> *Take a quart of white peas, a piece of neck-beef, and four quarts of fair water; boil them till they are all to pieces, and strain them thro' a colander; then take a handful or two of spinach, a top or two of young colewarts, and a very small leek; shred the herbs a little, and put them into a frying-pan, or stew-pan, with three quarters of a pound of fresh butter, but the butter must be very hot before you put in your herbs; let them fry a little while, then put in your liquor, and two or three anchovies, some salt and pepper to your taste, a sprig of mint rubb'd in small, and let it all boil together till you think it is thick enough; then have in readiness some forc'd meat, and make three or fourscore balls, about the bigness of large peas, fry them brown, and put them in the dish you serve it in, and fry some thin slices of bacon, put some in the dish, and some on the rim of the dish, with scalded spinach: fry some toasts after the balls are brown and hard, and break them into the dish; then pour your pottage over all, and serve to the table.*

Yet another way of cooking peas, along with other foods while keeping them separate, was to place them in a cloth bag set in a pot of boiling water. The result is a kind of pea pudding, which is served beside the contents of other bags. This was also the way groups of sailors could keep their food separate from others. On the HMS *Victory*, Nelson's flagship at the Battle of Trafalgar, each bag of peas was labeled with a wooden marker designating which group it belonged to. Related to this is a curious pea sausage invented by the Germans in the Franco-Prussian War. It apparently consisted of pea and lentil flour cooked, evaporated, mixed with bacon and seasonings. It could then be carried and quickly mixed with hot water to make a kind of instant soup. Here is Dr. Kitchiner's Pease-Pudding Recipe as recorded by Erroll Sherson, using the bag technique. The author says the only difference with those prepared in the British Navy is that the peas aren't sieved and despite this "it seems to be a favorite dish with sailors, and is a useful addition to the salted meats which, naturally, form a considerable part of the Navy's victuals."

> *Put a quart of split peas into a clean cloth; do not tie them up too closely, but leave room for them to swell. Put them on to boil in cold water slowly till they are tender. If they are good pease they will be boiled enough in about two hours and a half. Rub them through a sieve into a deep dish and add an egg or two, an ounce of butter, and some pepper and salt. Beat them well together for about ten minutes, when these ingredients should be well incorporated; then flour the cloth well, put the pudding in again, tie up as tight as possible, and boil for another hour. If eaten with boiled pork or beef, it is much improved by being cooked with the meat.*

One particularly scrappy little black pea from northern England deserves mention, the Carlin pea. It is actually a field pea rather than garden pea, and thus smaller, darker and tougher than green peas. They are also better for transport, which may be why Martin Frobisher buried them in caches in Baffin Island in the 1570s on his search for the Northwest Passage. There are many stories about their origin – they saved shipwrecked sailors on the holiday Carlin Sunday, a Dutch cargo (or maybe French) of Carlin peas rescued besieged Newcastle from the Scots during the English Civil Wars. Others trace their origins in the pagan past as a commemoration of the dead, later co-opted by the Catholic Church for their own festivities. Wherever the custom originated, they were indeed eaten on this Sunday in Lent before Easter. William Turner in his *Herbal* of 1562 says they were eaten in Northumberland in a napkin, like chestnuts, "being in taste not exceedingly unlike them." They are also sometimes called maple peas, though this may have been something quite different originally.

Peas were also at the center of one of the major technological revolutions of modern food supply. Apart from drying, there are not many ways to preserve delicate green peas. In the 1830s (according to *The Cook Not Mad*) peas could be preserved until Christmas if kept in a jar covered with mutton fat, covered with a bladder and stored in a cool place. But it wasn't until freezing that fresh peas defied the seasons. Concocting a wonderful story of how he learned to freeze

foods from Eskimos during his sojourn in Labrador, in the 1920s Clarence
Birdseye developed a way to quick freeze vegetables in a new container that
would keep them fresh. Although the idea did not catch on immediately, and
he sold the company, peas were his real success story. They are among the few
vegetables that hold up beautifully to freezing, and the Birds Eye label can still
be found in any US grocery store. Thus green peas escaped seasonality, before
so many other foods that followed in their wake.

Canned peas were an older invention, and arguably something passable can
be prepared at home in glass jars. The logic of peas in tin or aluminum cans
must elude any sane person, the fondness for "mushy peas" as a traditional/
industrial food in Britain notwithstanding. All these developments have meant
that we have almost completely forgotten that peas are a member of the bean
family – dried they only appear in the odd pea soup, which is mostly found
today canned or spewing out of the twisted demonically possessed mouths of
little children in horror flicks.

Chickpeas

Like peas, chickpeas through history largely escaped the ignominy of beans.
Though of course, they are hardly a pea at all. They are properly a bean, and the
Spanish name garbanzo bean is beginning to predominate in the US, where one
can find them sold (often by the same company) under both names. Remarkably,
the word garbanzo is unrelated to any Latin or Greek root, and seems to be of
indigenous origin. Nor is it borrowed from Arabic as so many Spanish food
words were. Garbanzo is really a rather robust and dashing name, befitting this
sturdy bean, and it is treated with much more respect in places where it is not
known by the silly and diminutive name chickpea.

The origin of chickpeas is once again in the Fertile Crescent and it is not
surprising that they still feature prominently in all the cuisines of Southwestern
Asia. In Arabic they are called hummus, also a stalwart name. We use the term
haphazardly for the dip which should be called hummus with tahini (sesame

paste). There are some forty species in the genus, five of which exist wild in this area. Only *Cicer arietinum* was domesticated though. Once again in Turkey and Syria the oldest carbonized chickpeas have been found, about 10,000 years old, but these are small and may have been gathered wild. Larger seeded, domesticated samples are found in Bronze Age sites in Israel and Jordan. They made their way to Greece by 6000 BCE and France a few thousand years later, and, like the other beans, eventually to Africa and India. They do not like cool weather at all, which is why they were fairly unknown in northern Europe. There are two distinct types of chickpea – the large smooth-skinned variety common in the Mediterranean called Kabuli and smaller darker chickpeas more common in India and thereabouts called Desi, the latter probably genetically closer to its wild ancestor. The latter can be bought in Indian shops and are called kala chana and look like tiny brown-skinned chickpeas. The chickpea also comes in every color, like other beans – red and, perhaps the most interesting of all, jet black.

In the classical world chickpeas were used mostly as an after-dinner snack, or tragemata, to be eaten with drinks or during a symposium. In fact in Plato's *Republic*, when asked what people will eat in his ideal city Socrates replies naturally wheat and barley; they couldn't do without wine, or olives and cheese. Nor does he omit these snacks – figs, chickpeas and beans. He doesn't want them to be miserable, but nor would he deny them the basic simple pleasures in life, as long as they don't over-indulge. In your typical symposium, not like Plato's where they do little but philosophize, but like Xenophon's where there are naked flute girls and heavy drinking, men would play a game called kottabos. It's the equivalent of modern-day quarters. Wine from a flat drinking vessel called a kylix would be flung at a target on the wall. Men would make crude jokes, argue about the latest Olympic games, and satisfy their appetites with the ancient equivalent of junk food – chickpeas. Some things never change.

The Greeks did not necessarily think of these as unhealthy though, quite the opposite. Galen thought they cause less flatulence than other beans and are more nutritious. He even described a few ways he had seen them prepared: not in town, but in the country they make soup from chickpeas, or chickpea flour cooked in milk. Others eat them whole, salted, or sprinkle on top a kind of dried cheese which resembles flour. They can be eaten fresh, unripe and green, or can be roasted, which makes them less flatulent, but harder to digest. His strangest pronouncement though is that "it has been believed to stimulate sexual urge at the same time as being generative of semen." This opinion was repeated by nearly every dietary writer for the next two millennia. The poet Eobanus Hessus a millennium and a half later penned this verse:

> *Exhaustis reparant genitalia semina membris,*
> *Nec Venerem vires deservisse sinunt*

> They restore the exhausted genital member with semen
> Nor do they permit men disservice to Venus

This may be why Pliny called the white round and smooth columbine chickpea the "pea of Venus." He also claimed that another variety resembles a ram's head, an idea expressed earlier in Theophrastus, but here accounting for the species name *arietinum* in Latin. Apparently they have two little curved projections which resemble horns. Though, it is also an article of fakelore that the word chickpea derives from the resemblance of the peeled seed to a little chicken's head – something which is easy to notice if you are looking for it – or drunk at a symposium. Chickpea is just a corruption of the Italian *ceci*. The Romans did to some extent look down on chickpeas as food of the poor, as with other beans. There was a saying "*fricti ciceris emptor*" – a buyer of roasted chickpeas, which meant a poor person.

Chickpeas appear in medieval cookbooks, naturally only in Italy and Spain where they grew. Although it would have been difficult to distinguish purely Christian Spanish dishes from Muslim and Jewish ones since these three cultures shared ingredients and recipes for centuries and the only real difference was that Christians used pork, there was one dish firmly associated with the Jews. A relative of the hamin made with fava beans, adafina, a slow-cooked stew of chickpeas served on the Sabbath and cooked the day before was a signature dish for observant Jews. There would have been no problem eating this dish until the Jews were formally expelled in 1492 and anyone remaining was forced to convert. The Spanish Inquisition, a branch of the older Roman Inquisition, though in Spain controlled by the state, was designed principally to root out crypto-Jewish practices among the *conversos* or "new Christians." The Inquisition previously had no authority over Jews, but now it was technically illegal to practice openly or in private. They thus sought to find ways to uncover the less than wholly converted ex-Jews. One simple means of discovery was a person's refusal to eat pork, or lighting candles on Friday night, but so too was an attachment to this adafina dish, or even for some reason serving chickpeas in any form. As recounted in David M. Gitliz and Linda Kay Davidson's *A Drizzle of Honey*, seeing someone serve adafina could be presented as evidence in an Inquisitorial court.

Although no Jewish recipes for adafina survive, a very similar stew, *cocido madrileño*, is served in Spain today, perhaps by people of Jewish ancestry. It seems that we can get a reasonable idea of what this dish was like by looking at the closest contemporary cookbook written a century after the expulsion but which perhaps reflects the customs of those who stayed behind. This is Domingo Hernàndez de Maceras' recipe for olla podrida, which means "rotten pot," probably so called for having been cooked so long. It is cognate with the word pot-pourris, meaning a hodge-podge, and similar recipes show up throughout Europe in the seventeenth century. It is also mentioned in Don Quixote. Just imagine that the pork and hare are replaced with kosher ingredients.

How to Make an Olla Podrida

To make an olla podrida, you must take meat: beef, salt pork, pig's feet, head, sausages, tongues, pigeon, wild duck, hare, beef tongue, garbanzos, garlic and turnips in season, and the meat of whatever you want; mix everything in a pot; and it must be cooked a long time: take your spices; and when it's well cooked, make plates of this, with grape must mustard, or another kind, and on top of each plate sprinkle parsley, so it will look good, and be very good.

One very interesting battle has been waging over chickpeas lately, specifically over the dish falafel. The Israelis have claimed it as a national dish since it is so popular and sold everywhere on street corners. A popular Israeli song written in the 1950s "And We Have Falafel" claimed that whereas new Jewish immigrants used to kiss the ground, now the first thing they do after getting off the plane is eat falafel. Palestinians claim that like the land itself, this dish was "stolen" and since it was used in the region for centuries it rightly belongs to Arab culture. The origins of the dish are of course unknown, but one could probably trace an ancestor back to an earlier cuisine, most likely to Egypt where a similar dish is made with fava beans (ta' amiyya). That any one people could own falafel is of course a ridiculous notion, but it nonetheless illustrates a very common tendency – to associate a people with a particular food and then claim it as an integral part of national identity. It were as if the US could claim frankfurters and hamburgers as quintessentially American, almost oblivious of the origin of their names, let alone even earlier examples of similar foods. This is not to downplay the seriousness of the conflict between these people; it is just fascinating that it is expressed in terms of food.

Throughout the Eastern Mediterranean distant relatives of fried chickpea balls can also be found. Chickpeas are commonly ground into flour and made into various flat cakes. Near the beach in Nice one can find peppery pancakes called socca and crunchy chickpea fries called panisses (from which Alice Water's famed Chez Panisse apparently gets its name). Socca is sometimes cooked on a griddle like a crepe, but it can also be baked in an oven, making it crisper. In Genoa a thicker and decidedly crunchier version is called farinata. Similar snacks can be found up and down the entire coast.

Panisses

Boil a pot of lightly salted water. Carefully shake in a bag of chickpea flour while stirring all the time to prevent lumps. Simmer slowly, all the time stirring, until the mixture becomes very thick which can take as long as 40 minutes or longer. Add some butter and if you like parmigiano and a lot of pepper. Thus far, this is made exactly like polenta. Pour this hot porridge

out onto a wooden board, straightening the edges into an even square. Let
this cool and solidify completely for at least a few hours. Next heat a deep
pot with vegetable oil. Slice the cold porridge into French fry shapes and fry
a few at a time in the oil until sublimely crispy. Drain on paper towels and
season to taste with Camargue sea salt. (If these ever caught on in the U.S.
they would give French Fried potatoes a good run for their money.)

Cajanus or Pigeon Peas

Among the lesser-known of so-called peas is *Cajanus cajan*, the pigeon pea,
Congo or gunga pea. Gandules, as they are known in the Caribbean, are born
of the blazing tropical sun. The voluptuous curves of each pea fairly bulge from
a small and sultry pod lined with dark purplish borders. Intense in flavor and
personality, they accompany a remarkable range of dishes from places across
the globe: Puerto Rico, Kenya, Malaysia. They can be found in Southeast Asian
shops, in farmers' markets fresh and in Latino groceries dried or canned. They
look something like peas, but gastronomically they make no effort to hide
their relation to the bean family. They probably originated in India, where they
are split, thereafter called toor dhal, and cooked down with spices until they
disintegrate, much like other dhals: chickpeas (channa dhal) and *Vigna mungo*
(urad dhal). To this day the majority are grown in India. From there they spread
basically to every dry tropical region where peas do not grow well. Thus in East
Africa they found a welcome home, though some speculate that they originated
here. They are also a favorite in the Dominican Republic where they arrived
with the slave trade.

The signature Latin dish is arroz con gandules, which usually calls for canned
beans and a "Spanish" flavoring packet, both concessions to modern convenience
and the marketing skills of manufacturers serving this community. But the pure
flavor shines through best using dried beans, fresh seasonings and a homemade
soffrito of onions, garlic, peppers and cilantro. This is my own recipe:

Arroz con Gandules

Boil the gandules verdes in a copious pot of unsalted water for about an hour, or until tender, without previously soaking. Drain beans and set aside, reserving about ½ cup of the cooking liquid. Then fry the ingredients for the soffrito, starting with chopped onion and proceeding slowly with garlic, green or red bell pepper and finally chopped tomatoes. Cook slowly until browned and intense. Push the soffrito to the side of the pan and add slices of chorizo and spices such as cumin, cayenne and pepper and let these brown too. Next add the rice, stir for a few moments to let the rice absorb the flavors. Add the gandules and the cooking liquid, 2 cups of water or chicken broth and a smidgen of achiote (also called annatto – found in Latino markets), just enough to color the dish yellow, and bring to a boil. Cover tightly and simmer on low heat for about 20 minutes.

There are similar recipes in Kenya and Uganda; among the Swahili they are cooked with coconut milk and spices originally imported from India.

All three "peas" mentioned here maintain a certain distance from beans, not biologically, but conceptually. Somehow their size and roundness makes us think they are something quite different from lowly beans. This and the fact that green peas occupy a completely different culinary niche, accounts for their steady popularity around the world and for why they have rarely been stigmatized as food of the poor.

6

Oddballs and Villains

Every family has its black sheep oddballs and criminal types. Beans are no different. They seem odd only by comparison to the respectable members of the Fabaceae family, and many have found very happy homes throughout the world. Some of these are real degenerates though, surviving on the very margins of the human food supply, mostly as famine foods. This is for good reason, as many of these species are toxic. Although in no way related to each other, these beans will be gathered together, mostly because few readers are likely to be acquainted with them. This rogues' gallery will include *Lathyrus* and *Lablab*, the Vetch clan, as well as the more obscure *Canavalia*, *Mucuna* and *Macrotyloma*, and the beautifully seductive *Psophocarpus tetragonolobus*, who takes the prize for the most outrageous bean nomenclature.

Lathyrus is known in English as the chickling vetch or grass pea and can be bought in very specialized Italian grocery stores as cicerchia, which fascinatingly enough have been revived in Slow Food circles as a traditional Umbrian food in danger of disappearance. They look something like chickpeas, but smaller and more recalcitrant. Oh, and poisonous. The country which grows them the most is India, where they are called khesari, and are there recognized as food of the poor. Since this tough little bean can withstand the severest of droughts, it is depended on in times of famine. This is when Lathyrus' true colors come out.

If surviving on a diet of these beans and not much else, a human, mostly young men for some reason, will develop the degenerative disease lathyrism. It begins as the neurotoxin causes degeneration of the spinal chord and lower limbs, leading to short difficult steps. These conditions are irreversible. In severe cases, it ends with convulsions, paralysis and sometimes death. In some states of India cultivation has been outlawed. Eating the beans now and then poses no danger, only excessive consumption every day for several months. Thorough soaking and cooking also purportedly leaches out most of the neurotoxin, discovered only in 1964, called OPAP or β-N-oxalyl L-α, β-diaminopropionic acid. It is still not entirely understood how the disease develops and strangely 95 percent of people who eat lathyrus are unaffected. Nonetheless, epidemics have occurred as recently as early 2000 during a famine in Ethiopia.

The ban on lathyrus, although ostensibly in the public interest, has had negative consequences. Since only the poorest of poor eat it when all other crops fail, bans may have little impact. Apparently they were banned in Europe in the late seventeenth and early eighteenth century, and then hundreds of years later during the Second World War people were found eating them in large quantities. Furthermore, when banned, research on improving the species tends to be neglected. There are some very ardent scientists in Western Australia who just developed a non-toxic variety called Ceora, though it is intended for cattle, not humans. Nostalgic Umbrians and impoverished Indians aside, lathyrus remains a hardened criminal. The close relative of these beans *Lathyrus odoratus* was smart enough to disguise herself in flouncy colorful petals and heavy perfume and can be found in many a garden. She is best known as the "sweet pea" but she's quite toxic too.

Lablab purpureus, hyacinth bean or bonavist, formerly classified as *Dolichos lablab* (one must be cautious with changes of identity and numerous aliases) is poisonous if eaten raw; the seeds contain prussic acid and cyanide. That is not to say with some stern correction in the form of a good cooking, they can't be used as food. In fact, they have been for centuries. They are native to Africa, but today are grown in many diverse places. The easiest place to buy them is in Chinese groceries; in China the pods are called pig ears, which they do resemble. The beans are large and have an attractive and unmistakable elliptical shape with a long white scar or belly-button along the side like an American football with its laces. The plant is a trailing perennial vine, mostly grown as an ornamental and has radiant purple flowers and pod, hence the name *purpureus*. They cook up exactly like any other bean, and retain their shape and firm meaty texture.

Under the name dolichos they were widely discussed in the ancient world. Hippocrates includes them among the beans that pass easily, cause less flatulence and are nourishing. Diocles, another dietary writer, claimed that "dolichoi are just as nourishing as peas, are similarly non flatulent, but are not so pleasant and pass less easily." Exactly what plant these texts refer to is not entirely clear, nor was it to Galen writing several centuries later. He remarks that it may be the bean commonly staked and grown for its pods called loboi, though some call it phaseoloi, not to be confused with phaselos, the black-eyed pea. Nonetheless, when he was writing in Imperial Rome, the beans dolichoi were grown like any other bean and Galen's own father grew and dried them for storage.

Centuries later this confusion persisted, especially when New World beans arrived and were given the name *Phaseolus* under the assumption that they were virtually identical to dolichos and beans now classified in the *Vigna* genus. It is only in the past few decades that botanists have separated these beans, reserving the ancient Greek word *Phaseolus* exclusively for New World types. This explains how under the heading of dolichus a seventeenth-century writer, Melchior Sebizius, could claim that varieties come from America, Africa, Egypt, India, etc. and that "our cooks" prepare the green pods by removing the string, chopping, boiling, straining and then serving with butter, vinegar, broth, pepper, salt, savory and leek. "This dish is most tasty and pleasing to the palate, and appears even on noble tables: so much so that for the most sumptuous and magnificent banquets piles quite avidly are prepared." Yet, we have no idea if he is referring to modern string beans or the Old World lablab, or even some other bean. In either case it is clear that green beans were an entirely different dish conceptually than dried and reconstituted beans, which were reserved for the common masses. What is equally interesting is how these beans were eventually replaced in the West by the newly arrived species, to such an extent that they are virtually unknown as food in Europe and the US.

The vetches, represented by dozens of species, are in the same *Vicia* genus as fava beans. They are nonetheless almost universally reviled as a human food – but have been used as such all the same. They appear spontaneously in wheat fields as weeds, stealthily invading gardens. *Vicia sativa* or tare in English, as well as its lowlife relatives, the hairy vetch and bitter vetch, have really only been consciously cultivated as animal fodder. Horses have stomachs that can digest them, unless they eat too many, but monogastric animals like rats and poultry eventually die if fed vetches. One percent of the vetch is composed of the toxin gamma-glutamyl-beta-cyanoalanine, which affects the metabolism of sulfur amino acids. Despite this, for humans, they have been the most universally recognized emergency food in Europe in times of famine.

Vetches were consumed in pre-historic times and are found in Neolithic sites in Turkey and the Balkans but there is no indication of how they were used since by historic times people generally found them unpalatable and only suitable for animals. Galen had this to say: "With ourselves and many other countries, cattle eat bitter vetch which has first been sweetened with water, but people absolutely avoid this seed; for it is distasteful and produces unhealthy humor. But sometimes in a severe famine, as Hippocrates wrote, from force of necessity they come to it." Hippocrates claimed that they cause pains in the knees and Dioscorides that they cause bloody urine. Yet in the *Regimen*, presumably a different Hippocratic author wrote that bitter vetches "are binding, strengthening, fattening, filling, and give a person a good color." This is at least evidence that people did eat them.

In medieval and early modern times, vetches continued to be grown for cattle, or could be gathered wild in times of famine. The monastic community of St. Bernard is said to have eaten bread made of vetches during the famine of 1135. The herbalist John Gerard tells a story about yellow vetches during a famine in 1555 wherein

> the poore people at that time there being a great dearth, were miraculously helped ... in Suffolk at a place by the sea side all of hard stone and pebble ... where nether grew grasse, nor any earth was ever seene; it chanced in this barren place suddenly to spring up without any tillage or sowing, great abundance of Peason, whereof the poore gathered (as men judged) above an hundred quarters.

Gerard notes that they had probably been growing there all the time, and were only noticed because people were starving. Vetches also found a place in folk medicine, and it was reported that women would steep the seeds in wine or milk and make a decoction thought to increase milk production.

Vetches in the modern era were used solely for fodder though. In the nineteenth century *The Rural Encyclopedia* of J.M. Wilson points out the importance of vetches as animal food. "In Gloucestershire and Worcestershire, they sow tares as pasturage for horses, and cut them early enough to allow turnips to be sown the same season. In Sussex tares are of such infinite importance that not one-tenth of the stock could be maintained without them: horses, cows, sheep, hogs, all feed on them."

The vetch, particularly the modern cultivar called blanche fleur, greatly resembles red lentils when hulled and split. Some unscrupulous Australian exporters even managed to sell them to India as such which caused an enormous row in the early 1990s when a scientist Max Tate pointed out the potential dangers. At the same time an Egyptian importer sued a US company for selling what they called "slow cooking" lentils, and this is really the only way to distinguish between the two. A lentil takes maybe fifteen minutes to cook, a vetch a good hour. All this led to a widespread ban on cultivation and exportation of vetches, though scientists have been developing varieties with low toxicity, mostly for use as animal feed.

The jack bean is another criminal type whose Latin name is *Canavalia ensiformis* – or sword shaped. We might call it Jack the blade, as its monstrous pods do curve like lethal scimitars. It is native to the Americas. Like the rogue beans, they're toxic: canatoxin and various others make them very dangerous if eaten raw. This is of course a protection for the plant, which keeps away predators and warns them with the first bite through a bitter unpleasant flavor. Leave it to human ingenuity to find a way around this. Prolonged soaking and boiling can leach out the toxicity. In Indonesia they also leave them in running water for several days, then ferment them, then cook them again. With such attention, nearly anything can be made edible. Not that toxicity should keep us from processing such foods; as we will see soy too might easily have been classed among this rabble were it not for the invention of ingenious ways to process it. Kidney beans also contain toxins if eaten raw. But people are occasionally poisoned by Jack, especially since the young tender pods are commonly eaten as a vegetable in Central America.

We shall not even dare to dwell on the most heinous of poisonous criminals, the Calabar bean (*Physostigma venenosum*) from West Africa, which is never used as food, but rather as an "ordeal bean" given to those suspected of witchcraft. Only the rare few who survive its lethal poison are exonerated. It is also said that people "duel" with these beans, chomping one and seeing who survives, a kind of all-natural Russian roulette.

Indigenous to India, and also highly drought resistant and extremely nutritious is the velvet bean, cowhage, formerly called *Stizolobium*, and now *Mucuna*. It is difficult to decide if this bean is a smooth talking swindler in fancy togs or a real lifesaver. The toxin it contains is L-DOPA, making up from 6 to 9 percent of the bare seed, more than is found in fava beans. As a therapeutic drug for Parkinson's disease, it has done wonders, though its lasting effects remain a matter of controversy. For others it causes nausea, and in quantity a range of neurological symptoms such as muscle spasms, irregular heartbeat and hyperactivity, and with continued use it may cause psychosis. Reportedly there was such an outbreak of mass psychosis in Mozambique attributed to the bean. With thorough cooking the drug deteriorates. *Mucuna pruriens'* Latin name may be thought to suggest its predilection, but actually means itchy.

Nonetheless, one can easily find it being sold in capsules as a sex enhancer. It has actually been used as such in Ayurvedic medicine for centuries. Recent studies have investigated its use in stimulating growth hormones and muscle-building, another reason for its popularity as an alternative drug. It is also claimed to increase testosterone levels. One person's poison is another person's drug, and yet another's food. As food it is found in Africa, where it is always boiled twice and the water discarded, and among the Ketchi in Guatemala and in Honduras, where it is eaten as a green vegetable, having been introduced to the area by the United Fruit Company as fodder for mules transporting bananas. In South America the beans are also roasted and used as a coffee substitute called nutria café or simply nescafé.

The horse gram is yet another of the Southeast Asian legumes living on the margins, both socially and literally in the worst of soils. It is reputedly the cheapest of all legumes among hundreds in India, and thus is particularly associated with poverty. *Macrotyloma uniflorum* or Madras gram also contains toxins which are destroyed by being first parched and then boiled or fried. In Myanmar they make a kind of soy sauce from it. It is not exactly toxic, but neither is it very good for you; it contains a large amount of oxalic acid, which binds with calcium and iron, making them unavailable for absorption. In Andhra Pradesh it is used to make a traditional dish called vulava charu, which is a kind of smooth bean puree eaten in cold weather, flavored with tamarind, onion, chili, mustard seeds, cumin and coriander. It is served over rice.

Among the beans, although we rarely think of them as such, are a number of tricksters and experts in the arts of disguise. They have all carefully hidden their ancestry by convincing us to consume them in decidedly unbean-like ways. The most notorious of these is *Arachis hypogaea*, which made its way from South America to Africa and from there to the US South where they constitute a major industrial crop. Though a bean, this maleficent legume hides his identity by burying his head in the ground and by appearing in jars roasted or pulverized into a fine paste. Of course, the peanut is merely masquerading as a nut in the modern world, but when eaten fresh or boiled they are decidedly leguminous.

Like their distant cousin soy, peanuts have also found a niche in modern food industries for their high quality oil. A lesser-known African relative, the bambara groundnut, jugo bean or *Vigna subterranea* has similar habits, but is consumed often as a bean, boiled fresh in the pod, or dried and ground into flour. There is also another groundnut, the Hausa or Kersting groundnut, related to the *Macrotyloma* (horse gram) mentioned above. Both of these are still cultivated but have largely been displaced by the peanut.

The tamarind is another bean in disguise, this time as a fruit. Actually it is the pulp that is eaten in this case, rather than the seeds, although they too can be eaten as an emergency food, roasted and boiled or ground into flour. Its botanical name *Tamarindus indica* is a complete misnomer, as the tree is native to tropical Africa, but it seems that when it arrived in Europe in ancient times they thought it came from India, and hence the redundant name "Indian date of India." The flavorful sweet and sour pulp is eaten fresh as a fruit, or it is dried and processed into blocks and then incorporated into a wide variety of vegetable, fish and meat dishes throughout the tropics, as well as candy. The fresh immature pods are cooked in India, and when grown but still unripe they are roasted in the Bahamas and called "swells." In Mexico and elsewhere it is made into a refreshing drink and tamarind is one of the signature flavors in Worcestershire sauce.

Ceratonia siliqua – carob or St. John's bread – is also a bean disguised as a flavoring. This tree bears a dark leathery pod with a rich flavor not unlike chocolate, for which it is often used as a substitute. It is normally this mature pod that is processed and eaten rather than the seeds, but these are apparently of such uniform size and weight that they were in ancient times used as a unit of measurement, or a keration – the word from which we get our word carat referring to diamond, equaling 200 milligrams. Carats are not to be confused with karats, which refers to the purity of gold, or of course with carrots. The bean is also called locust bean, once thought to be the "locusts" which St. John ate in the desert. From it a gum is extracted that is used widely in food technology as a thickener and to prevent crystallization in ice cream and "weeping" in pastry creams. It is also one of the foods traditionally eaten in the Jewish holiday of Tu Bishvat, and was also used in mummification in ancient Egypt. It deserves to be much better known, especially since the trees are marvelously productive. The beautiful tree across the street from my office must produce a good ton of pods every year.

The Mexican jicama, oddly enough, is also a bean. Although we normally eat the crunchy swollen tuber, raw or cooked, *Pachyrhizus erosus*, or yam bean, can also be consumed as a fresh string bean, as it is in Southeast Asia where it was introduced by the Spanish in the sixteenth century. The plant also has relatives in the Andes and the Amazon. When ripe, however, the beans contain rotenone, a nasty insecticide which is quite toxic to humans, despite the fact that it is considered a "natural" and "organic" substance. The bean developed the poison specifically to fend off predators, but little did it suspect that we would attack its roots.

Another legume who yields us its roots, not crunchy and refreshing like jicama, but intense, sweet and quasi-medicinal is *Glycyrrhiza glabra* or licorice – familiar to candy enthusiasts. Native to the Mediterranean and Asia, it has been used for centuries in medicinal concoctions, but in great doses it too can be dangerous, and recent studies have found that it lowers sperm count. In any case, its pods and beans are never consumed.

One would never think of fenugreek as a bean, but it is precisely the tiny beans dried and ground which make up this eastern spice. Its botanical nomenclature *Trigonella foenum-graecum* means little triangle, referring to the flowers, of Greek hay. It was used in ancient times as cattle fodder but the seeds were also used as medicine among the Greeks and Egyptians and it was an ingredient in the embalming of mummies. The dusky beige spice has an alluring odor reminiscent of maple syrup and indeed is used in making artificial table syrup.

After the disguised beans there are a great number which are merely not well known outside their native habitats. Many remain uncultivated, others are large trees; some are likewise toxic, which explains why few outsiders have found interest in them. Nonetheless, they deserve a place in the bean family biography, as the obscure distant relatives of whom few have ever heard.

Among these is *Erythrina edulis*, coral bean or basul, which grows on a tree native to South America in the humid subtropical forests of the Andes, particularly in Colombia. It has long tightly cinched pods and bright red flowers which protrude from the branches looking like coral. The Greek root of its name also means bright red. It is also sometimes called frijol de pobres, the poor man's bean, and thus fits in nicely with the others. Its seeds can be boiled or ground into flour which is used in cakes, sweets and soups. A relative is the official flower of Los Angeles, CA.

The outlandish name *Psophocarpus tetragonolobus* means "Noisy fruit" – the pods pop open loudly when ripe – "with four cornered lobes." It is also known as a winged bean because of these spectacular four-sided feathery pods. It deserves to be better known since every part of the plant is edible: leaves, stems, flowers and even the roots, which are eaten like potatoes. The light-blue flowers are used to color rice and pastries as well. The dried beans are round, white, black or red and resemble soy. They have comparable nutritional value with a high protein and oil content. Like soy, they are also made into tofu, tempeh and winged bean milk. Although native either to tropical Papua and New Guinea where numerous types are found or to tropical Africa (which linguistic evidence suggests), they are grown today through tropical highlands especially in India, Thailand and Indonesia.

There was a brief interest in winged beans in the 1970s as a wonder food that could stave off hunger in developing nations. Unfortunately, the bean is quite fickle, grows only with a specific amount of daylight and in the right tropical conditions with a lot of water, but good drainage. New day-neutral varieties have recently reawakened interest in the plant.

The *Acacia* is a familiar tree that bears pods that are unmistakably, if distantly, related to garden beans. Aboriginal Australians use many of these species such as *aneura, cibaria, longifolia, oswaldii* – whose seeds are ground into a nutty sweet and crunchy coffee-like condiment called wattle seed. Interestingly, modern

Australians are using wattle in a variety of new contexts, in baked goods and in confections. A chocolatier in Adelaide makes a gorgeous wattle seed crunch covered in chocolate. There are many other varieties around the world; *Acacia nilotica* from Egypt is a source of gum arabic, an extremely important thickener through history. It is also eaten as a vegetable in Sudan.

Astragalus gummifer is the source of gum tragacanth, an ancient thickener known to Theophrastus and native to the Zagros Mountains of western Iran. The name tragacanth means goat horn in Greek, which the sap oozing from the tree seems to resemble. Today it is used in a variety of industrially processed foods like salad dressings, mayonnaise, toothpaste, ice cream and syrups. The gum can be burned as incense as well. Since trade was cut off between Iran and the US in recent decades this gum is no longer as widely used as formerly, being replaced with guar and locust bean gums. A related species from China, *membranaceus*, has been used for centuries in traditional medicine as a laxative, aphrodisiac and for revitalizing orthogenic chi, which gives the body energy and ability to fight off infection. It has also received wide attention in modern Western medicine.

Cyamopsis psoralioides or bakuchi in Sanskrit is eaten as vegetable and legume in India. Bakuchi powder is used in skin ailments in Ayurvedic medicine. Although few people in the West are familiar with this bean, we eat it often in the form of guar gum, which contains galactomannin. This is a thickener which gels in water and is used in a range of processed foods, especially ice cream. It also has industrial uses in the manufacture of paper, textiles and even explosives.

Dipteryx odorata or tonka bean grows on large hardwood trees native to the rainforests of Guiana, Venezuela and Amazonian Brazil, where the seeds are fermented in rum, which causes crystals of the drug coumarin to form on the outside of the beans. Coumarin smells very pleasant and has been used in traditional medicine for snakebites and convulsions. It is also used today as an anticoagulant and antispasmodic and is processed into the drug Coumadin. It is also widely used in the perfume industry, once to flavor tobacco, and as an additive to vanilla in Mexico. This adulterated vanilla extract is suspected as a carcinogen and had been banned in the US along with all other tonka bean products intended for food. Another name in the Caribbean is the love wishing bean because it is used in voodoo love spells.

Entada phaseoloides comes from Southeast Asia and is also known as the St. Thomas bean or matchbox bean in Northern Australia. Its toxicity is removed with roasting, soaking, washing and then boiling. In Cambodia they play a part in traditional New Year's festivals when young adults form two lines and hurl the huge beans at each other in a game called *"da leing."* *Entada gigas* is a relative, the sea bean (Mackey bean or nicker bean) which grows on huge twining vines in the mangrove swamps or billabongs. They are collected in Northern Australia and painted by Aborigines (who have also used them as food) and sold to tourists. They are also called sea-hearts. To be made edible the beans must be leached in running water in a "dilly bag" for many hours. Then they are pounded and made into cakes and consumed as traditional "bush tucker."

Gymnocladus dioicus, which means naked branches because the tree has no leaves for half the year, is a native to the east coast of North America, and specifically to Kentucky. Since its beans were roasted, ground and reputedly used as a coffee substitute by colonial pioneers it is familiarly called the Kentucky coffee tree. Raw its seeds are poisonous, but when roasted for several hours the toxic alkaloid cystine is destroyed. The beans themselves are beautiful, and readers near the Bronx can find some of the most magnificent specimens on the grounds of the New York Botanical Garden on the path behind the education building.

Inga edulis or ice cream bean is a long pod from a tree native to the Brazilian Amazon. Always eaten fresh, the pods contain a sweet white pulp that is scooped out raw and is said to taste like vanilla ice cream. There are other similar species also called ice cream beans, though considered inferior. Native Americans in Colombia ferment the pulp into an alcoholic drink called cachiri.

Inocarpus fagifer grows in Samoa and Tahiti as well as in Indonesia. It is called the Polynesian chestnut, whose taste is apparently similar. They are boiled and roasted like chestnuts as well, but grow in pods like other legumes.

Leucaena leucocephala or lead tree is a shrub from tropical America. Mayans and Zapotecs have traditionally eaten the seeds, and when green they can be added to salsa. Today it is grown widely throughout the Pacific as well. In the Philippines they are cooked as a green vegetable. The ripe seeds can also be roasted and eaten as a crunchy snack and in the Caribbean they are often made into jewelry.

Parkia biglobosa is also known as the African locust tree of tropical West Africa. Its processed and fermented beans are used as a condiment in soups and stews, called dawadawa, which today is increasingly made from soybeans. Little sun-dried cakes or balls of this condiment are traditionally made by women on a small-scale basis and sold in the markets to supplement their income. *Parkia javanica* or sataw is a related tree and the pulp and seeds within each long black pod are eaten fresh in Southeast Asia.

Pithecolebium lobatum or Djenko bean comes from Indonesia. Raw they contain a toxin that causes cystitis and bloody urine. The long processing involves burying the seeds in the ground and letting them germinate. Then the sprouts are discarded and the bean is cooked. Raw they have an unpleasant smell which disappears when fried. *Pithecelobium dulce* or guayamochil, on the other hand, is native to Southern Mexico, whence it was brought to the Philippines and is now called Manila tamarind. It has a sweet acidic pulp eaten raw or made into drinks.

Prosopis encompasses a broad range of species native to North America. It is best known as mesquite in the US. And includes three major species: honey (*glandulosa*), screwbean (*pubescens*) and velvet (*velutina*) mesquite. Apart from its aromatic wood used for barbecues, in the Southeast the whole pods are ground into flour (pinole) and were one of the earliest foods used by prehistoric Native Americans. Remarkably, although quite sweet, the flour is slowly digested, and does not create a sharp spike in the blood sugar level as do other carbohydrates. And because the sugars are in the form of fructose, it can be used for controlling diabetes. In fact, it is speculated that the sharp rise in diabetes among the Native American tribes of the Southwest is in part due to replacement of mesquite with other highly processed carbohydrates and sugars. Mesquite flour is also among those traditional ingredients which interest the Slow Food set, and recipes for baked goods incorporating it are not difficult to find.

Psoralea bituminosa, also sometimes called the Arabian scurfpea, is a kind of trefoil or clover-like plant that grows throughout the Mediterranean. It is called the pitch trefoil because the crushed leaves smell like tar or bitumen, which is a kind of tar used in ancient times. *Bituminaria* is its more recent genus name. It is used principally as fodder, but also has medicinal uses to treat skin disorders such as psoriasis and vitiligo. An American relative, *Psoralea esculenta*, is known as the prairie turnip and was a major article of food used by the Indians of the Northwest. It was also one of the foods that sustained Lewis and Clark on their trek across the continent, after their stores ran out.

Sphenostylis stenocarpa or African yam bean grows and is gathered wild in the humid forests of Nigeria. In Ghana it is grown as a security crop and is used in puberty rites for girls. It is a vine whose roots are also sometimes eaten, as well as the leaves. The bean is said to be much like a black-eyed pea and is normally dried, ground into flour and then wrapped in plantain leaves and boiled. This is not related to the other so-called yam bean, *Pachyrhizus*, known in the US as jicama, whose tubers are eaten rather than the pod.

Tylosema esculentum or *Bauhinia esculenta* (Marama bean or camel's foot) is used in the Kalahari and southern Africa. The seeds are roasted and are said to taste like cashews, and are also used to make porridge and a drink somewhat like cocoa. The San people or Bushmen of Namibia traditionally ate both the beans and the huge root, which stores water in the desert and when eaten young is comparable to a potato or yam. It is probably the least studied of all potential legume crops in the world.

Finally, there are many foods we call beans which are nothing of the sort: coffee beans from Ethiopia now grown throughout the tropics, as well as cacao beans and vanilla beans from Mexico, the latter of which is an orchid bearing only the vaguest resemblance to a bean. But none of these shares the fate of beans, being sublimated into divine drinks and exotic flavorings. Nor is the Mexican jumping bean, alas, a bean but a shrub *Sebastiana pavoniana* whose seed capsule contains the larva of a small gray moth which causes the seed to jump around. Lastly, the alluring mottled castor bean, whose oil was unwillingly doled down the throats of Mussolini's political enemies with alarmingly laxative results; this is not a bean either. It is the source of one of the most deadly poisons on earth – ricin. Imagine stealthily wreaking destruction in the guise of a beautiful bean. And for those whose terror of beans remains steadfast, there are always innocent and now exotically flavored jelly beans.

7

Mung and the Vignas: India

India provides one of the few historical exceptions to the rule that beans are associated with poverty. As we have seen, there are some minor beans that are only eaten during famines or that are considered inferior, but in general there was never a social stigma attached to the consumption of beans. There is a very simple reason for this: lack of competition with meat. If the availability of meat provides the foil against which beans are measured, then it is obvious why a largely vegetarian civilization would not only come to depend on beans for protein, but also why conceptually they were highly esteemed. Whereas in Europe beans were a lowly and polluting food, beans were consumed avidly in India among the highest castes, including the priestly Brahmins.

How this came about is a fascinating story. There are native bean species in India found in archaeological sites among the indigenous Dravidian peoples. At some point the staples of Fertile Crescent agriculture either made their way here or closely related species of the lentil and chickpea were cultivated in prehistoric times. The earliest advanced civilization on the subcontinent was settled around the Indus River Valley of Pakistan and northwest India around 2500–1800 BCE. Extensive cities like Harappa and Mohenjo Daro were as sophisticated and densely populated as those of ancient Sumer and Egypt, with whom it is likely they had contact. They grew many of the same foods, including beans.

These people, however, succumbed to a series of invasions which swept through the ancient world around 1500 BCE. In this case it was an Indo-European people called Aryans whose language, Sanskrit, was closely related to Archaic Greek, Lithuanian and Celtic, which gives some indication how far these people spread. At first this was a cattle-based culture that consumed beef in prodigious quantities, much like other warrior cultures. How they came to be cow worshipers, which ultimately will explain the importance of beans in later Indian culture, is one of the more hotly debated topics in food history. Some scholars, like Marvin Harris, have argued that it was a simple matter of economic expediency. Cows are much more valuable for traction, fertilizer and fuel in the form of dung, and above all dairy products, a renewable resource. The laws banning consumption of cows stem from this practical consideration.

More plausibly, cow worship is rooted in cosmic ideas among the Aryans which eventually became the Hindu religion. In a nutshell, the ancient Rigveda explains that all life is a manifestation of the first primordial principle, atman, which means "self." Thus all creatures are equal offspring of the same original source, rather than a hierarchy of beings created in succession as in the Judeo-Christian tradition, which gives humans stewardship over other animals but also the right to consume them. In Indian civilization, this inherent equality means all beings deserve equal respect; murder of any creature is a crime. Ahimsa, reverence for all life, at least in principle, is rooted in the earliest religious texts. At this point, however, they still consumed meat, and a caste system was developing wherein the highest castes, the priestly Brahmins and warriors, ate a much richer diet than those below. All this would change around 600 BCE when famine and social unrest swept the land. The beef-eating Brahmins began to lose their hold on the people, and apparently decided to reinvent themselves to maintain their dominance. To do this, they implemented the full implications of their doctrines by becoming vegetarians and adopting other ascetic practices. By living more frugally and on fewer foods than the poverty stricken, they could maintain their moral as well as political superiority. Joined to this was the idea of reincarnation – that one's actions here on earth have a direct bearing on the form one will take in the next life, the highest form being a cow.

There was also an idea that some foods are inherently purer than others. Vegetables like garlic and onions were thought to be polluted or jhuta. Some foods like milk, ghee (clarified butter) and foods protected by a husk like beans are pure. Thus the veneration of cows and the valorization of beans went hand in hand.

About the same time as these ideas were coalescing, another figure, Siddhartha Gautama, later called Buddha, entered the picture with a doctrine of non-violence and a form of vegetarianism even stricter than that of the Brahmin caste, from which he sprang. Buddhism, although it did not survive in India, was adopted as the official state religion in the third century under the emperor Asoka, and this religion may have in turn influenced Hinduism to adopt a more rigorous form of vegetarianism, which is to this day strongest among Hindus in southern India, though ironically not among many Buddhists elsewhere.

These ideas catalyzed the valorization of beans in a way that was diametrically opposed to Western Civilization's denigration. Beans thus became an essential staple crop in India, the primary source of protein for the majority of people, to a greater extent than any other civilization in history, with the possible exception of cultures in the Americas. Although the majority of modern Indians are not vegetarian, dense population and the high price of meat has meant the majority still receive most of their calories from vegetables, primarily grains and beans.

As we have seen, Fertile Crescent legumes such as lentils and chickpeas were introduced at a very early date. But the subcontinent also had its own species, the most important of which are the Asiatic *Vigna* species or as they are known in India "grams": mung beans (*V. radiata* or green gram), urd beans (*V. mungo* or black gram) as well as moth beans (*V. aconitifolia*), and rice beans (*V. umbellata*). Step into any Indian grocery store and you will be overwhelmed by the profusion of beans. These are all among the quietest and smallest of beans – moth beans are miniscule, and rice beans roughly the same size as their namesake. They are all very mild mannered as well, cooking up quickly without the fuss that other beans demand.

In an Indian grocery store they can be found whole, but are normally bought split and labeled dhal. This word derives directly form Sanskrit and actually means split rather than bean. Dhal also signifies the dish from which these are made, a puree, either thick or thin, which is the almost universal accompaniment to Indian meals, spooned over rice, scooped up with flat bread or eaten on its own. The phrase "dhal and bread" is an Indian metaphor for sustenance. Along with vegetables and starch, these make up the basic triad of Indian cookery, which has only really been abetted by chicken and lamb in recent centuries, and in particular by the wealthy. Keeping in mind that dhal refers to any split legume, one will find practically anything under this name. There is yellow toor dhal (the pigeon pea *Cajanus*) normally coated in oil, which should be washed off before cooking. Split pink lentils are also called masoor dhal, and channa dhal is the hulled and split tiny chickpea, whose inside is yellow, so they too resemble split peas.

Here we will focus on the native *Vigna* species though. The urd bean is normally black (and in its whole form is called kali – meaning black) but split it is the tiny white urad dhal. It is this bean that is ground into flour and fried to make crispy pappadams and fermented in a batter to make the large pancakes of southern India called dhosas, which are wrapped around savory fillings. Moong dhal is the split mung bean, which is yellow when deprived of its green seed coat. Interestingly, the easiest place to find the other *Vigna* species is in gourmet shops where they are marketed under various trademark names as rice beans, aconite beans and so forth. Whole green mung beans are also easily found in Asian groceries.

The taxonomic distinction of the *Vigna* beans is also a relatively recent phenomenon. Many were classed as *Phaseolus* until that name was reserved exclusively for New World species and the former were then reclassified in the late 1970s with their closer cousins, the black-eyed pea and groundnut from Africa. These Asian *Vigna* species were also given a sub-genus classification called *Ceratotropis*.

The historic importance of beans in Indian culture stretches back to ancient times. The Vedic ritual of shraddha is the most important place beans play a role. The word means faith in Sanskrit and is related to the Latin word *credo*

– "I believe." The ritual is performed in various junctures in life, at births, weddings and to pay homage to the dead. It is essentially a reminder that death does not sever the ties of this world from the ancestors, which is why it is also performed at pilgrimages and during eclipses when the protection of the ancestors is evoked. But it is most important as funerary ritual. It involves an offering of balls of rice (panda) for ten days, which provides food for the soul of the deceased. This enables it to form a body in the process of reincarnation. In addition to rice, only pure foods are offered, vegetables, without salt, and beans. In northern India it is usually boiled mung beans, while in the south horse grams (lablab) are used cooked in milk and sweetened.

Mung beans are also mentioned in early Sanskrit literature. In the Yajurveda of about 1000 BCE, they are called mudga, along with masha and masura, the latter referring to urad and lentils. Archaeological evidence of cultivation is even earlier than this. Buddha includes mung as among those foods "full of soul qualities" and "devoid of faults." Mung beans cooked with rice, ghee and spices called khichri or khichdi was for centuries the typical evening meal, mentioned by travelers to India since the Middle Ages. Muslim traveler Ibn Batuta wrote that the "munj is boiled with rice, and then buttered and eaten. This is what they call Kishri, and on this dish they breakfast every day." The word and the dish were later corrupted into the British colonial kedgeree, a rice, fish and egg mishmash eaten for breakfast. This is my own very simple recipe for khichri, which attempts to approximate the original, in that it does not include chili, which is a New World import. Also note it contains only foods considered pure.

Khichri

Wash a cup or so of long grain or basmati rice in several changes of water until it is no longer cloudy. Set aside. Next pound a few slices of peeled fresh ginger, and a good pinch each of coriander, cinnamon, cardamom seeds (removed from the green pod), turmeric and pepper pounded in a mortar with one sliced onion into a paste. Fry the spice paste in a pan with ghee until fragrant. To make ghee slowly heat a stick of butter until the

milk solids brown and precipitate at the bottom of the pot, then pour off
the clear, nutty, clarified butter from the top. Next mix in the rice and fry
for a few minutes until it turns a vibrant yellow and then add the moong
dhal. Add enough water to fill the pan, plus salt, and bring it to a boil.
Cover the pan, lower the heat and gently simmer for about twenty minutes.
After cooking pour on more ghee, fluff with a fork and let rest for about five
minutes covered. Serve.

Urad or black gram is the sibling of mung since they share a common wild
ancestor. They are used principally in the south, especially ground into flour
and then made into a batter which is used to make idli, a steamed bean cake
mentioned as early as 920. Today idli as well as dhosa (flat pancakes) are made
with a fermented batter that includes rice flour, but the medieval original,
according to Indian food expert K.T. Achaya, appears to have been made only
with bean flour. A variant called kadubu is mentioned at a royal feast in 1485.
"The kings are relishing the kadubu made of black gram; it looked like a full
moon: like a mass of mist set together; as if heavenly nectar had solidified into
circles; or as if a drop of moonlight had hardened. The kadubu was attractive to
the eye and pleasing to the mind." Today the kadubu is still served, often stuffed
with a savory filling. Urad flour is also used to make crispy fried pappadams
and a variety of sweets drenched with sugar syrup. Dhosas are easy to make at
home given a little patience with the fermentation process and can be filled with
virtually anything, much like a burrito or crepe.

Dhosas (Bean Pancakes)

Today the proportions of rice and ural dhal are usually three to one or
more, but equal parts also produces an excellent pancake with a richer
bean flavor. First soak the beans and rice separately overnight. The next
day grind them in a mortar with the soaking liquid, which is hard work,
or put in a blender with sufficient water and a little salt, to make a
thick batter. Let this batter sit in a warm place for at least twenty-four
hours during which time it will increase in volume and ferment, taking
on a sourish smell. Then heat the largest frying pan available or griddle,
preferably non-stick and swirl a ladle full of batter onto the well-greased

surface. Carefully turn over when brown. The result will be crispy and flavorful but pliant enough to wrap around fillings.

The other *Vigna* beans are lesser known in the West, but are beginning to appear in gourmet shops for their sheer novelty: they are absolutely miniscule. New York's Gramercy Tavern has been serving them lately. Moth bean, pronounced "moat" or *mat* in Sanskrit is *V. aconitifolia*, sometimes sold as aconite bean. It is so called because its leaves resemble that of aconite or monkshood, a deadly poison, which is thankfully unrelated. The beans are sprouted or fried and salted as a snack. There is also another crunchy snack made in Bikaner in the northwestern state of Rajasthan, called bhujia made with a spicy moth bean dough extruded through a small brass press into hot oil. Although traditionally made on a small scale locally, large snack manufacturers have begun to process it in massive quantities, putting the cottage industry out of business. Although other species can be used much the same way as moth beans, the value of the plant is principally its resistance to drought, which it accomplishes with a long taproot and its tendency to lie low in dense mats, conserving moisture.

Another relative of the moth bean is the rice bean (*V. umbellata*), which is nearly as small, white and fairly looks like rice, but they also come in other colors and with interesting mottled patterns. The heirloom moccasin rice bean, which is trademarked, is red, longer and slightly curved, so they look like Lilliputian hot dogs when cooked. They also have a distinctive long eye or hilum. They were probably first domesticated somewhere in Southeast Asia, as wild forms are spread from northeast India as far as Thailand and Vietnam. Rice beans have among the highest calcium content of any bean, but are difficult to harvest by machine because the pod shatters and thus they have not been cultivated on a large scale for export. Nonetheless these too show up in "heirloom" bean catalogues and restaurant menus.

The importance of these beans and their value in Indian society was also further supported by medical opinion. As in the West, India has an indigenous dietary system known as Ayurveda, which means the science or knowledge of longevity. The classic text in this tradition is called the *Caraka Samhita*, which some commentators claim dates back nearly to the time of the Vedas, or around 1000 BCE, though the text that has survived probably dates to the first century CE. The system is based on a series of doshas which are basic forces governing physiologic systems, something like an energy principle. For example, the vata dosha governs movement, pitta digestion and metabolism, kapha the body's structure. The foods we eat each reinforce a particular dosha, and as in the humoral system, a balance of these forces maintains health. That is, too little pitta causes faulty digestion, an excess causes inflammations and dehydration. In this system beans are classified as a vata food, which aids physical movement in the limbs as well as breathing, circulation, nerve impulses and even the free movement of ideas. Too much vata however makes a person instable and hyperactive. Those born with a natural predilection for excess vata were thus told to avoid beans, while those who need energy and a pick-me-up should eat beans. For most people, they are an ideal and necessary form of nourishment and are suitable for everyday use. Despite the superficial similarity of this system to Western humoral physiology, its appraisal of beans is entirely different; here they are considered a positive food.

All factors, economic, religious and medical, conspired to keep beans highly esteemed in Indian cuisine and culture through its history. This has only begun to change in very recent times as Western modes of eating are challenging the traditional diet, particularly among the upwardly mobile. Other global forces have also had an impact.

For example, the face of Indian agriculture has changed dramatically since the so-called Green Revolution of the 1960s and 1970s. Modern technology was introduced in the hope of averting famine and supplying an adequate diet for a growing population by means of increased yields. Tractors, chemical fertilizers, hybrid varieties were all expected to solve the shortcomings in the nation's food supply. These well-intentioned strategies had unforeseen consequences though. It was only the larger farmers who could afford these new technologies, and to increase output they generally switched from subsistence farming and the production of many different traditional vegetables adapted to particular places over centuries, to monoculture of very few crops, which were sold as commodities. Some farmers profited immensely, but the majority fared decidedly worse. Moreover, the rich and varied combination of crops, including lesser beans like mung which could sustain drought, gave way to a narrower and less nutritionally diverse diet. Monoculture depleted the soils making dependence on chemical fertilizer greater, and it demanded machinery and fuel, all of which cost money. Farmers became even more dependent on foreign companies and capital because the use of hybridized, high-yielding and normally sterile seeds doomed the traditional practice of saving seeds for planting the next year. Ultimately this has caused a decline in the growth of traditional and native bean species. Despite the fact that scientists see great potential in these species and they understand the value of polyculture for human health and the environment, the needs of the global economy have taken precedence.

The ultimate irony, however, is that these tiny beans, once the staple of the poor, are being served in the West in trendy restaurants and gourmet shops. Indian farmers, now perhaps irrevocably tied into global trade networks, might do best to tap into these specialty niche markets with their traditional "heirloom" beans. For better or worse, the world is ready to pay for the authentic experience of local indigenous culture.

Adzuki

Although clearly thematically separate from the discussion in this chapter, there remains one more relative in this *Ceratotropis* sub-genus. He is much bigger than his brothers, and more boisterous, with his bright red coat. He is also a little sweeter and something about the adzuki bean (*V. angularis*) makes you feel like celebrating. This is a festive cheery bean that usually shows up, unsurprisingly, in sweets. No one knows exactly where he was born, but he is grown primarily in China and Japan, and in both countries is beloved in the form of sweet red bean paste.

In East Asia, the attitude toward beans is also very much different than in the West. There is no particular stigma against beans per se, but this is less a matter of the economic necessity of beans to survival of the poorest, as of a tendency to sublimate them into highly processed foods which bear little relation to what is conceptually the bean. Think of tofu, miso and soy sauce. Adzuki beans remain much closer to their true selves – decidedly more beany, and this is mostly due to the superior palatability of adzuki to soy. That is, adzuki beans are not ashamed to be beans, even though they normally appear mashed in sweet doughy casings.

This red bean paste is eminently versatile as well. It goes into steamed buns like Chinese baozi, and zongzi, which is a steamed rice dumpling filled with red bean paste, sort of like a Chinese tamale. It can also go into moon cakes, eaten in the autumn festival. In Japan they fill sweet mochi rice cakes called daifuku, and accompany little cold cubes of agar jelly called anmitsu. But their most celebratory form is in red rice or sekihan (sticky rice colored pink by the beans) and then topped with adzuki, served at weddings and birthdays. The red color symbolizes happiness.

Red bean paste (*anko* in Japanese) is also made into soups, and is even spread on toast nowadays. Adzuki ice cream is one of its more wild incarnations. It also fills a fluffy pancake called dorayaki in Japan. The story goes that a samurai warrior, Benkei, was fleeing his enemies and hid in a humble farmer's cottage. Upon leaving he left behind his gong or "*dora.*" The resourceful farmer promptly put the brass circle to good use, over the fire, forming a sweet pancake filled with red bean paste. The paste is simple to make and adzuki do not need pre-soaking.

> *Take a cup or so of red beans and put them in a pot with water. Bring to a boil and then drain. Add fresh water and a good handful of sugar. Boil for about an hour until the beans fall apart. You can keep them chunky or mash them with a potato masher until very finely textured. You can also press them through a ricer, a food mill or a processor for a very fine texture, which should be not unlike refried beans.*

One final, and perhaps the most fascinating thing to happen to a member of the mung genus is the transformation of a little bean into a gorgeous translucent "cellophane" noodle. The beans are ground and soaked, then the starch is drawn off, from which noodles are made. These are found in China (bai fun) and Japan (harusame – which very poetically means spring rain noodles – though these can be made of potato or rice starch as well) and also throughout Southeast Asia. They are among the most versatile of foods, as they can be soaked and briefly boiled, rinsed and treated like any other noodle. They can be fried until crispy, or tossed into soups, stir-fries, served cold in salads and even drinks. One would scarcely ever imagine any of these to be a bean product. Mung beans are also the most popular and familiar source of bean sprouts.

8

Black-eyed Peas: Africa, Soul Food

Vigna unguiculata, at least according to botanists, is a cousin to the Asian *Vigna* species. There is still disagreement about its exact origin either in West Africa or Ethiopia, but few still claim an Asiatic origin, which is why the name *V. sinensis* (Chinese) has become defunct. The black-eyed pea is, in any case, a resolutely and characteristically African bean. Archaeological evidence from the Chad basin suggests that the pastoral peoples who migrated into this area around 1800 BCE began to switch to an agricultural regime by about 1200 BCE replicating the pattern of domestication and permanent settlement seen elsewhere on earth but here with the staples of pearl millet and black-eyed peas. This bean has thus always played a central role in African agriculture and was brought with slaves to the Americas where it remains an indelible marker of African-American identity. This is a proud and hardworking bean, resolute through affliction and desperation, a true survivor. Its identification with black-eyed and black-skinned people has been both a result of historical subjugation as well as a source of pride and communal solidarity for African Americans for whom they have become an indispensable ingredient in Soul Food.

In the Old World, black-eyed peas spread northward and eastward in ancient times and the earliest recorded evidence of their use is not in Africa but among the Greeks and in India. No one really knew they came from Africa, and their origin was also effaced by the English term cowpea or *"caupi"* in Spanish. In older texts one also finds the word calavance, though that appears to be obsolete. In other European languages they were phaselos among the Greeks and phaseolus through European history up to the sixteenth century when that name was also applied to the New World species, creating taxonomic mayhem that has only been settled in the past few decades.

The ancient Greeks and Romans, as well as the Indians, did consume these beans, though they also used them as fodder. There is an interesting account in Galen of what can only be construed as an early example of the raw food diet, which featured cowpeas sprouted and dipped in fish sauce and a few other lowly legumes. A young man who practiced medicine in Alexandria lived only on these and raw fruits and vegetables simply seasoned, but "it has been his policy not even to light a fire." The example seems to be used to illustrate how even the simplest of foods can be nourishing. Athenaeus relates how the Spartans served figs, beans and phaselus as dessert at a certain festival, and everyone knows how, well, Spartan, Spartan tastes were. References like these seem to suggest that the black-eyed pea was merely classed among other lesser beans, as a food of austerity. They were grown by ordinary farmers and even in Virgil's magnificent poem on farming, *The Georgics* (I.227), we are given some practical planting advice for these beans. This is my very literal prose translation. Most older authors translate phaselus as kidney bean, which obviously it was not.

> *Si uero uiciamque seres uilemque phaselum*
> *nec Pelusiacae curam aspernabere lentis,*
> *haud obscura cadens mittet tibi signa Bootes:*
> *incipe et ad medias sementem extende pruinas.*

> If truly you would sow the lowly bean and vetch
> Nor spurn to care for Pelusiacan lentil,
> A hardly obscure sign will be sent you by setting Bootes:
> Begin and seed half way through the frosts.

There are also medieval European recipes calling for fagioli, which again then meant black-eyed peas. This Venetian recipe of the fifteenth century is for a tart of fresh beans, shelled. The combination with pork belly or fat back is of course perennial. Lardo is merely cured solid fat.

Torta de Faxolli Freschi

Take the beans and let them cook with pork belly, then pound the beans in a mortar and the belly with a knife, then add the best spices you can have and add enough cheese so that it is a half or at least a third of the other mixture, and add aged lardo and make the tart and it is most perfect.

Africa, however, is the real home of black-eyed peas and West Africa still produces roughly 90 percent of the world supply. They also figure prominently in African religion. Among the Yoruba black-eyed peas are one of the principal ingredients used to feed the gods or Orishas, who protect the community. This religion was carried to the New World where it took various forms such as Candomblé in Brazil and Santeria in the Caribbean. There too the Orishas are fed with their favorite foods. Obatala, for example, prefers yams, rice flour paste, corn meal dumplings and black-eyed peas. Yemaya, the mother of the Orishas, also eats black-eyed peas, watermelon and fried pork rinds, while Oxun prefers them in savory dishes with shrimp and palm oil. The specifics of each sacrifice differ among various forms of worship, but black-eyed peas are one of the most important, traditional foods these discriminating gods demand.

So crucial are black-eyed peas to African culture that a Yoruba proverb, "You do not know what black-eyed peas are like for dinner," refers to a person so stupid and negligent that he is totally unmindful of the consequences of his actions.

In African cuisine black-eyed peas appear in some of the most delicious contexts. In Nigeria moin-moin (which means basically yum-yum) is a steamed bean cake wrapped in banana leaves. It is said to have seven lives because it can have incorporated seven different ingredients including smoked fish, eggs, tongue or corned beef, or leftover meat plus a range of vegetables. Nowadays it is often steamed in a tin can. Apparently, as one website claims – you know you're Nigerian if "u kno wut chin chin, puff puff, or moyin moyin is." These snacks are respectively fried squares of flat dough, deep fried dough balls and these steamed bean cakes. When the bean batter is fried in palm or vegetable oil it yields a delectable snack called akara. This is my recipe as bared to its most basic quintessential form. For the basic technique I am grateful to Fran Osseo-Asare. It sounds like an absurd amount of labor for such a simple dish, and be forewarned it is only for the preternaturally patient and there are no shortcuts. But it is well worth the effort.

Akara or Blind-eye Bean Fritters

First soak the beans in cold water in a big bowl for about fifteen minutes but no longer. Then rub them vigorously between the palms of your hands under water, breaking them in the process so the skins come off. The skins, with their "eyes" float to the top of the bowl and can be carefully poured off when the bowl is placed under the running tap. After about twenty minutes at this (or longer) you should have a disconcerting sink full of eyes and a bowl of blinded beans. If you are truly mad, pound the beans in a huge mortar with a little clean water until they form a smooth paste. Alternately put them in a blender with just enough water so they can be processed into a thick batter. Add some salt and let this sit overnight in the fridge. The next day place spoonfuls of the batter into a deep pan of hot oil. Turn the blind eyes when browned on the bottom and when done drain on paper towels and sprinkle with salt. They turn out fluffy and delicate. The batter can be abetted with chopped onion, crushed chili or whatever you like, but the simple taste of bean works fine on its own. They can be served with a spicy sauce of lime, jalapeno, ginger and palm oil, as they are in Brazil where they are called acarajé.

Black-eyed peas were brought with African slaves to the Caribbean, South and North America. We often have this image of slaves secreting their favorite seeds in their pockets before being forced across the Atlantic. Even if a few stray beans arrived this way, more likely slave owners began to import African crops after their captives refused to eat. According to Judith Carney, this is the way rice was imported to the Carolinas, and at first only Africans knew how to grow it. So too arrived okra, another African plant. Black-eyed peas may also have been stowed on board to feed the slaves during the Atlantic passage and any leftovers sold and planted.

The slave diet was meager at best, but since slaves often cooked for their white masters a number of foods and culinary techniques were introduced into Southern cuisine more broadly. Grits is nothing more than an American adaptation of African fufu – a staple porridge. Well-cooked greens also have African roots and the panoply of traditional Southern foods including fried chicken, chitterlings and hush puppies have ties to Africa rather than Europe.

Although this kind of cooking, what later came to be known as Soul Food, was associated with African Americans, as were black-eyed peas, beans were not denigrated in the way they were in the Old World. This might seem strange that a society so divided racially would nonetheless freely share a cuisine. This happened, it seems, precisely because the lines of difference were so starkly and indelibly drawn. That is, there was no possibility of a white person, rich or poor, being mistaken for a slave. There was no possibility of social denigration on the basis of diet. Eating beans in no way threatened your social category, the way it might in Europe. Of course such divisions were entirely socially constructed and there were certainly many people of mixed heritage, but having fixed categories ensured that identity was stable despite what one ate. Black-eyed peas are thus both characteristic of Soul Food as well as Southern cuisine on the whole. Thomas Jefferson grew them right alongside his treasured European imports and in 1774 his garden journal reads "black eyed peas come to table." Mary Randolph's *The Virginia Housewife* of 1824 includes a fried cake of "field peas" descended from the akara mentioned above, although it is made with fresh boiled beans, mashed.

The most revered dish in this tradition is called Hoppin' John. There has been a great deal of nonsense written about its origins, which are without doubt unrecorded, as well as its name. One theory suggests the name is an invitation to "hop in John" and join us for dinner. Though why Betty and Harold are not so invited is unclear. Perhaps the beans themselves hop in the pan when heated – but no one in their right mind would try to cook a bean that way. Another theory insists that children would hop around the table in tantric fits at the mere mention of the dish. A third theory has a crippled black man selling it on the streets of Charleston, South Carolina in the year 1841. Lastly, maybe more plausibly, the name is a corruption of the French "*pois pigeon*" even though this is an entirely different species – but if this were true, the dish is a cousin to arroz con gandules.

It doesn't really matter what the dish means or when it was first mentioned, it's the attention lavished on Hoppin' John as the food that must be eaten on New Year's Eve for good luck and wealth that interests. The beans supposedly represent coins, greens are dollar bills, and corn bread in some accounts is auspicious for obtaining gold in the coming year. There was probably something very much like this eaten in Africa long before fakelore explained it in such terms. Here's a recipe, which will probably arouse vociferous protest, as indeed any recipe for Hoppin' John would since the proper dish is as hotly debated as the best barbecue, political party or form of worship.

Hoppin' John

Soak beans overnight and drain, though this is not strictly necessary. In a capacious pot add the rinsed beans, fresh water, a chopped onion, bay leaf, thyme and a smoked ham hock. Simmer long and as slowly as possible until the beans are toothsome. Remove the hock, finely shred and return to the pot. Add a little salt and pepper and some rice, with a little more water if necessary and cook about twenty minutes longer until the rice is cooked through. Garnish with unspeakable quantities of serious hot sauce and for the effete a flourish of parsley or other such nonsense. If you are in a Creole mood substitute red beans and say "red beans and ricely yours" and pretend you're Louis Armstrong.

Strangely, although to our modern sensibilities brazenly racist, there was a decided nostalgia, particularly in the early twentieth century for an imagined happy Southern past where Mammy would be doing some of her magic in the kitchen. This is the only way one can explain *Miss Minerva's Cook Book: De Way to A Man's Heart* published in 1931. It was the last of a series of novels written in mock dialect and illustrated with pictures of Miss Minerva herself, a stereotypical cartoon black woman cook. This is very difficult to read today, but will give a good taste of this kind of entertainment, almost certainly aimed at white readers. Appropriately, this appears before the first recipe in the book, for bean soup.

> Bean soup air col' weather eatin's an' if it air made right it air sho' eatin's an' not drinkin's. I done hear O' Miss time an' agin call the chilluns ter they manners when they'd say eat soup 'stidder drink it, but when it was bean soup she'd leave 'em alone, when they said eat fer drink. If bean soup ain't think it air as po' as a houn' dawg.

What is truly perplexing about the book is its recipes many of which are hardly homemade traditional favorites. Her bean recipe in fact comes from a can. "I ain't never been one er these here hide-boun' folks what thinks nothin' good can't come outer a can ... I ain't sayin' boughten baken beans don't need boostin' up a bit ter make 'em mo' tastified...". To this end she adds ketchup, Worcestershire sauce and bacon, another indication that this is intended for an audience who cares to reenact only a cartoon version of traditional African-American cooking.

Such dishes, and in particular black-eyed peas, were eaten by pretty much everyone in the South; they were nonetheless reappropriated as a dish expressive of black identity in what came to be called Soul Food, particularly after the black diaspora of the twentieth century. As families moved north to find jobs in industrialized cities, there was a real nostalgia for black-eyed peas as appropriate for family gatherings, church socials and special occasions. Not that they were eaten every day though. Increasingly and especially among more affluent black people, this was not a food they wanted to be reminded of all the time. Only poorer urban families depended on the pot of beans day after day. Anyone who could afford to ate meat and other foods associated with mainstream culture, especially modern convenience foods. So this became a class issue within the black community itself. You even see this among such unlikely cookbook authors as Nation of Islam leader Elijah Muhammad, motivated partly by Muslim values, but also inherent class tensions. He says in *How to Eat to Live*, "Do not eat the swine – do not even touch it. Stay off that grandmother's old fashioned corn bread and black-eyed peas." These were specific reminders of what he called the "slave diet," designed to oppress and weigh down black bodies. He also said to stay away from sweet potatoes, collard greens and pinto beans, as unfit for human consumption. Now why Elijah Muhammad thought small navy beans were fine, and how bean pies came to be sold by Nation of Islam devotees, is a mystery.

In any case, Muhammad's comments were made in a specific context, just at the point that the black power movement began to valorize traditional cooking and African-American culture. Especially among those who could afford to eat otherwise, this new Soul Food was a reassertion of a once denigrated cuisine as something authentic and binding for the community – much as was traditional African music and apparel. The spate of Soul Food cookbooks in the latter part of the twentieth century attests to the conscious appropriation of this cuisine as something uniquely and originally black. It was also a cuisine which tied people back to their roots in the South, as these books were largely written for transplanted African Americans in the North, and it seems largely for middle-class African Americans. This is evident even in a fairly recent *Soul Food* cookbook by Joyce White. The recipes are all taken from churches where cooking traditions were carried on by extraordinarily talented and usually elder cooks who still had connections to their Southern upbringing. In every story that accompanies the recipes the author makes a point of explaining how the cook and her family have "made it," praising their economic success, the academic degrees of their offspring and their community service. Their preservation and sharing of traditionally black dishes, even the most lowly of foods such as black-eyed peas, is tantamount to being authentically black.

The fascinating part of this story is that these dishes were anything but healthy. With relative affluence also came larger portions, and with sedentary jobs came problems of obesity, heart disease and diabetes. The slave diet, it turns out, is not ideally suited for modern lifestyles. Interestingly, many of the Soul Food cookbooks published recently take an entirely different tack. They are obsessively health conscious. In *Neo Soul* by Lindsey Williams, the son of Sylvia Woods (one of the acknowledged experts of this cuisine, who owned a restaurant in Harlem), the recipes are trimmed down for a modern health-conscious audience. The author writes "'There's nothing that captures the 'soul' of soul food more than black eyed peas. I consider it the African-American signature dish." So it may be, but here it appears in a healthy salad with peppers and celery tossed in a light vinaigrette. Another cookbook by the pastor of the Abyssinian Baptist Church in Harlem (Rev. Dr. Calvin O. Butts III) is a classic story of before and after: See how I went from a size XXX to my now slim healthy figure by changing my diet – while still eating authentic Soul Foods. And of course beans feature prominently here too – as an inherently health-promoting food when cooked without the hog fat. Obviously these attitudes are tempered by changing cultural ideals of body size and beauty, but their interaction with the desire to preserve traditional culinary culture, shared meals and spirituality makes this one of the more interesting cases of the reappropriation of beans. It is more than a simple recovery of one's ethnic roots; it's also an assertion of middle-class values – as long as one tinkers with the traditional recipes, and in the case of black-eyed peas, only if one leaves out the ham hock.

In contemporary culture there is still a strong association of black-eyes peas with both the South and African Americans. Just a few years ago the Dixie Chicks recorded a hilarious song called "Goodbye Earl" about an abused housewife who decides to kill her husband by feeding him poisoned black-eyed peas. Interestingly, poisoned foods are almost always also comfort foods, those we trust most and are least likely to refuse, which of course makes the poisoning all the more dastardly. In this case the beans came from a can (at least in the music video), which may have been a further assurance of purity in the mind of the victim.

There is also a rap/hip hop group from L.A. called Black Eyed Peas, whose recent hit "My Humps" is apparently the single most frequently downloaded song in history, and can be heard on errant cell phones across the US. Not that this reveals anything about beans, but it is interesting that the group would choose such a name.

Among the strangest things that have happened to this bean over the centuries was its transplantation to East Asia where its tendency to gigantism was consciously exploited. The so-called "yard-long" beans sold fresh in Asian markets are none other than the black-eyed pea grown berserk and eaten fresh. They are the same species, but are given the sub-species name *sesquipedalis* meaning a foot and a half in Latin. Maybe they should be half-yard beans. There is another related *Vigna* species – *V. vexillata*, offering swollen tubers which are eaten like sweet potatoes in Africa. These are also called zombi peas. *V. lanceolata* is another similarly eaten in Northern Australia among indigenous peoples.

9

Phaseolus vulgaris: Mexico and the World

Think of the epitome of bean, the bean that embodies absolute beanity and it will almost certainly be a variety of the single species, *Phaseolus vulgaris*, the common bean. This species has done a better job than perhaps any other plant at insinuating itself around the globe in the place of traditional indigenous species. Moreover, these beans come in so many shapes and colors, are so infinitely adaptable and versatile that we rarely think of them as manifestations of a single ancestral progenitor. In many respects, *Phaseolus* is most like our own species – spread around the globe in every imaginable climate. The white navy bean, mottled pinto bean, red kidney bean, black bean, green flageolet, as well as fresh green beans or string beans, haricots and so forth are all the same species. They are all quite different characters too, some homespun and honest, others rugged as the untamed West, others boisterous and flamboyant.

To understand these beans we must begin with their origins in the Americas. The wild ancestor of *Phaseolus* is spread from Northern Mexico to Argentina and it was domesticated independently both in the Peruvian Andes, from the *aborigineus* sub-species as well as in Mexico from the *mexicanus* sub-species. In the course of millions of years in the wild and several thousand more in cultivation, their forms diverged significantly and when crossed today they produce mostly infertile hybrids, which is decent evidence of independent domestication. The changes experienced through human interaction and selection constitute what is called the "domestication syndrome." This involves developing pods that will not shatter and disperse seeds, seed dormancy which allows them to be stored for later use as food or to plant, tolerance of differing light conditions which allows them to be grown at different latitudes and locales outside of the tropics where days are relatively short, and development of sturdy stalks whose beans mature all at once and can be harvested at the same time rather than trailing vines which mature irregularly. This may have been the result of selecting vines which grow up corn stalks. Lastly, there is the amazing variation in size and color. All these are the result of human intervention.

Exactly when these events took place is more difficult to determine, partly because archaeological remains are sparse in the humid environment of Meso-america, unlike the dry Fertile Crescent of Southwest Asia. Remains of *P. vulgaris* from a cave in the Peruvian Andes have been radiocarbon dated at about 6000 BCE and they may have been domesticated well before that, perhaps contemporaneous with or even before Old World beans. Their domestication, again independently, occurred in Mexico only a few thousand years later, if the surviving archaeological remains can be trusted. Carbon 14 dating has proven fairly erratic and is being called into question with newer Atomic Mass Spectrometry methods, so it is probably safest to say that these beans were domesticated several thousand years ago, without indicating a precise chronology.

Beans were one of the principal crops among early New World civilizations. Here we will focus on Mesoamerica and pick up the Andes in the next chapter with lima beans and other *Phaseolus* species. The staple grain of these civilizations was corn. On its own corn is very nutritious, but it lacks vital amino acids like lysine, isoleucine and tryptophan. But in combination with beans it forms a fairly complete protein package, especially when the corn is nixtamalized, or soaked in lye (wood ash) or lime (calcium hydroxide, not the fruit) which frees up the niacin. Presumably this was discovered merely as a way to remove the seed coat and more easily grind the corn into dough, the swollen grains or hominy become soft. Those cultures which treated their corn were in consequence better nourished and probably reproduced at a greater rate than the others. Cooking beans was also a distinct advantage, as kidney beans in particular contain toxic lectins, which are phytohaemagglutinins – that means they cause red blood cell membranes to rupture. These lectins are only destroyed with cooking, so again, those who adopted these procedures survived at a greater rate.

With a comparative paucity of large domesticated animals, Mesoamerican civilizations came to depend on a largely vegetarian diet. Although this point is usually overstressed, as they did have turkeys and ducks, guinea pigs, domesticated dogs for the table and various wild animals, a large population demanded alternate sources of protein as well, and this explains the importance of beans. In combination with squash, beans and corn were cultivated together in the same plot, the squash providing ground cover to keep the soil moist and intact and to discourage weeds, the corn providing stalks for the beans to climb, and the beans providing nitrogen for the others. Along with tomatoes, chili peppers, amaranth, spirulina (a nutritious kind of algae), and the occasional bit of human flesh if accounts are to be believed, this diet left little to be desired. But arguably without beans the land would never have been able to support a large population.

These crops and methods of agriculture were in place among the early civilizations such as the Olmec, Maya and the people of Teotihuacan and more recently the Toltec in Central Mexico. In an account of Mayan cuisine, Sophie Coe, quoting Bartolomeo de Las Casas, describes a bread made of maize mixed with ground beans, which looked something like lupines. These may have been *P. vulgaris*, or its cousin the Lima bean, judging from the size and shape. In other accounts black beans are mentioned, in the Mayan language called buul, which are definitely *P. vulgaris*. Coe further describes bean dishes with toasted and ground squash seeds and green onions, others with chili and seasoning of epazote or garnishes of greens. The importance of beans among the Maya is a direct result of the infrequent use of meat. Interestingly, the descendents of the Maya in the Yucatec peninsula still eat a dish called sabe boul made of black beans, onions and epazote.

Beans were equally important in the Aztecs' diet. This group arrived in Mexico relatively late and claimed to have originated in the north, in a place called Aztlan. This makes sense as their language and culture is related to the Apache and Shoshone who remained in what is today the Southwestern US. Upon arrival, they soon adopted the crops and farming methods of their neighbors. From a small nomadic tribe settling on the shores of Lake Texcoco in Central Mexico sometime in the fourteenth century, they quickly grew and eventually filled the power vacuum left in the wake of the collapse of the Toltec state a few centuries earlier. Within a century they came to dominate the entire region from their capitol in Tenochtitlan, a sprawling city built in the middle of the lake connected by causeways to the mainland, and covering about 5 square miles, with a teeming population of about 150,000. Aztec agriculture was also highly advanced. Terraced farming was practiced with intricate irrigation systems and large floating islands or chinampas were built on rafts covered with dirt and planted with crops like corn and beans.

The Aztecs not only grew their own food but also demanded corn and beans as tribute from their subject states. When population pressure forced them to find greater quantities of food, as it did in the severe famine of the 1450s, they merely intensified their farming or conquered new peoples. Rather than turn to cannibalism as a solution to their increasing need for food, as has been suggested, they merely required greater tributes of corn, amaranth, chia and of course beans – an essential source of protein.

Apart from archaeological evidence, written accounts of Aztec bean use come primarily from Spanish interpreters. One such account is by Francisco Hernández who was sent by King Philip II of Spain in 1570 to record all the plant-based medicines in use by the Aztecs. Hernández generally interpreted what he witnessed in light of his European medical training, which leaves his observations somewhat skewed. Nonetheless it provides an extensive account of native flora. In a section of his book on atolli, a kind of corn-based drink taken both for pleasure and medicinally, one version includes chili (chillatolli), taken in the morning as protection against cold. Another type called ayocomollatolli uses beans. Ayacotl is the Aztec name for bean. "This one is made by adding chillatolli, epazotli, and the pieces of dough when it is all half cooked, and finally when it is nearly done, whole cooked beans. It constitutes a splendid and most pleasant food, and by virtue of the epazotli, it purges the blood and raw humors." He also describes how beans are added to their translucently thin tortillas.

Aztec cuisine, largely based on corn and beans, as is Mexican cuisine today, naturally lacked all the Old World imports, wheat, pork and beef in particular. Nonetheless it could be extraordinarily complex – no less than that served in the courts of Europe at the same time. In fact, the Aztecs had a socially stratified society based on conquest not at all dissimilar to those across the Atlantic. This is probably why Spanish observers understood their dining ceremonies so readily, or at least they believed they did. For example, Bernal Díaz gives a description of a banquet thrown by Montezuma that includes elaborate hand-washing ceremonies, hundreds of dishes of wildfowl and game accompanied by tortillas, followed by fruit, bowls of chocolate and tubes of tobacco. With a switch of key ingredients he could have been describing a banquet in Italy. Unfortunately he makes no mention of beans in this Imperial banquet, but they do appear in another description, a celebration of a baptism for a merchant family. There beans are mixed with toasted corn in a mulli, or sauce. With the absence of contemporary cookbooks one can only guess at what this would have been like, and here is just that, taking into account available ingredients and cooking technology:

Ayacotlimolli

Begin by lightly toasting some dried chili peppers over an open flame. Put these in a bowl to soak for about fifteen minutes until soft, then place them in a molcajete or mortar with some of the water and mash into a paste. Next put into an earthenware pot some pre-soaked pinto beans, some hominy (posole or whole swollen corn kernels treated with lime – which can be bought dried or canned) and some turkey legs (or if you like dog meat or human limbs), some finally chopped scallions, a few skinned and seeded tomatoes, a square of bitter sweet chocolate and the chili paste along with some salt and a pinch of epazote (a dried herb not unlike oregano but with a distinctive odor and apparently the ability to reduce the gaseous effects of the beans). Cover the contents of the pot with water and simmer gently for several hours. Serve in deep bowls.

Beans also played a role in Aztec religion. The sacrifice of a statue formed of corn to Huitzlipochtli is fairly well known, but Brother Bernardino da Sahagun in his vivid if extremely prejudiced account of Aztec festivals mentions many others involving beans. One called Vauhquiltamalqualiztli involved a statue of the fire god, before whom were laid sacrificial loaves made of corn dough encasing whole beans, perhaps a kind of large tamale. These macuextlaxcalli were later eaten by the devotees, washed down with pulque, a mildly intoxicating drink. Sahagun also gives a complete account of the Aztec markets and the many bean dishes served by street vendors.

Phaseolus vulgaris was equally important to American Indians in what is today the US and Canada. It arrived in the Southwest or may even have been independently domesticated there about 1,500 years ago, and archaeologists surmise that beans were the principal source of food there. Beans are believed to have arrived along the east coast about 1,000 years ago and made their way as far north as the St. Lawrence River; Jacques Cartier reported their presence there in the 1530s. Among the Iroquois the so-called "three sisters," – corn, beans and squash – were as central to the diet as they were in Mesoamerica. *Phaseolus* were also grown in the center of the continent among the Mississippians, who flourished between 750 and about 1350 and whose city Cohokia was probably the largest settlement north of Mexico. Interestingly, beans did not make their way up the west coast into California where there was never the pressure to adopt agriculture.

The earliest European accounts of the Southwest also emphasize the import-ance of beans there. Alvar Núñez Cabeza de Vaca mentions corn, beans and pumpkins grown among all the peoples he encountered in his trek through Texas in the 1520s and 1530s. Francisco Vásquez de Coronado in his search for Cíbola in 1541 in what is now New Mexico indicates that "They grow maize, although not that much, and beans and calabashes; they also live on game: rabbits, hares and deer." In every city he visits, Coronado mentions that all they need for subsistence is corn, beans and calabashes, although the last are properly squashes.

Almost all explorers to the east coast of North America, if they mention agri-culture or foodways, pinpoint corn and beans as the most important staples. In the earliest detailed account of American Indian cultures of the coast, Giovanni da Verrazzano, a Florentine explorer employed by France in the 1520s, mentions several times that "On the whole they live on pulses, which are abundant and different from ours in color and size, but are excellent and have a delicious taste..." Of another tribe he encountered at 40 and ⅔ degrees parallel to Rome (which puts him in Manhattan), he claims that the people here cultivate beans more systematically than the others, "when sowing they observe the influence of the moon, the rising of the Pleiades, and many other customs derived from the ancients."

A fuller account is found a few decades later by Thomas Hariot, an Oxford mathematician sent on the aborted first English attempt to settle in the New World. In *A Briefe and True Report of the New Founde Land of Virginia* he describes not only the crops grown but also their names in the Algonquian language of Secotan and Pomeiooc plus how beans are cooked.

> Okindgier we called beans, because they are like beans in England, except that they are flatter, more varied in color, and some are pied. The leaf on the stem is also different. However, they taste as good as our English peas. Wickonzowr. We named these peas to distinguish them from the beans, because they are much smaller. They differ little from the beans, though they taste different and are far better than our

English peas. Both the beans and the peas ripen in ten weeks. The natives boil them in a broth, where the beans are reduced to small pieces or boil them whole until they are soft and begin to break, as we prepare them in England. These peas are either cooked by themselves or mixed with wheat. Sometimes after they have been boiled whole they are pounded in a mortar and made into loaves or lumps of doughy bread.

By wheat he means corn, which he had just mentioned.

A relative of these bean loaves survives among the Cherokee, who now live mostly in the West, but at the time were neighbors to the south of these tribes. This Cherokee Bean bread is still served in October for the harvest festival. It is basically boiled beans mixed with corn meal into a stiff dough which is then wrapped in hickory leaves and boiled.

A slightly later account of native agriculture in Virginia is found from 1612 in William Strachey's *Historie of Travaile into Virginia Britannia*. He describes how trees are uprooted by removing a ring of bark and scorching the roots. In the remaining holes three or five grains of corn are planted with one or three grains of beans. About the native legumes he explains, "Peas they have, which the Natives call assentemmens, and they are the same which in Italy they call fagioli. Their beans are little, like a French beane, and are the same which the Turks call garvances, and this kind of pulse they much esteem for their daynties." By this point the English were probably familiar with *Phaseolus* from Mexico, so it is not surprising that they recognized these beans as similar.

To the north we have an account of Abenaki agriculture from the French explorer Samuel Champlain written in 1605 and published as *Les Voyages de Sieur de Champlain* in 1613. Along the Saco River in Maine he describes Indian corn.

> This they grow in gardens, sowing three or four grains in one spot, after which, with the shells of the aforesaid signoc, they heap about it a quantity of earth. Then three feet away they sow as much again, and so on in order. Amongst this corn they plant in each hillock Brazilian

> beans, which come up of different colors. When fully grown these plants twine around the aforementioned corn, which grows to a height of five to six feet, and they keep the ground very free from weeds.

He also mentions squash, the third sister. Champlain, who would thereafter found the city of Quebec also discusses the Huron methods of horticulture and cookery, and the women who practiced them. "Their principal food and usual sustenance is Indian corn and red beans, which they prepare in several ways. They pound them in wooden mortars and reduce them to flour ... of this flour they make bread with beans which they first boil, as they do Indian corn for soup." This appears to be yet another version of the aforementioned bean bread.

In describing the American Indian foodways these explorers unwittingly recorded a way of life that would soon be confronted with disease and destruction as settlers poured in not only from England, but also from France, the Netherlands and Spain. The settlers also introduced Old World species of beans, and to understand the impact of this exchange on both Worlds and the importance of *Phaseolus* in it, we must start back in 1492.

The Columbian Collision

The year 1492 was one of momentous importance in the history of our species, as it was for *P. vulgaris*. The great exchange of plants, animals and pathogens, between the Old World and the New began in this year. In his journal entry for November 4, Christopher Columbus, in his frantic search for spices (which was the intended goal of the voyage), mentions as an aside that "These people are very gentle and timid; they go about naked, and as I have said without arms and without law. The country is very fertile. The people have plenty of roots called zanahorias (yams), with a smell like chestnuts; and they have beans of kinds very different from ours." The translator here should have said sweet potatoes, as the true yam is African. As far as beans are concerned, the words Columbus used were faxones and fabas or as we would say phaseolus (which to him meant a black-eyed pea) and fava beans – which were the beans he knew. From that point on, the name phaseolus stuck to the beans just as the name Indian stuck to the people, by accident. As Lawrence Kaplan succinctly put it "Had herbalists and botanical authors of the succeeding three centuries taken account of Columbus' recognition that these New World legumes were different from those of Europe, some of the confusion might have been avoided."

Many explorers to the New World speak of beans and apparently many brought them back home, just as they sent chickpeas, fava beans and other Old World species to the Americas. The initial reception of *P. vulgaris* in Europe went largely unrecorded, which suggests that it happened fairly easily. This is odd considering that most new species were first treated with dire apprehension. Tomatoes did not find a place in European cuisine for centuries, nor did peppers, and corn only in a few areas such as northern Italy where they were ground and cooked as polenta. Potatoes likewise took ages to find a culinary niche. These were all strange and unfamiliar plants, some with poisonous relatives in Europe (the Solanacea). Why then were beans grown without much fuss? Europeans didn't recognize them as foreign species. They thought they were just new varieties of the beans they were used to growing and eating, and they referred to them with the same name – phaseolus. That is, they already had a place in European cookery and over time they gradually and quietly worked their way among the Old World species, but it would be many years before they recognized these as new beans.

The only ones to really notice the botanical distinction of New World beans were the herbalists, who by chance were in the middle of a botanical revolution of sorts, partly because they were busy trying to account for legions of new species unheard of by the ancient authorities, which forced them to rethink taxonomy, but also because printing and illustrations disseminated their findings quicker and more broadly than ever before. That is, they carefully described and depicted the new beans and people read about them throughout Europe. Not that they knew where they came from, and even the great father of modern taxonomy, Linnaeus, thought they came from India, but at least we can be certain of their appearance. *Phaseolus* probably arrived in the early sixteenth century, but it was several decades until it was discussed in print.

The earliest botanical description as well as artistic rendering of *Phaseolus vulgaris* is said to be found in the groundbreaking herbal of Leonhart Fuchs, *De historia stirpium commentarii insignes* of 1542. Fuchs does not mention America in his entry, nor does he even call the bean *Phaseolus*, but rather *Smilax hortensis*. *Phaseolus* is merely offered as a synonym, as is the Greek *Dolichos*, and German *faselen, welsch* or *"wild Bonen."* Welsch here means foreign rather than Welsh. This nomenclature certainly doesn't clarify anything, as *Smilax* today is a genus including the greenbriar and sarsaparilla, not even legumes. What the ancients, whom Fuchs cites, called *Phaseolus* is now a *Vigna* and *Dolichos* is *Lablab*. As was the fashion in the sixteenth century, no opinion was considered legitimate unless it could be backed up by classical authority, but obviously none of them could have known about this bean. The description perhaps leads us a little closer: leaves like ivy, fruits like fenugreek – that is, a long pod, "in which the seeds are similar to kidneys, not of one color, but in parts rather red." This to him sounds like Dioscorides' smilax; to us it sounds quite like a kidney bean. He continues that there are also white ones and they can have whitish, red or purplish flowers. Apparently he examined specimens for this description, and says that they are grown in gardens. Fuchs then goes on to quote Galen, the Byzantine Aëtius and Arab Symeon Sethi, which of course leads us off the trail as all these people wrote well before 1492. It can only be on the basis of the startlingly clear and accurate illustration that the identification is made.

The earliest description of pole beans, those that climb rather than bushy varieties, was made a decade later by another German, Hieronymus Bock, or as he Latinized his name Tragus. According to Agnes Arber, author of the classic history of herbals, Bock was one of the first botanists to free himself of dependence on ancient authorities and to look with his own two eyes.

By this point it was clear to the botanists that a new species of bean had arrived. Flemish botanist Rembert Dodoens, in *Frumentorum, leguminum, palustrium* ... (Fruits, legumes, marsh plants...) printed in Antwerp in 1566, makes a pointed argument that beans must be distinguished from favas, even though people commonly use the terms interchangeably in the vernacular. The seeds of what he calls Boona are not round like favas, but rather longer and larger. Although he doesn't know where they come from, he insists that "among the ancients these are found nowhere, for instance in Galen, or other writers of his age…" "Beans therefore are not favas, but altogether another legume" which are also to be distinguished from the faselus of the ancients. Here at least is a clear recognition that a new species had arrived in Europe.

Later in the century it was also recognized as an American bean. Castor Durante, in his *Il tesoro della sanita* (Treasury of Health) of 1586, notes that now fagioli "are found from the Indies." The red ones are particularly hot (in humoral terms) and therefore help generate sperm and "excite coitus." These benefits notwithstanding, Durante still believed that no legumes are tasty "and for this reason are not used by all nations, nor by all persons, and among Princes are not used at all…" Likewise Englishman John Gerard reports on *Phaseolus* that

> the fruit and cods of Kidney Beans boiled together before they be ripe, and buttered, and so eaten with their cods, are exceeding delicate meat, and do not engender winde as the other Pulses doe. They doe also loose the belly, provoke urine, and ingender bloud reasonably well; but if you eat them when they be ripe, they are neither toothsome nor wholesome.

Comments such as these may explain why these beans are not found in elite cookbooks.

Despite the recognition of a new bean by the herbalists, other culinary literature of the sixteenth century is relatively silent on the topic. One would suspect that Spain and Portugal would be the first place to find references, and one often reads that Columbus brought back beans with him from his second voyage, but what became of these is unknown. There is little indication that anyone apart from the botanists recognized *Phaseolus* as a new bean, even if they were eating them. For example, Gabriel Alonso de Herrera's *Libro de agricultura* first published in 1513 and then in many subsequent revised editions has lengthy entries for garbanzos, favas and lentils, but no mention of any new beans. Luis Lobera de Avila's *El vanquete de nobles cavalleros* of 1530, even though it has a whole section on the proper foods to eat on sea-going voyages, says nothing about any New World plants. Slightly later in the century, Francisco Nuñez de Oria does have a section on these new foods in his *Vergel de sanidad*, first appearing in 1569. There are descriptions of sweet potatoes, cassava and "mayz" but beans are not included. Again, it seems that no one in Spain considered these a different plant, or worthy of mention. All these authors were far more interested in their agricultural inheritance from the Arab world, and what they could learn from the recently conquered Kingdom of Granada.

References to New World beans are far more prevalent in Italy, and, as we know, Italians eventually came to be mad about fagioli and the Tuscans still proudly refer to themselves as *mangiafagioli* or bean-eaters. The species must have arrived unrecorded, or at least not in words. There are, however, some startling images of New World species adorning the palace of wealthy Sienese banker Agostino Chigi, now called the Villa Farnesina across the Tiber from downtown Rome. In the festoons and swags adorning the loggia painted by Giovanni di Udine around 1515 to accompany the myth of Psyche painted by his master Raphael, there are the first depictions of corn, squashes and what are almost certainly *Phaseolus* beans, distinctly longer and more slender than the fat fava pods also painted there. One might even imagine that these beans were growing in the garden which was then adjacent, for Giovanni to use as models.

It was not for another fifteen years that we have written evidence of *Phaseolus* in Italy, and thereby hangs a tale. There is a specific variety called the lamon, a large mottled red bean grown today around a little village of the same name near Belluno in the Dolomites. So locals claim, it was introduced here by native humanist and hieroglyphics expert Piero Valeriano in 1532, who got it in Rome from Pope Clement VII, who in turn was given it by the Emperor Charles

V (also king of Spain), who apparently got it directly from the conquistador Hernán Cortés as a present, who would naturally have gotten it from the Aztecs. Whether this is true or not is entirely beside the point, but rather it is interesting that such rapt devotion would be afforded such a simple legume. Valeriano even composed an ode to the bean in 1534, sealing its fame, if not his own. These are the immortal verses in which Valeriano waxes rhapsodic:

> *Ipse Pater Clemens dono mihi quam dedit ultro,*
> *Et dixit donans, ditabis tu quoque colles*
> *Fruge nova patrios, Belluniaque arva beabis.*
> *Ergo ego ut in patriam redii, data semina sevi*
> *Non agris tamen haec, aut hortis credita, verum*
> *Fictilibus tectum ornarum, phialisque fenestras.*
> *Scilicet hinc minimae quid sperans messis; et ecce*
> *Ingentem primum foliorum surgere sylvam,*
> *Innumeras passim voilas florere per omne*
> *Virgultum, et siliquis praegnantibus omnia plena*

> Father Clement himself gave me a gift from far far away,
> And giving it he said, "You shall enrich your homeland hills
> With a new fruit, you shall gladden the fields of Belluno."
> Therefore, I, when I returned to my homeland, sowed these given seeds
> Not in fields, however, nor entrusted them to gardens, but rather
> To adorn my dwelling with earthen pots, and my windows with saucers.
> Surely hoping for some very small crop from them; and, behold!
> First there arose a prodigious forest of leaves,
> Everywhere flowered countless violet blossoms throughout every
> Tendril, and all of them full of pregnant pods.

Celebrated as lamon beans are in the north, it is the Tuscans who pride themselves on being bean-eaters and arguably it is they who have perfected the art of bean cookery. But this art did not develop in the great courts where cookbooks were written. Rather it was in humble peasant kitchens. With caution, we can get some sense of what may have been happening in these kitchens by comparison with subsequent practices. For example, beans are mashed into a puree and served on bruschetta, slices of garlicy toast, and drizzled with extra virgin olive oil. They are cooked in a justly revered soup called ribollita made with cavolo nero, a species of black cabbage, and leftover bread, also redolent of olive oil, and "reboiled" or sometimes baked in the oven so it forms a crispy crust. But the most famous method of cooking them is fagioli in fiasco. Here the beans are carefully placed in a chianti bottle (with the raffia removed) or a flask along with salt, olive oil, garlic cloves and pepper corns. The bottle is then filled with water and is placed in hot ashes for several hours until all the water is absorbed. The top, however, must not be corked, or you would indeed have a fiasco (which is where we get that term) when it explodes. Rather it is tied with a piece of cloth. Then the beans are poured out and served with another drizzle of oil. Today the beans are more often baked in a terracotta *coccio*, which connoisseurs insist is infinitely preferable to a metal pot. We can't be sure how far any of these methods go back and they may just be nostalgic recreations of the past, but they do suggest that an entirely unique range of bean dishes was developing in the early modern period among the poor which at some point substituted New World beans for the older species.

As was the case with fava beans, elite cookbooks in the past were reluctant to offer many fagioli recipes, as the association with poverty and rustic living usually also stuck to these beans. For example, Florentine Luigi Alamanni in his magnificent Vergilian ode to agriculture (*La coltivazione* printed in 1546) can only associate beans with rustic simplicity. Whether he is thinking of the new or old *Phaseolus* is hardly important.

> *Or prendendo il Villan (che l'ora è giunta)*
> *Dal chiuso albergo, e la famiglia insieme,*
> *I semplici legume, e l'altre biade,*
> *Che nel felice Agosto in seme scelse;*
> *Cerer chiamando, e chi de i campi ha cura*
> *Alle fatiche sue larga mercede;*

Già commetta al terren la sua sementa.
Sian la fava pallente, il cece altero,
Il crescente pisel, l'umil fagiuolo, ...

Now Rustic takes (when the time is ripe)
From the enclosed dwelling, where the family is gathered
The simple legumes, and other grains,
Which in happy August were chosen as seed;
Ceres is called, and who takes care of the fields
For his labors – a great gift;
Thus is rendered to the earth its sowing
Whether the pallid fava, the proud chickpea,
The waxing pea, the humble bean, ...

When *Phaseolus* do appear in cookbooks, they are usually in the form of green beans, dried beans being normally left for peasants. For example, Domenico Romoli, called Panunto, lists "fagiuoli fritti con la scorza" or beans fried in the pod, as a possible Lenten dish as well as "fagioli verdi, & secchi" in the form of a soup. There is no way of knowing for sure if these are New World beans, but it is possible since his *La singolare dottrina* was first published in 1560. In any case, he gives us a fuller description in book 10, which focuses on legumes. There he offers the usual warnings about their cold and dry nature, causing bad dreams and so forth, but also some culinary advice. "Mustard corrects greatly their harmful nature, and similarly vinegar with salt, pepper and oregano, and you must drink with them powerful, strong wine." On the other hand, "they are good for rustics, and men who work hard, but not for those who repose, nor the delicate."

In 1611 in his *Trattato della natura de' cibi et del bere* (The Nature of Food and Drinks) Baldassare Pisanelli explains that fagioli are "much worse than favas, but among them the red are the best, because hotter and less windy." Cooking them with mustard helps correct them or with vinegar, salt, pepper and oregano. But "fagioli don't last very long, and this happens because they cannot be perfectly dried." "The white are rather humid and slow to digest.

Which is why fagioli offer a great deal of nourishment, but nonetheless are a meal for country folk, and not the delicate or students." Quite clearly the stigma attached to all beans was easily transferred to the new species, though not as decisively with fresh green beans which he says can be seasoned with salt, oil, cumin and pepper. This seems to have been the only way they appeared on wealthy tables in the seventeenth century.

Salvatore Massonio soberly describes the various forms and uses of salads among rich and poor in a remarkable book, *Archidipno overo dell'insalata* of 1627. He says that fagioli have been used for many years in salads and that they are very pleasant. He also describes how they should be "boiled in water and then seasoned with oil, salt, vinegar and pepper; or with oil, garum and pepper; or with orange juice, oil and pepper." His mentioning the ancient Roman condiment garum, a fish sauce, is rather surprising since it had gone almost completely extinct by this period. Massonio also warns to be careful to remove the string from the beans, which is difficult to digest, and to chew them very well for fear of choking. Such anxieties, compounded with flatulence, meant that green beans did not take a place among the most elegant of vegetables in this era, namely artichokes and asparagus. Dried New World beans did not appear at all.

In the early eighteenth century a Jesuit priest named Francesco Gaudenzio living in Arezzo wrote a cookery manuscript called *Il panunto toscano*. In it there is a recipe for mature fagioli as an antipasto, which probably reflects common eating habits better than the earlier courtly cookbooks. It provides some evidence that this method of cooking them dates back several hundred years, whether with the old fagioli or the new.

> *Take fagioli and place them to cook in cold water: when they are cooked, drain them from the water, chop onions with aromatic herbs, place in a pan with the same fagioli, pepper, salt and enough oil; fry them for some time and at the end add a little vinegar. In the same way you can cook fresh fagioli with the addition of a little garlic. And if you have to serve soup, when they have been fried, put in boiling water in proportion and in this*

*case don't add vinegar. You can also make them by putting them a night in
cold water in a warm place; in the morning throw away the water and put
them to cook in hot water, and season as above, first frying the said things
and you can bring it to the table.*

Later in the century Vincenzo Corrado in his *Il cuoco galante* of 1786 gives a
recipe for a Florentine soup based on dried fagioli. His book, although written
for the court at Naples, more closely resembles the modern conception of
Italian cookery as it finally makes use of New World ingredients like tomatoes
and peppers. Along with several recipes for fresh green beans and fagioletti, by
which he probably means small black-eyed peas, there is this now classic soup:

*Of dried fagioli you make a soup with oil, seasoned with chopped herbs,
and simmered in oil, with beet greens, borage, and parsley adding chopped
onions. You season alla Fiorentina with a sauce of oil, anchovies, lemon
juice, and pepper after the fagioli have been cooked in water and salt.*

In his earlier *Del cibo pittagorico,* Corrado gives other variations such as alla
Vicenzina (from Vicenza), which involves first frying onions, garlic, peppers,
tomatoes, parsley, anchovies, oregano and bay leaf, then adding fish broth.
When this becomes thick, the pre-cooked beans are added. Fried in butter
and herbs with a squeeze of lemon juice, they become all'Inglese, and his own
creation (all Corradina) is made with sour sorb apples, botargo (salted dried fish
roe), anchovies, garlic, oregano, basil, oil, vinegar and fish broth all made into
a sauce passed through a sieve and then used to season pre-cooked beans. These
recipes do not necessarily suggest that beans were being accepted more readily
in upper-class circles; the intention of the book is to feature vegetarian dishes
as a matter of health, something which had come into vogue a few decades
before, inspired by a medical book by Antonio Cocchi called *Del vitto pitagorico*
(1743).

To round out the Italian bean dishes, there is a fagiuoli a guisa d'Uccellini, or
beans in the style of little birds, which Pellegrino Artusi, the author of the great
nineteenth-century Italian cookbook *La scienza in cucina e l'arte di mangiar*

bene, says he saw in the trattorie of Florence. The beans are first cooked in water and then strained. These then go in a pan with oil and sage leaves, salt and pepper. Over this goes some plain tomato sauce. It is only in works like Artusi's that we begin to get a glimpse of what had been by then common culinary practice among ordinary people for generations. Not that Artusi included himself in their cast; he was firmly bourgeois and wrote for a similar audience, but recording local traditions was for him an act of nostalgia as well as nationalism. Nonetheless, he keeps an arm's length from the common folk for reasons he prefers not even to mention directly in polite society. Here are his comments about a zuppa di fagioli:

> One says, with reason, that fagioli are the meat of the poor, and in fact when the worker rummaging through his pockets notices with a melancholy eye that he cannot buy a piece of meat large enough to make a good meal for his family, he finds in fagioli a healthy aliment, nourishing and of little expense. Moreover, fagioli stay a long time in the body, quelling for a bit the pangs of hunger. But ... and this is a big but, as are so many things in this world – I think you understand. For partial protection, choose fagioli with a fine skin or sieve them; those with an eye have less of this fault than others.

Despite this apprehension, Artusi does thereafter offer a Tuscan peasant soup, a "modest" soup made with stale bread, white beans, oil, cabbage, potato and a bit of prosciutto – essentially a form of ribollita. At the very least, this provides a record of a dish that would never have been found in elite cookbooks before.

Historically this fondness for beans in Tuscany stems partly from dealing with rural poverty, but it is also the result of an innate sense of the importance of frugality and simplicity. This might seem strange in a place where Renaissance culture blossomed and material wealth was legendary. But that was largely a phenomenon of the late Middle Ages and up into the sixteenth century. By the seventeenth century the Italian economy began to wither as northern Europeans, particularly the Dutch and English, muscled their way toward financial dominance of the continent as well as its colonies. The Agricultural Revolution in the north also provided a consistent base to support a larger population and eventually industries and capitalism. In contrast, by the nineteenth century the Italian countryside was comparatively impoverished.

In Italy, there were some wealthy people at the apex of society and a small bourgeoisie, but in general most people, especially in rural villages, lived at the subsistence level. Carol Helstosky in her book *Garlic and Oil* argues that the frugal Mediterranean diet was not an ageless way of eating but rather the result of dire circumstances mixed with bad agrarian policies. Tracing the disastrous consequences of rural policies from unification in 1861 through the economic boom of the 1950s and 1960s, she shows that this simple threadbare diet was the result of politics, most notoriously Mussolini's plan for self-sufficiency or autarky, which prevented the importation of food, and which left Italians surviving mostly on pasta, vegetables and of course *Phaseolus* beans. As we shall see below, this lifestyle would be romanticized in the latter twentieth century, and the lowly bean ennobled. But for now, let us see how these beans fared elsewhere in Europe.

France

The reception of New World beans in France was less straightforward than in Italy. There is a long-standing legend that Catherine de Medici, when she was betrothed to the dauphin of France in 1533, the future Henri II, brought with her Tuscan chefs who taught the French about fine cookery and Italian vegetables. There is little evidence for this apart from a few Italian names among her retinue, nor evidence that in her trousseau she brought with her beans, phaseolus no less, so she could enjoy familiar dishes from her homeland. If she did bring *Phaseolus* with her, there is little evidence of them being eaten or grown in France for a very long time after her arrival. When they were finally, the French also contrived their own name for these beans to distinguish them from favas. The word haricot, first appearing in French in the seventeenth century, is supposedly a corruption of the Nahuatl word *ayacótl*. Strangely, haricot originally meant a medieval fricassee of chopped up mutton, a hericot or harrico, from the word *harigoter*, to cut up, which in turn is a word with Germanic roots. That a bean could accidentally take the name of such a dish seems unlikely, and haricot was still being used in this original sense in the late seventeenth century. It also seems unlikely that beans went into such a dish and then adopted its name. Maybe the French just used a familiar sounding word arbitrarily as the Aztec term was corrupted.

Recipes for haricot do not appear in sixteenth- or seventeenth-century French cookbooks at all, nor in the great agricultural texts like Olivier de Serres' *Le théâtre d'agriculture*. Fresh peas make a sudden appearance at the court of Louis XIV and to a lesser extent fresh green fava beans, but no mention is made of haricot and certainly not in dried form. It seems as if the stigma against beans in general also attached to the haricot here too.

Nonetheless, people eventually began to grow *Phaseolus* in France, possibly as a garden ornamental, which is how tomatoes and potatoes were grown. But they were also eaten as green beans. Late seventeenth-century French gardening authority Nicholas de Bonnefons gives explicit directions on how to grow *Phaseolus*. This is the English translation by John Evelyn: "The small haricot, or kidney beans, are of two sorts, white and colored, amongst which, there are also some white, but they are lesse, and rounder than the great white ones." These, he advises, should be sown in beds in four rows. When they fruit, some are eaten green and others left on the plant to ripen for seed. Keeping in mind that these beans are self-sowing, he knows that the next year they will come back true to form. Furthermore, "The painted, and the coloured Beans which are a lesser sort, are commonly sown in the open ground, newly dug and raked over, without any further care, then what you take of such seeds as are sown abroad in the Fields..." "But the Red are to be esteemed above all the rest, because of their delicateness, much surpassing the white, though they are most accounted of at Paris."

That gentlemen reading this text would be interested in growing their own beans reflects a fashion in early modern Europe for enjoying the delights of the countryside, a kind of mock-rustic aesthetic which has little to do with actual farming for the market, but is instead a leisurely activity for those who have land and spare time to cultivate vegetables and fruits. Such gentlemen-farmers not only avidly read gardening guides but also traded seeds and of course served their produce on their own estates. This pastime held a strong appeal especially for Britain and its colonies, where the most familiar example would be Thomas Jefferson, who grew many varieties imported from Europe.

The appeal among the French was not merely one side of the gardening craze which swept through Europe in these centuries, it was partly a real botanical curiosity and in a sense a desire to connect with the land in a meaningful way among those who in their starched wigs and ruffles were growing increasingly unfamiliar with actual farming. This probably explains why these beans are found in gardening books before cookbooks, although the fact that they bear beautiful flowers has a lot to do with it too.

When haricot beans finally do make their way into cookbooks, it is exclusively fresh green string beans, and this is only at the very end of the seventeenth century. Very revealingly it is also in books that consciously appeal to middle-class audiences. François Massialot, who had previously published the *Cuisinier royal* in 1691, came out with a revised book *Le nouveau cuisinier royal et bourgeois* in 1712. Here haricots are listed among the possible salad ingredients. They are also described in what would become the two classic treatments of the eighteenth century – conservation of green beans, one a form of pickling, the other dried. (A variation of what is called in the US leather britches.) Normally green beans would have been expensive garden vegetables available only in a short season in spring, but these new methods made their use possible throughout the year and by a broader social spectrum of people.

Haricots Verds, the Way to Conserve Them

One can conserve them in two fashions, either in a brine of vinegar, water and salt, like cucumbers; or equally dried, after having been cleaned and blanched. One lets them dry in the sun, and when they are good, you place them in a place which is not humid. To revive them, you soak them for two days in warm water; and they regain their greenness, just as when they were picked. You next blanch them and prepare as usual. For those who preserve them in brine, when they are well seasoned in a pot, with some cloves and a bit of pepper, one must cover them well, for fear that they will spoil, with some melted butter on top. The quantity that you want to use, you must soak in water like the others; and after you can serve them, either for a salad, or for a side dish, after having blanched them and seasoned with cream.

Variations on these two recipes show up throughout the eighteenth century in both French and English cookbooks. Vincent La Chapelle, for example, in *The Modern Cook*, published in both languages, further refines the cooking method. He suggests that the dried string beans, after they are reconstituted, be gently boiled in a small kettle with water, butter, salt and an onion. They are then sautéed in a pan with more butter, a little flour, chopped onions and some of their own broth, and thickened with egg yolks and a dash of vinegar so they "be of a good Relish." They can also be stewed with ham, bacon or sausages. What is truly interesting about these recipes, on both sides of the Channel, is that dried beans are nowhere to be found in cookbooks. The social stigma was so powerful that only fresh or preserved green beans were considered worthy of elite tables, or of those who aspired to eat like them.

It appears that the first place dried haricots are mentioned in a major French cookbook is in François Marin's *Le dons de comus*, a monstrous work of three tomes printed in an expanded version of 1742. Their appearance here appears to be a reflection of the author's attempt to reach a broader audience, other than aristocratic households. There is even a section explaining "the idea of cuisine and bourgeois economy" and how people of "mediocre fortunes" such as artisans and other persons of the third estate who live simply can also enjoy good food. This may explain why we suddenly see toasted bread topped with haricots blancs as a side dish, puree of white haricot soup as well as this simple bourgeois recipe. In his shorthand, the author appears to have left some steps a little unclear; all the ingredients go into the marmite, or little pot, to simmer on the coals.

Mutton Cutlets with Haricots

Sauté your cutlets in lard or butter. Remove them and sauté your chopped turnips. When they are colored, remove them and dry them well. Place them in a little marmite with the cutlets, a bouquet of fine herbs, salt and pepper. Make a roux with what remains in the pan. Cover it with water, broth or bouillon. Let your haricots simmer on the hot cinders. To finish degrease, place very dry croutons, a dash of vinegar. Haricot with mutton breast do the same way.

We can also get some indication of how beans were used among the common people on the eve of the Revolution from a study of vegetables by Antoine Augustin Parmentier, the *Recherches sur les végétaux nourissans* of 1781. Parmentier is renowned as the great promoter of the potato, both as food and as an additive to bread, so his comments here are perhaps not surprising, but they point to the fact that beans were commonly used as bread extenders when the price of wheat was high. He admits that leguminous plants furnish nourishment to all of Europe, but "they are infinitely less appropriate for bread making." The introduction of vetches, féveroles (Horse bean or *Vicia faba equina*) or white haricot "results in nothing but a heavy indigestible aliment, of the worst taste." The only natural way to cook them is in water, as green beans or in a puree.

It is not really until the nineteenth century that cookbooks specifically catering to the poor included recipes for dried beans. As in Italy, and as we shall see in Britain too, these records were normally written by elite chefs condescending to describe peasant foodways, or those with a social conscience who are honestly trying to help poor families cope. Pierre-Joseph Buc'hoz in 1803 gives us a hint that haricots have all along been eaten by the poor in a manner quite different than in cookbooks for the wealthy. He describes the usual preservation methods, which he thinks ruin the fresh flavor, but also that "the seeds are eaten fresh and dried, cooked in water, or in a stew, then appreciated with meat or lean, or seasoned with oil and vinegar; they enter into soups; one makes of them excellent purees; of them one can also make bread." The sudden change or willingness to describe common foodways is almost certainly the result of a transformed cultural milieu. After the fall of the French monarchy, the concerns of ordinary citizens, and especially their daily nourishment, was of real political concern. Revolutions could, and of course, would happen again, often triggered by famines. Buc'hoz also offers a very simple recipe for white haricot beans, one appropriate for the kind of frugal virtues promoted by the Revolution.

White Haricot in Roux

You cook them in water, you make a roux of butter and flour, where you place a chopped onion, you fricassee the haricots, with parsley and chopped onions, a dash of vinegar; you moisten with bouillon, salt and pepper; and serve as an entrée, or in place of butter use fine oil.

The monarchy was, however, reinstated and along with it grand dining on a magnificent scale in France. It might seem odd that the great, celebrated chef Antonin Carême, known as the chef of kings and king of chefs, would serve something as lowly as a bean soup while the aristocrats were ogling at his towering architectural masterpieces. But indeed there is a red bean soup recorded as appearing on the table in the Chateau Rothschild in 1829. Only the name reveals the aesthetic involved. It is called Potage à la Condé. The Prince de Condé had the great Vatel running his kitchen in the seventeenth century (the same Vatel who committed suicide when he thought his orders of fish would not arrive.) That is, this dish is the homage of one great chef to another, but also his reconstruction of what he thought would be a seventeenth-century dish. Of course, he was entirely mistaken about that, but the appearance of bean soup nonetheless is meant to be a historic dish and probably better reflects ordinary cuisine of the time. It is quite simple. Three pints of red beans are boiled in a pot for three hours with a bundle of vegetables (carrot, leek, turnip and celery) a lean piece of ham and a partridge (probably intended to give some elegance to the dish). Just the beans are then rubbed through a sieve, consommé is added and it is simmered for another two hours. It is served with fried bread. Without the complicated pureeing it could easily furnish a table less elegant than the Rothschild's.

But we must not forget that beans still remained in many people's minds a coarse food, fit for ordinary and coarse people. In Brillat-Savarin's mind, even the great celebrated Soissons bean was something one would most likely find fat people indulging in. There is a hilarious dialogue on obesity in his *Physiologie du goût*. He is seated among various fat people who are calling for stodgy bread, potatoes and so forth. One calls for Soissons beans and the author hums sarcastically the well-known tune "Les soissonnais sont heureux, Les haricots font chez eux" for which he is upbraided. Do not laugh, Paris pays large sums for them, to which Brillat-Savarin can only exclaim "Anathema on beans!" Brillat-Savarin was basically a devotee of an ancestor to the modern low-carb diet. In his mind beans were not only uncouth, but fattening.

Beans would eventually find their way into haute cuisine though. Arguably, the French apotheosis of *P. vulgaris* is found in the celebrated cassoulet of Languedoc. Originally it would have been made with favas. The legend posits that the dish, originally called "estofat," was created during the siege of Castelnaudary during the 100 years war. Throwing everything they had into a huge ceramic cassole, the town chefs were able to feed the army who thereafter had the strength to repulse the invading English. At some point haricot beans were introduced into the dish. Today it includes the distinctive haricot tarbais, a big white, thin-skinned, pole bean. The story of this variety involves a Monsignor de Poudenx, Bishop of Tarbes, who found them in Spain and brought them over the Pyrenees in 1712, where they are still cultivated in the Adour Valley.

There are actually three different versions of cassoulet, each claiming, if not priority, then superiority. Prosper Montagné said "Cassoulet is the God of Occitan Cuisine: the Father of Castelnaudary, the Son of Carcasonne and the Holy Spirit of Toulouse." Each version is made in an earthenware cassole, from which the dish gets its name, and never in a metal pot. The first includes beans, pork loin, sausages, pork skin and confit leg of goose, all of which are baked slowly in an oven, the crust on top being periodically pushed down and then finished with a breadcrumb topping. Some even specify the number of times the crust must be submerged. The second version uses mutton and sometimes partridge, while the last includes fresh lard and a combination of sausages, mutton, duck or goose. These are the formulas according to the *Larousse Gastronomique* but there are infinite variations from kitchen to kitchen.

Much simpler than all these and perhaps closer to the peasant-like original is a recipe for *haricots au lard à la villageoise* offered by Alexandre Dumas, the same of musketeer fame.

> *Begin by having a good stomach, armed with a good appetite. When you're not sick, you never lack one except through alimentary indulgence, or by lack of exercise. Rise at a good hour and go out with an empty stomach for a good while: promenade on horseback or trot on foot; they must think that you are quite fit, since you read cookbooks. Then cook about 2 liters of big white haricots with a kilo of good bacon; cut into slices, so that all the morsels are equally fatty. To this add the necessary quantity of water so that it should not need to be stirred nor removed during cooking. All the water and all the fat during this drenching will be found absorbed by the starch, in a manner that it will be thoroughly cooked and perfectly good without having been boiled, and that's it.*

Britain

Cookbooks in seventeenth- and eighteenth-century Britain make no mention at all of dried New World beans or any dried beans for that matter. As in France, they appear only as immature green beans or, as they are called in England, French beans or kidney beans. The usual treatment is either pickling or drying as in France, or laying them up in salt the way capers are preserved, a related form of preservation. John Evelyn offers a pickling recipe in 1699 (in *Acetaria*), which is fairly simple and may be regarded as an ancestor of nearly all English recipes that follow in succeeding centuries.

> *Take such as are fresh young, and approaching their full growth. Put them into a strong brine of white-wine vinegar and salt able to bear an egg. Cover them very close, and so will they be preserved twelve months: but a month before you use them, take out what quantity you think sufficient for*

your spending a quarter of a year (for so long the second pickle will keep them sound) and boil them in a skillet of fresh water, till they begin to look green, as they soon will do. Then placing them one by one (to drain upon a clean course napkin) range them row by row in a jarr, and cover them with vinegar, and what spice you please; some weight being laid upon them to keep them under the pickle. This you may preserve French beans, harico's, &c. the whole year about.

By the mid-eighteenth century it was clear to agronomic writers that certain varieties of the *Phaseolus* came from America. What is interesting is that these did not appear to be grown as often for the table as were Old World varieties except for cattle fodder, or for eating fresh and green, as we have seen. For example, Philip Miller's *Gardener's Dictionary* (third edition of 1748) explains that enumerating all the varieties of *Phaseolus* or kidney bean would be pointless "since America does annually furnish us with new Sorts, so that there is no knowing what varieties there may be produced in England: besides, as they are not likely to be much cultivated here, since the old Sorts are preferable to any of the new ones, for the Kitchen." He believes they are mostly grown for their ornamental flowers or as curiosities and describes the scarlet runner bean and the *P. vulgaris* varieties in precisely these terms. Of those eaten the common white, or in his time called the Dutch kidney bean, had fallen out of use and he preferred the lesser garden kidney bean or "Battersea" bean which he insists is "the best bean of all the rest for eating." It is also clear from the context that he is talking about green beans and that only some beans are left on the plant to mature for seed.

In the eighteenth century nearly every cookbook has a recipe for pickling green beans and normally all the authors stole from each other, so the origin of this recipe is probably elsewhere, but here is Mrs. Raffald's version published in 1787. It is decidedly more spicy and interesting than Evelyn's and reflects the changing tastes of the British Empire. The Jamaica pepper is what we now call allspice, long pepper is a relative of regular pepper in the form of a little spike-like catkin, and alegar is malt vinegar (a much less accurate term).

To Pickle Kidney-beans

Get your beans when they are young and small, then put them into a strong salt and water for three days, stir them up two or three times each day, then put them into a brass pan, with vine leaves both under and over them, pour on the same water as they came out of, cover them close, and set them over a very slow fire till they are a fine green, then put them into a hair sieve to drain, and make a pickle for them of white wine vinegar, or of fine alegar, boil it five or six minutes, with a little mace, Jamaica pepper, long pepper, and a race or two of ginger sliced, then pour it hot upon the kidney beans, and tie them down with a bladder.

Apparently to keep the beans especially fresh looking and green, it was a common practice to put a copper coin in with the boiling water. Dr. Hughson in his *The New Family Receipt Book* (1817) warns against the practice and explains how it causes verdigris poisoning. Other cookbooks recommend alum instead, which can still be purchased for keeping pickles green.

The Age of Industry

In the late eighteenth and nineteenth centuries Britain would be the first place on earth to experience the technological and social transformation known as the Industrial Revolution. This was in part only possible because of the Agricultural Revolution mentioned in the fava bean chapter, a rise in population and availability of cheap labor that could be concentrated in factories. All these factors worked together in concert with the development of new fuel sources such as coal, used in the new steam engine. In a nutshell, people abandoned the countryside in unprecedented numbers and moved into urban tenements. They were employed in factories long before there were any regulated working conditions, minimum wages or even child labor laws. The unwillingness to regulate labor was on the one hand the effect of implementing the economic theories of Adam Smith who believed that the less a government meddled with the economy (hence a "liberal" or free economy) the greater the wealth that would accrue to the majority of people. On the other hand, the capitalist owners of these factories were also the ones making the laws, and clearly it was they who stood to benefit most from this new arrangement. In practice it was indeed new; formerly governments routinely set prices for foods, wages were determined by guild statues, and trade was firmly controlled. Suddenly the economy was left to its own devices under the assumption that the free play of supply and demand – the so-called "invisible hand" – would set everything aright to the benefit of everyone. This is a simplification of Smith's theory; nonetheless this principle ensured that the government would not tamper with the economy.

The effect was unprecedented prosperity for the factory owners and misery and oppression for the majority of workers. As the lowest possible wages were paid, the proletarian's diet narrowed significantly, with meat becoming a rare luxury and the greater proportion of the household income being spent on bread, tea, sugar and starchy foods like potatoes. Nor were there any food purity laws, so manufacturers frequently adulterated food. The effect on the health of working-class Britons was equally deplorable with rickets, a vitamin D deficiency, becoming common. In this milieu, beans also played a significant role in the working-class diet. It may be no coincidence that suddenly cookbooks were published catering to this class and they always include affordable bean dishes. This is already apparent in William Kitchener's enormously popular if eccentric *Apicius Redivius or the Cook's Oracle* of 1817, in which he offers a white harrico bean soup. Kitchiner's goal was "render Food acceptable to the Palate, without being expensive to the purse."

> *To make three quarts of this soup, wash and thoroughly cleanse a quart of white harrico beans in lukewarm water; let them boil very gently for a couple of hours, till the beans are tender; work them through a cullender into a clean stewpan, put in a large bunch of parsley, a quarter pound of butter, and the inside of a three-penny loaf crumbled to pieces, season with white pepper and salt, and keep it simmering slow for an hour and a half longer, and pass through a sieve.*

In 1825 an English physician living in France for many years, Louis-Ustache Audot, published his *French Domestic Cookery, Combining Economy with Elegance and Adapted to the use of Families of Moderate Fortune*. Like books elsewhere, there is a social conscience involved, not only in the marketing of the title, but the simple rustic recipes as well.

Dried French Beans à la Provençale

Put into a small earthen vessel dish a quartern of dried French beans, with four spoonfuls of oil, a small piece of butter, two sliced onions, some shred parsley, a bunch of fine herbs, the leg of a goose, or a bit of salt meat, some pepper, salt, and a little nutmeg: let them stew nearly four hours, more or less, till the sauce is sufficiently thick.

Audot offers many other frugal haricot recipes, including white haricot à la bourgeoise, which is simply boiled then tossed in a pan with butter and seasonings. There is also a recipe for stewed red kidney beans, which include wine and butter in the boiling water, and which is served with bacon. Again, it was only in the nineteenth century and among the professedly economical cookbooks and in periods of social distress that dried bean recipes were published. No better example of this exists than the cheap paperback *Soyer's Shilling Cookery for the People*. Soyer was quite a character, but one with a deep social conscience. He set up soup kitchens in Ireland during the Irish potato famine and worked in the Crimean War developing a portable stove for soldiers to use on campaign. But it was perhaps his cheap cookbook that sold over a quarter of a million copies by mid-century that is his lasting testament. Here is his simple economical recipe for beans.

Haricot, plain boiled, should be first washed, then put into the black iron pot one quart of them, with four quarts of cold water, one ounce of butter or fat; boil them gently for three hours, or till tender; the water will be nearly absorbed, if the haricots are good; draw off the remainder; mix in a pint of it, three teaspoons of flour, half ditto of pepper, add it to the haricots; boil for ten minutes, keep stirring, and serve, adding three teaspoons of salt; an ounce of butter is an improvement. A little meat of any kind can be cooked with them, just the same as dried peas, only these are to be eaten whole, and four onions in slices, fried, may be added with the seasoning, when the haricot or lentils are nearly cooked, the broth, if ample, when strained from them, may be used as soup, with bread in it.

Soyer's concern was driven by his impression that few young housewives knew how to cook anymore. Often having grown up working, they never had a chance to learn the basics at home, and thus he gives basic advice for setting up a kitchen, how to buy inexpensive utensils and so forth and how to make a meal stretch to feed a hungry family on a tight budget. It is also very revealing to note that Mrs. Beeton's *Book of Household Management* of 1861, which is written for a decidedly middle-class audience, still only has recipes for fresh green beans and fresh shelled broad beans (favas) but nothing on dried beans, which were still, it seems, stigmatized as lower-class food.

The invention that would truly revolutionize the humble *Phaseolus*, making it not only cheap, but also for the first time in history quick and convenient, was canning. Invented by Frenchman Nicholas Appert early in the nineteenth century, canning in glass was first used for gourmet items, fruits and vegetables out of season. The basic principle was not understood until Pasteur, but through trial and error Appert figured out a way to seal food in jars and then boil it, which kills the bacteria and creates an enclosed vacuum into which no other contaminants can enter. He explains that "I take the precaution of putting the beans in bottles as soon as shelled. When the bottles are full, the beans having been filled up, I add to each bottle a little bunch of savory; cork them quickly in order to give them one hour's boiling in the water-bath." While he actually preferred small fava beans, he also canned Soissons and haricots blancs.

With this new technology, beans in jars were tried as provisioning for the navy, but glass is neither light nor durable. It was the British who perfected metal canning methods, first one Peter Durand who used iron coated with tin. He was awarded a patent which he then sold to Bryan Donkin and John Hall who proceeded to mass manufacture canned goods at Bermondsey in 1812. By the next year they were supplying the British Army and Navy. Not that cans were at first cheap or easy to make, but in the long run they transformed the way beans would be eaten. They could be a food that required very little heating expense or could even be eaten cold straight out of the can.

Ironically, Britain's love affair with canned beans comes by way of the United States. The Heinz Company began in 1869 in Sharpsburg, Pennsylvania, at first making pickles. By the late nineteenth century they expanded their line to condiments and baked beans. With aggressive marketing campaigns they eventually expanded sales to Britain in 1886 and a factory at Peckham started production in 1905. The British became paragon bean-eaters, especially of Heinz canned baked beans. Just think of the Who song entitled "Heinz Baked Beans" that includes the lyrics "What's for tea, Mum?" The answer is the title. According to the *Guinness Book of World Records* the UK is the country with the highest per capita consumption of baked beans in the world (in 1999 consuming 11 pounds; 10 ounces per person). The Heinz Corporation estimates that 1.5 million cans are eaten per day, and they report that a 1998 poll voted baked beans one of the products that best represents Britain. London's Business Design Centre houses a time capsule that contains Heinz Baked Beans. Although the context seems odd to most Americans, Heinz Baked Beans are commonly eaten in a traditional breakfast of fried eggs, Cumberland sausages or black pudding (i.e. blood pudding), a roasted tomato and fried bread. A quick and less fussy version just includes the beans on toast, for breakfast or a light meal anytime.

There is also a definite nostalgia connected with Baked Beans (or "Baked Beanz" as it is now spelled after the Heinz Meanz Beanz campaign). In Britain it is a quintessential homey comfort food that recalls youth or student days on a budget. Though of late, many people contend that they're not quite the same as they used to be. Some claim they're watery, too sweet or the beans mushy. Whether the recipe has actually changed or whether memory has embellished the taste over time is uncertain, though the company has reduced the salt content recently.

The modern obsession with canned beans aside, late in the nineteenth century the more typical way to cook beans in Britain was in a soup or as the classic dish "pork and beans." Mrs. Frederick's *Hints to Housewives* of 1880 gives us a good idea of how these were made, in this case by a household cook rather than the reader, who is told how to best instruct her domestic servants. For example, regarding a bean soup she insists that the beans not be cooked haphazardly, and they must be strained. "The excellence of this soup depends upon the way in which it is done and the care bestowed upon it. The cook often spoils it for want of straining – of which she is not over fond; witness the lumpy potatoes and stringy spinach we frequently have to endure." Servants were not uncommon among the middle classes and this was probably the audience for which this book was intended. Here is her pork and beans recipe; the bacon is not in thin strips as in American bacon, but a cured smoked hunk of pork meat.

> *Put a quart of haricot beans to soak in cold water overnight, pour off the water in the morning. Put them in a saucepan with enough fresh cold water to cover. Add a pound and a half of bacon or salt pork and let all simmer gently until the beans are quite soft, adding more water if they boil dry. Remove the pork, scoring it neatly, and place it in the centre of a deep dish. Pour off the water from the beans, leaving them only enough to keep them moist and soft, and let them boil until nearly a mash. Now turn them into the dish containing the pork, around but not over the pork, and put the whole into the oven to bake for about twenty minutes, until it is a nice brown. This is a hearty and very satisfying dish, and one could make a satisfying lunch from it alone.*

There is also a British tradition of the "bean feast": a celebration thrown by bosses for their workers, in which beans were served. It could also be a celebration for a working-class club or society, and this seems to be how the word was first used in print. According to the O.E.D. in 1789, "The annual bean feast at the long-established house in St. George's-Fields, which for so many years has been celebrated under that title, will be held on the 22nd of this present July..." According to legend, King George III made an incognito visit to Woolich

Arsenal and ate some beans and bacon alfresco with the workmen, and enjoyed himself so much that he instituted an annual bean feast to commemorate it. The legend aside, the bean feast did become a kind of working-class holiday spree or "beano" in which raucous behavior and heavy drinking turned everything briefly upside down. This is probably why the popular British comic strip was called *The Beano* – it had a decidedly working-class appeal, with the villains usually upper-class twits and snobs.

The class-associations of the bean feast are made apparent in a hilarious episode in Jerome K. Jerome's novel *Three Men in a Boat*. The men decide to row slowly on a long journey up the Thames, but are often disturbed by steam-driven pleasure boats whizzing past with wealthy passengers. This was a calculated mode of insult: "Another good way we discovered of irritating the aristocratic type of steam launch, was to mistake them for a bean feast, and ask them if they were Messrs … Cubit's lot or the Bermondsey Good Templars, and could they lend us a saucepan." Taking the luxury yacht for a working-class party boat was highly demeaning, to say the least.

The popularity of beans among working-class Britons did not, however, extend to those with taste and discernment. Edward Spencer in his decidedly snotty *Cakes and Ale* of 1897 put it pretty bluntly. "Curiously enough, among the vulgar folk, at the present day, there would seem to be some sort of prejudice against the vegetable; or why should 'I'll give him beans' be a synonymous threat with 'I'll do him all the mischief I can?'" He then discusses the haricot bean "as the idiotic French call it" and says "few people in Europe besides Frenchmen and convicts eat the dried seeds of this form of beans, which is frequently sown in suburban gardens to form a fence to keep out cats…" Furthermore, he adds that "An English 'bean feast' (vulg. beano) is a feast at which no beans, and not many other things, are eaten. The intelligent foreigner may take it that beano simply means the worship of Bacchus." That is, it had become merely an opportunity to get plastered.

Despite such prejudice, through the twentieth century, the British remained addicted to baked beans, especially as an object of working-class pride. One brief if extraneous anecdote may shed some light on this. Actually, it is only a single line in a song from the first version of the movie *Willy Wonka and the Chocolate Factory*. American audiences who saw the movie were fairly perplexed when the spoiled daughter of a wealthy and clearly nouveau-riche nut processor (Verucca Salt) breaks out in song and demands that she wants a "bean feast." Given the working-class northern English roots of her family, it makes perfect sense.

As for the British and green beans, until very recently they were treated with the same violence afforded fresh peas. W. Teignmouth Shore, writing in 1929, put it succinctly: "There ought to be an English Society for the Prevention of Cruelty to Vegetables. So quite appropriately, this recipe for French Beans." The reader is then advised not to slice or chop them, but simply tail, top and string, and then stew gently with butter, some stock and a few drops of lemon juice.

The United States

If cookbooks are to be trusted, colonial North Americans of English descent essentially ate a diet not much different from that in the mother country. In fact, the cookbooks can't be trusted, as they were written mostly for the wealthy and if not outright editions of British works like Hannah Glasse, they still tried to replicate British cookery. The first true American cookbook is said to be Amelia Simmons' *American Cookery* of 1796, which does include American ingredients like corn and dishes such as turkey with cranberry sauce, which people had been eating since colonial times. Most of the book, however, is not terribly different from British cookbooks of the same time, and it is revealing that she only has string bean recipes, but not baked beans.

A better indication of the colonial diet can be found in contemporary accounts such as that of William Douglas, whose report on the British settlements in 1749 related that "in New England ... the general Subsistence of the poorer People (which contributes much toward their Endemical Psorick Disorders) is Salt Pork and Indian Beans, with bread of Indian Corn meal."

The ailment he speaks of is an itch thought to be caused by salty food. There is also documentary evidence in the records of colonial Williamsburg that kidney beans were regularly grown alongside favas, in fact, many different varieties and colors mostly eaten as green beans. Their seeds were carried in stores up through the revolutionary period: Canterbury, a kind of kidney bean and White Dwarf kidney beans, the Turkey snap bean, which probably gets its name from the mistaken origin in Turkey, as well as the Dutch bean also eaten in the pod.

The many varieties and these locales aside, the quintessential American bean dish has always been baked beans, and no place in the United States is more consistently and proudly associated with them than Boston, whose nickname is Bean Town. Before the Red Socks, there were the Boston Bean Eaters, who won the championship in 1897 (they later became the Braves and moved to Milwaukee). The city of Boston has also held regular bean feasts, sometimes connected with political campaigns. There is perhaps no city so firmly associated with a single food in the US, or so proudly eaten by its inhabitants as a matter of civic pride and tradition, which they believe stretches back to their Puritan founders.

There are many hypotheses about the origin of Boston Baked Beans. Some contend that the basic method was learned from the local Indians in the seventeenth century. They apparently baked their beans underground flavored with maple syrup and bear fat, though there is little convincing evidence that they boiled down maple sap to make syrup. The colonists, so the story goes, merely adapted the dish, using molasses and pork fat, and cooked it in a traditional ceramic bean pot in the oven. Another theory contends that the pilgrims, like observant Jews, would bake a pot of beans the night before the Sabbath, in this case Sunday, so as to avoid labor on the day of rest. The beans could be eaten for supper on Saturday night and then again in the morning on Sunday. Although this did become a tradition in later centuries, there is no record of colonial settlers doing this. Another theory has New England sea captains learning the process in North Africa from Spanish Jews who cooked a dish called skanah, which appears to have been a variant of the adafina made with chickpeas. Were this true, then it is not a coincidence of two different people inventing the same Sabbath tradition accidentally but a real historical connection, which seems unlikely. Another possible, if far-fetched theory, has its origins in France, whose cassoulet was introduced to Quebec, which does have as strong a tradition of baking beans as New England.

One thing is certain: there was no tradition of baking beans back in England. Even in the late nineteenth century baked beans seem to have been unknown there. Ella Kellogg, wife of Dr. John Harvey, relates a revealing story in her *Science in the Kitchen* of 1893.

> Beans to be baked should first be parboiled until tender… We mention this as a precautionary measure lest some amateur cook, mislead by the term "bake," should repeat the experiment of the little English maid whom we employed as cook while living in London, a few years ago. In ordering out dinner, we had quite overlooked the fact that baked beans are almost wholly an American dish, and failed to give any suggestions as to the best manner of preparing it. Left to her own resources, the poor girl did the best she knew how, but her face was full of perplexity as she placed the beans upon the table at dinner, with "Well, ma'm, here are the beans, but I don't see how you are going to eat them." Nor did we, for she had actually baked the dry beans and they lay there in the dish as brown as roasted coffee berries, and as hard as bullets.

Maybe the girl was just stupid and another cook might have fared better. In either case, baked beans do not appear in British cookbooks of the time, nor in those stretching back to the seventeenth century. The current British obsession with baked beans, as we have seen, dates only to the early twentieth century.

So, baked beans are indigenous and American. But there are no recipes in colonial America. Amelia Simmons says nothing of baked beans or dried beans of any sort. The first published recipe dates to 1829 and is found in Boston-based cookbook author Lydia Marie Francis Child's *The American Frugal Housewife: Dedicated to those who are not ashamed of economy*. The cheap small-format book was specifically designed to help poor families suffering through an economic depression in the 1820s, and it is hardly surprising that baked beans appear first in a book of this sort. It evidently enjoyed great success and went through thirty-five printings up to the middle of the century.

> *Baked beans are a very simple dish, yet few cook them well. They should be put in cold water, and hung over the fire, the night before they are baked. In the morning, they should be put in a cullender, and rinsed two or three times; then again place in a kettle, with the pork you intend to bake, covered with water, and kept scalding hot, an hour, or more. A pound of pork is quite enough for a quart of beans, and that is a large dinner for a common family. The rind of the pork should be slashed. Pieces of pork alternately fat and lean are most suitable; the cheeks are the best. A little pepper sprinkled among the beans, when they are placed in the bean-pot, will render them less unhealthy. They should be just covered with water, when put into the oven; and the pork should be sunk a little below the surface of the beans. Bake three or four hours.*

In a similar vein Sarah Josepha Hale, the woman largely responsible for promoting the celebration of Thanksgiving in the US, included a pork and beans recipe, in fact baked beans, in the section on "cheap dishes" of her *The Good Housekeeper* of 1841. Though more condescendingly, she writes that "this chapter is *not* written for the *poor*," either the miserable poor who are made so through their dependence on alcohol, or those she calls the "luxurious poor," who are so because they live beyond their means. Rather it is for the frugal and industrious – those who are "growing rich." One also denotes her discomfort with presenting such lowly fare, admitting that "it is an economical dish; but does not agree with weak stomachs." Furthermore, "The beans will not be white or pleasant to the taste unless they are well soaked and washed, nor are they healthy without this process."

The term "Boston Baked Beans" does not seem to have been current until the mid-nineteenth century; Mrs. A.L. Webster's *Improved Housewife* of 1853 is the first recorded appearance in print. It was not until about this time that molasses became an indispensable ingredient in baked beans, its ubiquity having been assured as a by-product of the sugar refining industry. Sweetening beans by any means certainly goes back much further though, and the Quebecois version using maple syrup probably better reflects the dish's early history. In French it is called Fèves au Lard au sirop d'érable, even though it was made with white phaseolus beans rather than favas.

> Soak navy beans or Great Northern beans in water overnight. Drain and rinse. Boil covered with 2 inches of water and simmer until the beans are somewhat tender. Place in a bean pot with the cooking liquid, maple syrup, mustard, thyme, a hunk of salt pork and a chopped onion. Bake for about six hours at a low temperature. Add a little more syrup and serve.

That bean recipes first appear in the nineteenth century is not surprising. Bean recipes of all sorts seem to proliferate most in periods of economic depression, especially when authors pen small inexpensive cookbooks for modest households. This would explain Lydia Child's cookbook (and perhaps also those of the 1930s). As the cheapest form of protein available, they were recommended as the ideal way of making ends meet – that is, assuming one has the time and fuel to cook them, let alone a kitchen and the right equipment.

There was also a certain connotation of beans in nineteenth-century America as a simple frugal food that one would choose not out of necessity but to escape the over-refinement of modern life and the threats it poses to health, spirituality and autonomy. Think of Sylvester Graham, the tee-totaling vegetarian minister who lived in Northampton, Massachusetts, who gave us whole wheat (or Graham) flour and the eponymous crackers, both unsullied by mechanical processing and additives. Graham can be considered the first of those we might call Food Luddites, those who reject modernity for a simpler diet, historical forerunners of our modern health food movements.

These nineteenth-century Luddites and vegetarians also supported their ideas with the latest scientific evidence. In 1842 Justus von Liebig published his *Animal Chemistry* as well as other food-related studies in which he had identified the substance in all food, which we now call protein. By extracting glutens from flour and comparing them with animal proteins he proved that there was no basic chemical difference between them. Of course, he was wrong about that, not knowing about all the amino acids, but in any case, this scientific argument lent weight to the claim that one could live on a vegetable diet, and once research was conducted on specific foods, it was consistently shown that beans have the highest protein content in the vegetable kingdom. It is no wonder then that beans figured prominently in vegetarian diets, which began to spring up mid-century, as did the word vegetarian itself, and vegetarian societies on both sides of the Atlantic.

In the midst of this turn to basic simple foods William Alcott (a New England physician and uncle of author Louisa May) published his *Vegetable Diet* (1849). In it are all sorts of testimonials from individual vegetarians and physicians who attest to the benefits of abstaining from meat. As much as it disparages meat, it also glorifies beans in a way that is almost wholly unknown in Western Civilization. He offers passages such as "no careful inquirer can doubt that bread, peas, bean, rice, etc. are twice as nutritious – to say the least – as flesh or fish." Quoting a study by Percy and Vaquelin, he insists "In bread, every one hundred pounds is found to contain eighty pounds of nutritious matter; butcher's meat, averaging the different sorts, contains only thirty-five pounds in one hundred; French beans (in the grain), ninety-two pounds in one hundred." This is indeed a reversal of fate. More valuable than any other food, he puts beans at the top of a list of nutritious foods with 86 percent solid matter, 14 percent water, and in chemical composition 31 percent flesh forming principle (by which he means protein – and this figure is pretty close), 51 percent heat forming matter (which would be carbohydrates) and 3 percent ash for the bones (which seems to mean calcium).

But all these encomia notwithstanding, there was still a social stigma against beans, mostly the result of gas. Alcott concludes "Beans, whether ripe or green (unless in bread or pudding), are not so wholesome as peas. They lead to flatulence, acidity and other disorders. And yet, eaten in moderate quantity when ripe, they are to the hard, healthy laborer very tolerable food. Eaten green, they are most palatable, but least healthy." In another book for young housekeepers Alcott also warns against beans, regarding the flatulence issue especially, and of all odd things recommends that they should only be cooked in pure water with a little salt and they "should also be eaten for breakfast; and alone or with bread. Those who are vigorous, and who dine as early as twelve o'clock, may eat them at dinner, if they prefer it; but breakfast is the *best* hour; and they should never be eaten in the evening."

Simple frugal diets with or without beans enjoyed a vogue in the mid-nineteenth century, and through them we may be able to make sense of one of history's more intriguing bean stories and begin to understand why Henry David Thoreau decided to abandon civilization, and camp out as a hermit on Walden Pond in 1845 for an experiment in essential living through planting beans. We should not make the mistake of thinking of Thoreau as a kind of back-to-nature type in the mold of wild John Muir, appreciating nature for its own sake. Quite the opposite, he wanted to conquer nature, to plant it, with his own hands rather than with horses and machinery. The chapter of *Walden* entitled "The Bean-Field" records his resolve, "I was determined to know beans." This may have been a self-deprecating joke – to know beans is to know nothing and may be a jibe at erudite learning, but on the other hand he read Homer in his solitude and constantly described his labor in classical, even Herculean terms. The beans "attached me to the earth, so I got strength like Antaeus" (whom Hercules conquers only by lifting him off the ground). There is also something philosophical about his resolve to eek out a living on his own. Independent of civilization (though he did go to town for salt pork and yeast) he could have direct contact with the earth, which perhaps makes beans a logical choice. We can never really know why he chose beans per se and he himself admits "why should I raise them? Only Heaven knows" and "What shall I learn of beans or beans of me? I cherish them, I hoe them, early and late I have an eye to them; and this is my day's work."

And hard work it was. Thoreau sowed 7 miles of bean rows, by one estimation, some 25,000 plants. Then there was staving off the varmints and picking off weeds like Trojans. He did taste the beans, but strangely admits himself "by nature a Pythagorean, so far as beans are concerned" and preferred to trade them for rice. (Though he did serve them to Joseph Hosmer, who came to visit him in 1845 and wrote "our bill of fare included roasted horn pout, corn, beans, bread, salt, etc.") But for Thoreau it was not a trial to live directly off the land. What was the point then? For his investment of $14.72½ he made a net profit of only $8.71½. And the labor appears to have thoroughly worn him out; he didn't do it the next year and later left the pond for good. It wasn't for the sake of profit that he grew these beans but rather to commune with the elemental forces of the earth, the ancient beds where natives once farmed. His aim was to draw in the energy or "virtue" from the earth by walking barefoot and expending his labor. This was something lost when farming became a business, no longer a "sacred art" but merely raising crops efficiently for the sake of selfish profit through which "the landscape is deformed, husbandry is degraded with us, and the farmer leads the meanest of lives. He knows Nature but as a robber." But at Walden it was different. Not a monoculture of wheat, but also food for the woodchucks, and room for weeds to grow which bear seeds for birds. His vision of everything that had gone wrong about farming was an eerie prognostication of the industrial agriculture of the twentieth century.

Navy Beans and Beans for Traveling

Beans have also long been associated with navies, as the name navy bean suggests. They were probably the food the crew was forced to endure once the fresh food ran out. Once the beans themselves were gone that would have been the end, and the saying in French "*la fin des haricots*" meaning the absolute end of everything may derive from this recognition. Another similar saying "*passage du cap Fayot*" may have a similar derivation. (*Fayot* is the French form of the word *fayol* in Provençal, *fajol* or *fagiolo*.) Again, once you pass the Cape of Phaseolus, it's time to break into the bean cask. After that you're done for.

It might seem odd that beans would find a place where fuel would be a precious resource and cooking time would have to be kept to a minimum. But according to Pablo Pérez-Mallaína, beans (chickpeas mostly at first) were a regular provision on Spanish ships crossing the Atlantic from the earliest voyages. The brick stoves would be kept on the lower deck away from wind and set in sand to prevent anything from catching on fire. And with plenty of time, there was little problem with soaking the beans. A typical week's rations for a sailor in the US Navy in 1799 would include 7 pounds of bread in the form of hard tack, 2 pounds of pickled beef, 3 of pork, 1 of salt fish, and one and a half pints of peas or beans, plus potatoes, turnips and the daily half pint of rum. The term navy bean comes from the fact that since the mid-nineteenth century, they were issued regularly to US warships. Pease were the typical legume in Admiral Nelson's Navy, though according to Janet MacDonald, in the Mediterranean and West Indies "calavances" or dried haricot beans would be substituted.

For similar reasons, beans made an ideal army food. Here is one diverting anecdote from the Civil War, surprising only because it took place in the wake of the Battle of Fredericksburg in 1862 after an overwhelming defeat of the Northern troops. Nonetheless, this is what a soldier there remembered in his memoirs. It is also revealing that soldiers often cooked haphazardly for themselves outside of the organized mess (i.e. food prepared by army cooks). This was in a letter from Edward Bridgman to his brother.

> We had a man in our company named Bishop, who was rather odd. He once put a pot of beans on his fire and then was called away for an hour. After he left it occurred to him that he had forgotten to salt the beans. So, on meeting a man of the company, he said to him "Wont you go into my tent and put a little salt into my beans?" A little later he met George Clapp and said to him "Doctor, wont you salt my beans a little? I know Jim will forget to do it." George did not go directly to camp, so meeting a man of the company, he told him that Bishop wanted his beans salted and asked him if he would not do it. He did; and George on his return, also salted the beans, and that, too, with

a double dose! When Bishop returned he prepared to sit down to a square meal. He was a man who could use words of emphasis as of piety, and with the first taste of the beans came "-------- that George Clapp; he must have emptied a barrel of salt into these beans!" George was a brick.

In the mid-nineteenth century beans were also considered one of the ideal foods to take on long cross-continent journeys, the ideal pioneer food because of their durability. Indeed, Lewis and Clark in their first foray across the continent early in the century brought with them 100 pounds of beans from St. Louis. Later they traded for more beans among native tribes, and they ate the beans along with buffalo. Later the migrants would give beans the nickname "prairie strawberries" or "whistle berries" for the musical consequences of eating them. In the provisions for one party on the Oregon Trail, there are listed 1,200 pounds of flour, 400 of bacon, 100 of dried beef, 40 of lard, 200 of corn meal and 150 pounds of beans. But they also brought with them what might be considered luxuries: dried fruit, sugar and coffee, and brandy. One has to wonder though, how could a food that takes so long to cook possibly be useful to those constantly on the move? Beans can certainly be soaked in transit, but as for cooking? They can be simmered while biscuits are being mixed. But it is claimed that another method made even more sense.

One of the best ways to cook beans without a lot of equipment, and which is still practiced in New England and westward across the US, is to put the beans and other ingredients into a cast-iron covered pot or "Dutch oven." This is then set over charcoal embers in a deep pit and then covered with more embers, and sometimes completely buried in dirt until the next day. In a sense, this may replicate the original Indian way of "baking" beans, as the dirt acts as insulation and the embers stay hot all night. But it would also be ideal for traveling in a chuck wagon, as the cooking is done while everyone sleeps, and there is a hot meal in the morning. This method may explain how people on the move could manage to cook a food that takes so much time, as it would be impractical to start a meal of beans late in the day for that evening.

Beans were also legendary foods in the mining camps of California. Here they could be cooked easily even though the habitations were ramshackle. Consider this verse of the popular "Oh Susannah":

> In cabins rude, our daily food
> Is quickly counted o'er;
> Beans, bread, salt meat, is all we eat –
> And the cold earth is our floor.

One must remember though that most miners came to California without honed culinary skills, and an inexperienced cook could easily ruin a pot of beans or worse. Charles Warren Haskins penned a memoir of his experience as a '49-er that contains a great bean story. The dialect of the speaker here is left in the original and is intended merely to record the story as it was told, although obviously it may be regarded in extremely poor taste by our standards. Take notice though that it is a "venerable colored individual from the city of Boston" named Julius speaking, as one who does know how to cook beans.

> Yes, sah! now I spose you is jes' gwine to spress yer ignorance on de bean cooking question sah! jes' as all ob dem gemman did who was ignorant ob de cookin' art, sah; an' who am deficinent in de high culture necessary for de casion, sah. I tells ye dat de ignorance ob de gemman in de early days was mos' stonishing when dey fills de pot chuck full ob de beans, an' den, as dey swell up an' fill de pot chuck full, dey jes' scoop 'em out, 'til dey fills all de old pots an' pans about dere house wid dem half-cooked beans. Yes sah! one ob dose uncu'tivated individuals way down in Calaveras, one day in '50, jes' filled his dinner pot chuck full ob beans, an' when dey undertook for to swell up, he jes' takes a big chain an' lashed de kiver down to keep 'em in de pot. But I tole him dat it wernt no use to do dat, kase de swellin' proclivities ob dem beans am so powerful, sah! dat you raight jes' as well try to spress wid a big chain dem gentle swellin' proclivities ob! ob! --- "Of what Julius?" "Ob de ocean, de ocean sah." "Well Julius did the pot cover blow off?" No, sah; but de whole pot kiver an' all, jes' blowed up froo de roof, an' away it went sailin'

froo de air ober de country towards Bosting, sah, wid dem beans jes' er streamin' along after it. De miners tink it am a comet, suah, wid a long tail jes' er scatterin' de fire an' de grabel stones all ober de country.

About as close as one can get to a taste of miners' beans is a recipe published in 1885 in San Francisco entitled Puree of Dry White Beans, Pioneer Style. It was penned by Jules Arthur Harder.

> *Take a quart of dry white Beans. Wash and pick them well, allowing them to soak overnight in cold water. Drain them, and put them into a saucepan with three quarts of broth, and one pound of salt pork (that has been previously washed and parboiled for five minutes), a piece of raw ham bone, two onions and two carrots. Cover the saucepan and cook slowly until well cooked. Then take out the pork, ham bone and carrots, and pound the soup through a fine collander. Put it back into the saucepan and season with salt and pepper, adding a piece of butter. Cut the pork into small square pieces and fry it, and when serving add it to the soup with small fried bread crumbs.*

Although no particular variety was associated with the mining camps, there is a uniquely Californian bean favored by ranchers and grown in the Santa Maria Valley near the central coast. As an indispensable component of the Santa Maria Barbecue (which includes grilled tri-tip, salsa, sometimes macaroni and cheese) the pinquito is a local star. The name appears to be a Spanglish invention, taking the word pink and adding something that sounds like the word *poquito*, meaning little, because this is indeed a petite pink bean, and particularly fetching. Normally it is cooked with bacon and chili sauce. The only serious Californian contender for bean fame is the King City Pink bean introduced to the Salinas Valley to the north after the area was irrigated at the turn of the century under the instigation of legendary newspaper man Frederick Godfrey Vivian through his newspaper *The Rustler*. It is this bean that is featured in John Steinbeck's *East of Eden*, as the main character, Cal Trask borrows $5,000 from his mother to start a bean venture, hoping to win his father's love by striking it rich. Aficionados still argue over the superiority of these two beans; little pinquito just seems to have had a better publicity agent.

Along with miners and soldiers, among the most renowned bean eaters were loggers and those traveling in the back woods. The US Department of Agriculture Bulletin by Mary Hinman Abel printed in 1906 puts it perfectly:

> There is a general opinion that while they are suitable for robust people leading an active, outdoor life, indispensable to the soldier's outfit and to the logging camp, welcomed by the hunter and woodsman, and a necessary part of the food of the hard-working poor, they are, on the other hand, unsuitable for people leading a sedentary life, and are generally avoided by the invalid and convalescent.

The author even describes a remarkable way to transport beans in the dead of winter. In New England when a woodcutter left for the day he brought along a bowl with cooked and frozen beans inside. In the beans there was a string so he could pull out the beans and drop them in a pot for defrosting.

Not everyone was so enthusiastic about this bean-laden diet, even for lumberjacks. Otto Carqué in a book purporting to be about natural foods nonetheless warns that beans should not be eaten by the sedentary more than twice a week and only in small amounts combined with green leafy vegetables. For the robust – "In lumber and mining camps where beans are served almost daily and often combined with pork, the workers become afflicted with gout and rheumatism." In all these contexts beans were food fit for hardworking outdoorsmen, but there was an entirely different set of people who would come to be associated with beans – the immigrants.

Immigration

In the late nineteenth century and up to 1932 when quotas were first set, America received an unprecedented outpouring of immigrants from Southern and Eastern Europe, and in particular those places which had not yet industrialized and whose teeming population made life increasingly precarious. These poor huddled masses, "the wretched refuse of your teeming shore" naturally arrived with their own foodways, which in many cases featured cheap economical bean dishes. From southern Italy came pasta e fagioli, Jews from Poland and Russia brought cholent, Scandinavians their pea soup. While first generation immigrants tried to hold on to their food habits as best they could, their children were often pressured to assimilate. Some groups resisted this better than others and in some cases "ethnic" foods went mainstream – think of spaghetti, bagels and so forth. But by and large, food habits of the old world were lost or transformed beyond recognition, or merely reserved for holidays. Nutritional science of the time was complicit in this assimilation. As Harvey Levenstein points out, people were advised "that the essence of European economical cooking: the *minestras* and *pasta-fagioles* of Italy, the *borschts, gulyashen*, and *cholents* of eastern Europe were uneconomical because they were mixtures of foods and therefore required uneconomical expenditures of energy to digest." Strong seasoning, especially garlic, was equally derided.

Especially interesting, and what will account for the awakened interest in bean dishes later in the century, are the children of these second generation assimilated immigrants who tried to recover what had been lost. For them food provided one of the most tangible connections to their ancestry, which became especially important as old neighborhoods disintegrated, people spread around the country, intermarried and felt that their heritage was being lost. Below is a discussion of some bean dishes as they were prepared among immigrant groups, or as they have been reconstructed by later generations. Although many of these dishes have changed in transition and with new ingredients, they give some idea of the amazing range of ways *P. vulgaris* has been used.

From Europe, there came a wide variety of peoples with their own culinary traditions and ways of cooking beans, many of which have since been lost. Ironically, many of these reintroduced the bean back to America, or merely substituted *Phaseolus* for bean dishes familiar at home. This traditional soup comes from Hungary.

Bab Leves (Hungarian Bean Soup)

Take small white navy beans and soak overnight. Then boil gently covered in water with a smoked pork knuckle, pig's feet or a ham hock, until the beans are tender. Taste the cooking liquid, if it is too salty replace some with fresh water. Add chopped onions, parsnip, carrot, leeks and garlic and continue to cook. When the vegetables are cooked thoroughly, remove the meat from the bones, chop and add back to the soup. Then make a roux of a spoonful of lard, a spoon of flour and a heaping spoonful of Hungarian paprika. Mix this with a cup of sour cream and add to the soup, stirring and reheating gently. Serve. Or if you are lardophobic, just add paprika-laden sour cream.

Another European group who arrived in the US, not large in numbers, but with a fascinating history, are the Hutterites. There is also a Hutterite bean, a lovely pale greenish-white heirloom with a kind of eye surrounding the seed scar, which often goes into soup. It was introduced to the US in the 1870s after the Hutterites were exiled from Russia and is still grown among the Hutterites in Montana and over the Canadian border in Saskatchewan. The Hutterites themselves were followers of German Anabaptist Jakob Hutter who in the sixteenth century espoused pacifism and communal living. Their industrious communities were formed around "bruderhof" or house of brethren, where property was held in common in imitation of the apostles, and cooking was done in a communal kitchen. After persecution they moved from Moravia to Russia and from there to the US and their cooking is an amalgam of German and Russian traditions.

The Amish or Pennsylvania Dutch are a related group, in terms of religious identity, although they arrived much earlier from Germany. They too have a distinctive set of beans cultivated using traditional methods. There is a distinctive Amish bean soup, or Preaching Soup as well, which uses a ham bone, potatoes, celery and carrots. One particular variety is grown among the Amish, the gnuddlebuhn – which roughly translates as turd bean because of its squared off ends that make it look like rabbit droppings. They also grow the bizarre pretzel bean, thus called because the green pods curl and twist just like a pretzel.

From Eastern Europe there are a number of traditional bean recipes. In Serbia there is a kind of baked bean dish called prebanac and a soup called pasulj, which includes tomatoes, carrots and sausages simmered with beef bones and sometimes served with dumplings. To the north in Trieste, now part of Italy and neighboring Slovenia, comes a bean and sauerkraut soup flavored with bacon, called la jota. It can also be made with pickled turnips. We have already discussed the cholent made with beef brought by Ashkenazi Jews.

Bruna bönor is a Swedish dish of brown beans using a distinctive meaty *Phaseolus* developed in Europe and reintroduced to the Americas. It is popular especially in the Midwest where many Scandinavians settled. They are cooked much like other beans, except they are flavored with brown sugar, vinegar, cinnamon and nutmeg and in the end are very sweet. The more common Great Northern bean can also be used in this dish, and in fact has become one of the most important beans grown in the US.

Of all the ethnic cookbooks published in the immediate wake of immigration and intended to hold onto Old World traditions, none speaks so eloquently of the ability of food to retain identity than *Treasured Armenian Recipes* of 1949. In this particular case, survival, literally, as a people was at stake.

> We entertain two purposes in gathering and publishing these Armenian recipes. Our primary hope is to perpetuate and honor old Armenian customs and pass them on to the growing generation of young Armenians in this country... A race of people who've lived through twenty-five turbulent centuries does not give up trying. Our hope is that young Armenians will seize upon these recipes ... as an heirloom and make them their own.

Appropriately there are many bean recipes, including one for plaki made of dried beans with carrots, green pepper, celery, garlic, parsely and dill simmered in tomato sauce.

Of all immigrant groups, Latino culture has naturally made the most extensive use of the bean that belongs to the Americas. In fact these people were so closely associated with a diet of beans that a derogatory slur for a Mexican was "frijolero" or just "beaner." Many people of Mexican descent didn't technically immigrate though. Rather the place where they lived was a Spanish colony (and then the independent state of Mexico after 1821) that was later annexed by force by the US. In turn, many of these people were of Native American descent and were engulfed by the Spanish only a few centuries earlier. On the other hand, many people of Mexican ancestry also immigrated into the Southwest, Texas and California.

It would also be incorrect to say that Mexicans in the US lost their indigenous cuisine. Rather, it was assimilated by mainstream US culture, and was transformed to fit Anglo taste. Justifiably, many argue that Tex-Mex should be considered a unique cuisine in its own right, a historical development rather than a bastardization. Chili con carne is one invention that belongs to this tradition, and as purists insist, "chili ain't got no beans." But in this context, and faced with such adaptations, authentic Mexican food, or what was construed as such, did become a matter of cultural pride, something which held the community together along with traditional mariachi music and dances. Whether re-fried beans belong more properly to the newfangled or authentic tradition is a matter of debate, but it is the quintessential way to serve beans among Mexican Americans. The name re-fried is actually a misnomer, since the beans are only fried once. Literally frijoles refritos means fried over. This recipe makes no claim to authenticity, but is at least typical. These can be eaten with tortilla chips, used to fill rolled burritos or eaten as a side dish. Or it can be layered in a casserole with tortilla chips, salsa, cheese and cooked meat, a decidedly US invention.

Refried Beans

First bring a pot of pinto beans to the boil. (Pinto means colored, just as the horse is mottled brown and white.) Boil for five minutes then drain. Return beans to the pot and add fresh water, chopped onions and garlic, chili powder, cumin and oregano, and a few soaked and chopped ancho chili peppers or canned chipotles in adobo if you like, and boil gently for about two hours or until tender. Then add salt to taste and continue

to cook until thick. Serve these beans and save the leftovers. Next fry a
chopped onion in lard until brown, and add the cold leftover beans and fry
them gently in a cast-iron skillet, and mash with a sturdy fork or a potato
masher, adding a little water or chicken stock if necessary.

Beans have been equally important among other Latino groups in the
US. Normally each group uses the bean variety preferred in their country of
origin. Among Hispanic groups on the east coast even the term for a bean can
separate communities. Among the longer-established Puerto Ricans, a bean in
"Nuyorican" is called a habichuela. Among more recently arrived Dominicans it
is a frijol. Among Cubans, the black bean takes precedence. There is a company
called Goya, which caters to the specific culinary traditions of each of these
groups with a huge range of canned beans, probably the best source for *Phaseolus*
varieties in the US. Among the large Cuban community in the United States
there are several dishes that incorporate beans, such as Moros y Christianos,
which is rice and black beans. The most popular dish, however, is Cuban black
bean soup of which there are many variations.

Sopa de Frijoles Negros Cubana
Soak black beans overnight, discard water. Make a soffrito of onions, garlic
and green peppers with a bay leaf and cumin, fried in olive oil. Add beans,
a hunk of ham and cover with water. Simmer for about an hour or until
tender. Remove ham and dice. Return to soup. Add salt and pepper to taste.
Mash some of the beans to make a thick soup. At the very end add a good
dash or two of sherry or vinegar. Serve on top of a mound of white rice,
garnished with a chopped egg, chopped raw onions and chopped cilantro.

Another country whose history has been tied to Spain since conquest in
1571 is the Philippines, and since 1898 and the Spanish-American War, the US
has been a destination for a large community of immigrants. Their food culture
is a brilliant amalgam of Asian, Spanish and American traditions. Halo-halo
comes from the Tagalog language and means to mix. It can be combined with
a wide variety of ingredients but usually includes shaved ice, condensed milk,

sugar, sweetened cooked beans and a mix of tropical fruits and coconut, as well as sweetened plantain, yam or tapioca, often topped with ice cream or flan. It is served in a tall glass as a dessert or snack. Pre-mixed halo-halo ingredients can be bought in jars in shops serving Filipino communities, and eating it is a singular way of reconnecting to tradition and homeland.

Although their numbers are proportionally small, the Brazilian communities in the US are fervently passionate about their national bean dish, one of the most hallowed in the bean repertoire: the feijoada. It is always featured at family gatherings, as a vivid reminder of their homeland. Traditionally it is served at midday with a good caipirinha (a drink of cachaça, lime juice and sugar) and followed by a sound nap. Ideally it is made with the entire pig, every part including ears, snout and tail. It is said to have originated among African slaves using the cheapest cuts of meat, but clearly it is also an amalgam of Portuguese, Native American and African elements. Versions also exist in Portugal, made with red or white beans, and in Angola, a former Portuguese colony.

Brazilian Feijoada

Begin by soaking black turtle beans over night. The next day brown in a skillet various cuts of pork, ideally Brazilian linguiça and carne seca, and ribs but smoked ham hocks and any smoked sausages will do. The adventurous can add pig's feet and any other part. Set the meats aside and in some of the remaining fat brown a chopped onion and garlic. Simmer all the ingredients together for about two hours or until beans are tender. During cooking check for salt, which will depend on what kind of meat you are using. Add a shot of vinegar at the end and hot sauce if you like. Serve garnished with slices of orange, along with white rice, sautéed mustard greens and farofa (seasoned toasted manioc meal, which can be sprinkled on the stew or eaten as a side dish).

Mid-twentieth Century

Periods of economic depression quite understandably force beans into prominence as meat becomes expensive and families have to find cheap alternative sources of solid nourishing food. Not that this was done with glee. It is also in such periods through history that the stigma of beans intensified and their association with the lower classes or working classes became stronger. This association of beans with working-class culture is beautifully illustrated by a song written by Frank Loesser (of *Guys and Dolls* fame). In it a self-proclaimed "working girl" laments her life as a "weary dreary drudge" who spends her hours doling out beans to customers in a cheap "beanery."

> Beans, beans, Marching up and down again. Beans' beans, Served with Boston brown again. Lima beans, kidney beans, Butter beans and soy beans… But ah, my friends, and ah, my foes, You don't know what it means To be raised from the cradle With a ladle in your hand. To fish 'em up and dish 'em up For all the world to swish 'em up – It's more than any mortal can stand. That gooey sticky, icky, Picky family of greens Known as beans, beans, beans.

She dreams of a better life married to a millionaire or as a star in Hollywood, but instead is stuck with "Those tootin', tootin', hootin', Shootin', nasty little fiends Known as beans! Beans! Beans!" The song was meant to be in the 1938 film *Stolen Heaven*, but perhaps one can understand why it ended up on the cutting room floor.

A better fate awaited the song by Hoagy Carmichael which was immortalized by Ethel Waters in a 1939 recording. It tells a story of perseverance through the depression and redemption through financial security and being able to "keep up with the Joneses." Ironically security means being able to eat beans, much better than nothing at all.

> Bread and gravy, lots of bread and gravy,
> Beans and bacon, lots of beans and bacon,
> No more lay-offs, no more frettin'
> Full day pay offs, since I'm getting
> Lots of bread and gravy all the time.
> Peace and quiet, lots of peace and quiet,
> Friends and money, lots of friends and money

No more ramblin', through with gamblin', scramblin'
Right up with the Joneses all the time.

As long as we are on the topic of bean tunes, the most popular of these is Louis
Jordan's "Beans and Cornbread." This is a traditional combination throughout
the South, the cornbread is often crumbled on top of the stewed beans. It has
been suggested that the song may be a commentary on race relations. In it
beans and cornbread get in a fight and the former taunts "meet me on the
corner tomorrow night" to settle it once and for all. The refrain is "I'll be ready."
In the end they decide that they really work better together, but not without
the unveiled threat "it makes no difference what you think about me, but it
makes a whole lot of difference what I think about you." In their tenuous peace,
the chorus agrees they should hang out together like chitterlings and potatoes,
like strawberries and shortcake, corned beef and cabbage, liver and onions, red
beans and rice, bagels and lox, sour cream and biscuits – all classic combinations
that really don't work without each other.

No verse better captures the association of beans and poverty than Gwendolyn
Brooks' *The Bean Eaters*, first published in 1960. In it an elderly couple looks
back on better days from their rented back room. "They eat beans mostly, this
old yellow pair." It is a quiet, sad poem, and the figures are perfectly delineated
"as they lean over the beans" much as Carracci's bean-eater in the painting did
several centuries before. There is perhaps no food that better describes social
standing than a lowly bowl of beans.

All the same, beans have been exalted too; they are even a hallowed fixture
in the US government. There is a long-standing tradition in the US Capitol
that august senators should be able to dine every single day on common bean
soup. Its presence has become the stuff of legend and various legislators are
given credit for inaugurating the dish. Joseph G. Cannon, Speaker of the House
from 1903 to 1911, has the most colorful claim, having burst out one day in
protest after perusing the menu "Thunderation, I had my mouth set for bean
soup! From now on, hot or cod, rain snow or shine, I want it on the menu

every day." With this demand, the cooks willingly obliged and apparently all eleven Capitol dining rooms have served it every day ever since. The reason, so eloquently defended by Senator Everett Dirksen, a republican from Illinois in the 1960s, is as follows:

> It was many years ago that a very dignified and slightly belligerent senator took himself to the Senate Dining room to order some bean soup, only to discover that there was no bean soup on the menu. This dereliction on the part of the Senate Dining room cooks called for an immediate declaration of war. So the senator promptly introduced a resolution to the effect that henceforth not a day should pass, when the Senate was in session and the restaurant open, that there would not be bean soup on the menu. It has, therefore, become an inviolate practice and a glorious tradition that the humble little bean should always be honored. There is much to be said for the succulent little bean – any kind of bean, be it kidney, navy, green, wax, Kentucky, chili, baked, pinto, Mexican, or any other kind. Not only is it high in nourishment, but also it is particularly rich in that nutritious value referred to as protein – the stuff that provides energy and drive to the bean eater and particularly the senators who need this sustaining force when they prepare for a long speech on the Senate floor. I venture the belief that the marathon speakers of the Senate going back as far as the day of the celebrated "Kingfish," Senator Huey Pierce Long of Louisiana, and coming down to the modern marathoners in the forensic art such as Senator Strom Thurmond of South Carolina and Senator Wayne Morse of Oregon, both of whom have spoken well in excess of twenty hours and felt no ill effects, would agree the little bean had much to do with this sustained torrent of oratory.

Presumably the senator had some himself to sustain his own prolixity. But the question remains, why bean soup of all foods? Beans are indeed little and humble and they send just the right message of simple square homespun honesty that these populist politicians wanted to project. If they're good enough for my constituents, they're good enough for me. This was very much the tack taken in the presidential campaign of Bill Clinton, which focused on his own humble roots. Although known for his weakness for french fries, in his memoir he was willing to point out a particular joint called McClard's which serves "unquestionably the best barbecue beans in the whole country." Oddly, in an earlier campaign, a TV ad featured this jingle "If you're tired of eating beans and greens and forgotten what pork and beef-steak means, there's a man you ought to be listening to... Bill Clinton's ready, he's fed up too. He's a lot like me, he's a lot like you." Everything depends on the context. When addressing a rural audience who actually has to eat beans, you make a promise of beefsteak. When you're trying to show everyone else that you're common folk, you let them know you eat beans. In either case, the association of beans with the masses and poverty is crystal clear.

It is also clear in this brilliant recipe by Russell Baker. The context was a legendary 4,000-dollar dinner thrown by gourmet Craig Claiborne in 1975. As a rejoinder Baker devised this bean dish, which he claims to have perfected in 1937 in his *cuisine du dépression* phase.

> *The dish is started by placing a pan over a very high flame until it becomes dangerously hot. A can of Heinz's pork and beans is then emptied into the pan and allowed to char until it reaches the consistency of hardening concrete. Three strips of bacon are fried to crisps, and when the beans have formed huge dense clots firmly welded to the pan, the bacon grease is poured in and stirred vigorously with a large screw driver. This not only adds flavor but also loosens some of the beans from the side of the pan. Leaving the flame high, I stirred in a three-day-old spaghetti sauce found in the refrigerator, added a sprinkle of chili powder, a large dollop of Major Grey's chutney and a tablespoon of bicarbonate of soda to make the whole dish rise. Beans with bacon grease is always eaten from the pan with a tablespoon while standing over the kitchen sink. The pan must be thrown away immediately.*

But even this beautiful recipe pales beside the perversity of one conjured by the Michigan Bean Commission sometime in the 1960s, obviously out of creative desperation. It wins the runner's up award for the most deranged use of beans:

Bean Fudge

4 c. Michigan sugar	*1 ¼ milk (part canned)*
½ c. cocoa	*½ c. karo syrup*
¼ t. salt	*½ bean puree*

Boil to 235° – Add ½ cup butter. Cool to 110° then add 1 cup peanut butter, 1 tsp. vanilla. Beat until creamy. Pour in large buttered cakepan. Cool. Cut in squares.

First place for perversity goes to the Idaho Bean Commission. The Berkeley Co-op had the guts to distribute this in all seriousness to their customers in the 1970s. This is something you give your enemies at Christmas.

Pinto Bean Fruit Cake

2 cups well-cooked pinto beans	*½ teaspoon salt*
¼ cup cooking liquid from beans	*1 teaspoon cinnamon*
½ cup butter or margarine	*½ teaspoon ground cloves*
1 cup sugar	*½ teaspoon allspice*
2 teaspoons vanilla	*½ teaspoon mace*
1 egg, unbeaten	*2 cups finely chopped peeled apples*
1 cup sifted all-purpose flour	*1 cup seedless raisins*
1 teaspoon soda	*½ cup walnuts or pecans chopped*

Mash the beans with the bean liquid thoroughly, using potato masher or electric mixer. Cream butter, add sugar gradually, beating until fluffy. Add vanilla and whole egg. Beat well, then beat in the mashed beans. Mix thoroughly. Sift together flour, soda, salt and spices. Add half the flour to the batter and stir until just mixed. Spoon into buttered 9-inch tube cake pan. Bake at 350° for one hour. May be served with a hard sauce if desired, but it is very nice served plain.

Notwithstanding the publication of such recipes, in the end, Americans are not great eaters of beans, and this is largely the result of the central place of meat in the diet. Most cultures place beans not at the periphery but at the core, beside the staple starch. Americans consider beans a side dish; that is, something easily dispensed with, or replaced with corn, pasta or something else. And then there is the persistent stigma of beans. Helen Black put it very well in this make-believe food diary, also published in the *Berkeley Co-op Food Book*. Recalling 1954 she writes: "Beans are cheap, but so low in status. Should never have served them at my last dinner party. Loud cries of indignation by the men, the trouble-makers. They feel affronted with cheap food, no matter how delicious." Of course in the 1970s the author was still trying to promote beans, though apparently faced continued protest.

The US does grow a lot of beans though, mostly soy as we shall see, but dry beans for consumption as well. The USDA reports that among dry bean producers, the US ranks sixth behind Brazil, India, China, Burma and Mexico. Between 2001 and 2003 Americans ate 6.8 pounds of dry beans per capita, which is 11 percent lower than a decade before. According to the Bean Education and Awareness Network, a large consortium of smaller regional groups, as of 2004 the leading states growing beans for the table in the US are in the Midwest, with North Dakota clearly in the lead with 475,000 acres planted (which includes black-eyed peas, limas and garbanzos, but not soy, which far outstrips production of all bean varieties). Next is Michigan with 185,000 acres and Nebraska and Minnesota slightly behind with 110,000 and 100,000 respectively. Idaho, Colorado and California trail behind, with Washington, Wyoming and Texas behind them. The majority grown are kidney, red, navy, Great Northern, black, pinto or cranberry beans. If Americans aren't consuming them in great numbers, one can only presume they are for export.

Phaseolis Redux

Of all strange twists of fate, the vulgar bean, or at least certain varieties have found a niche in late twentieth-century gourmet circles. This is partly the result of Slow Food ideology, which seeks to rescue threatened traditional foods, but also a valorization of what was once considered homely peasant fare that takes a long time to cook. Beans fit the bill perfectly.

Perhaps the *P. vulgaris* variety with the greatest claim to tradition hails from the American Southwest, the Anasazi bean, named for the ancient ones as they are called by modern-day Indians. Today they are cultivated in Arizona around the remarkable ancient cliff dwellings such as those at Mesa Verde. In the 1980s (or by some accounts in the 1950s) an archeological team from UCLA working in this area uncovered a clay pot sealed with pine tar containing a mottled red and white bean which they carbon dated to about 500 BCE. Remarkably, some of these beans sprouted, so the story goes, and some intrepid businessmen decided to market them. At first called New Mexico Cave Beans, they were later trademarked by the Adobe Mills Company under the name Anasazi beans. Apart from the fact that beans lose the capacity to germinate after about fifty years maximum, and that the beans were probably really obtained from farmers in the area, the story makes great publicity. For consumers hoping to capture the authentic flavor of ancient Anasazi cuisine or a reasonable confabulation of it, this was an ideal product and remains so for American Indian enthusiasts.

Marketing schemes aside, the Hopi, descendents of the Anasazi, still use beans in their daily diet, and they figure in their religion as well. The Powamuya or bean dance is held in February as a kind of initiation rite for young boys. During this boys are assembled in a ceremonial kiva, an underground chamber which reenacts creation from the navel of the earth. The men of the village then appear dressed as kachinas, human personifications of the spirits; they frighten and ceremonially whip the boys, later giving them gifts of sprouted beans that have been grown in the kiva, and instruct them in their duties as members of the community. The ceremony ensures a bountiful harvest of both sturdy beans and young men. Not that this is some kind of tourist attraction; outsiders are not invited.

We have already met the lamon bean introduced by the humanist Valeriano. This bean is today treated with reverence in northern Italian cuisine, particularly in pasta e fagioli. They are also cooked in soup with cabbage, mixed with potatoes in a dish called pendolon, in a consistency like polenta and served sliced hot or cold, and cooked with pork in various stews. Since 1993 there has even been a Syndicate for the Protection of the Lamon Bean and a festival held every September in Belluno. The European Union has awarded the bean and its four different forms (spagnolet, spagnol, calonega and canalino), IGT status (Indicazione Geografica Tipica), which essentially legally protects the name in marketing. One can construe all this as a marketing ploy, but it is truly a gastronomic phenomenon too. For those who regard the modern global food system as corrupt, a simple locally grown bean attaches people to place and community, and their pride in it is earnest.

The same is true of the sorana in Tuscany. They too have a festival and IGP (i.e. "protected") status for this milky white pearly gem. Near the little hilltop town of Sorana north of Florence the bean is cultivated along the sandy banks of the Pescia River. The moist and gentle climate, and hills which give this area the nickname of "La Svizzera Pesciatina" or Little Switzerland, yield beans with almost imperceptible skins when cooked, and a firm but delicate texture. There is no colorful story about their introduction, but these beans have been so beloved that the composer Gioacchino Rossini is said to have made a deal with his fellow composer, Giovanni Pacini. In exchange for some of these precious beans, he would correct a score for him. A bean festival is held regularly in September and is a major tourist attraction, as with the lamon, emphasizing the bean's history and traditional uses.

Vying for attention with these is the magical zolfino bean, another New World fagiolo with a sulfurous yellow color – *zolfo* means sulfur. Grown in the Pratomagno region between Florence and Arezzo along the Val d'Arno it is prized as being the most buttery of local beans with a dense and smooth texture and an extraordinarily thin seed coat. So the farmers claim, it was only rescued from near extinction in recent decades by the minions of Slow Food. The bean is protected by the organization's "Ark of Taste" and is grown using only organic methods. The cynic might see this hoopla as merely a matter of good marketing, and since they are fairly hard to find even within Tuscany, the zolfino is expensive – all the better then as the object of passion for gourmets seeking traditional historic ingredients.

This Italian rapture over beans is easy to understand. For current generations in the wake of economic success compounded with the changing structure of society and abandonment of the countryside for cities, eating in traditional ways has become more a matter of nostalgia, trying to recapture an imagined past, abetted by a lively tourist trade seeking out the indigenous and authentic. Not surprisingly, people will pay a lot for a bag of lowly beans, as long as they can picture the happy farmer growing them – the zolfino, lamon or sorana, following traditional methods that stretch back to antiquity. Of course neither the methods today nor these beans go back so far.

Among all these Tuscan beans, perhaps the only one which can truly claim an ancient pedigree is the fagiolina grown only to the southeast around Lake Trasimeno near the same spot where Hannibal decimated the Roman Army. Its ancestry is confirmed because unlike these others, this one is *Vigna unguiculata*, the original phaseolus rather than a New World bean.

France also has its revered *P. vulgaris* types. The haricot tarbais is considered the ideal bean for cassoulet. There has been a cooperative association growing and marketing these beans since 1988 and in 1992 a Brotherhood of the Tarbais was formed to protect and promote the threatened bean. In 2000 the bean was awarded IGP (Indication Géographique Protégée) status, which delimits where it can be grown, with what fertilizers and pesticides and protects the name legally.

There are other heirloom beans in France which are marketed under the rubric of traditional varieties. In the Vallée de Lys around Calais there is also a Lingot du Nord, advertised with the "Label Rouge" a designation of quality control and legal status for the name. They are claimed to have a skin so thin that no soaking is necessary. There is also the tiny green flageolet or chevrier, which looks pretty much like the tiny beans one finds inside green beans, dried. They are served traditionally with gigot d'Agneau (leg of lamb). The Mogette de Vendée (pronounced mo-het) is another protected bean as of 1996, white with strangely squared off ends. It is typically served with a ham from the Vendée. As elsewhere, there is a Nuits de la Mogette festival promoting the bean.

In coming decades, one can only expect a greater profusion of designer beans, traditional heirloom varieties, mammoths and miniscule dwarf varieties, in every brilliant color and coming from every corner of the globe. And perhaps if these beans fetch decent prices, the developed nations of the world may once again turn, even if slightly, back toward their historical bean-eating roots. Beans may just rise again.

10

Limas and the Lesser Phaseoli: Andes

In the *Phaseolus* genus there are fifty-five separate species, and aside from *P. vulgaris*, the other commonly eaten domesticated species include *P. acutifolius*, the tepary bean of the American Southwest, *P. coccineus*, the scarlet runner, and *P. polyanthus*, the year bean. There are also some other minor wild species used as food. The most important member of this group is *P. lunatus*, the moon-shaped or the lima bean. Its name does come from the Peruvian capital of Lima, even though perversely it is pronounced "lime-uh" in English. It is among the largest of beans and for those who were subjected to them when young in the form of canned limas, the memory of their pasty texture, bitter metallic aftertaste and lurid green color can only evoke the gag reflex. This is a pity, for when fresh or even dried they are among the most pleasant and affable of beans, hulking in proportions, gentle and sweet. There is a smaller tender variety called the sieva or butter bean, which was domesticated around 800 CE in Mexico or Guatemala according to the archaeological record.

The large lima, however, is native to the Andes. Those found at the Guitarrero Cave in the highlands of Peru were domesticated even before both the common bean and corn. This cave is among the most remarkable sites because it contains textiles and red decorated pottery as well as the oldest cultivated plants in the New World, found in layers dated about 8,500 years ago, although by some accounts they are even older. They are thus roughly contemporary with many Old World sites of bean domestication.

Like the Aztec Empire, that of the Incas was formed only about a century before the first contact with Europeans and it stretched thousands of miles down the western flank of South America from modern-day Ecuador down through Peru to Bolivia, Chile and Argentina, from the highest points in the Andes down to the flat coast. This posed unique challenges for farming at radically different altitudes and latitudes and may explain why so many plants were adapted to varied conditions, and why complex systems of terraces and irrigation were developed. The Incas were conquered by Francisco Pizarro in the 1530s much the same way the Aztecs were conquered by Cortés. The record the conquistadors left of Inca agriculture at the point of contact suggests a highly organized system of state mandated distribution of food and an extensive system of accounting using knotted strings. They also had huge storage centers to prevent famine in the case of crop failure. The Inca staples were corn, quinoa and amaranth, as well as their primary contribution to the rest of the world – the potato. These were grown in countless varieties including chuño, a kind of small mountain freeze-dried potato that can be stored. Beans were equally important in the Inca diet, particularly the lima, even though they did have domesticated sources of animal protein from llamas, ducks and guinea pigs.

The original method of cooking lima beans, or pallares as they are called in Peru, is difficult to reconstruct, but this salad is a good example of how Spanish ingredients and methods combined with native ones. It is still popular today in Peru.

Ensalada de Pallares
Soak the dried lima beans overnight, and boil until tender. Chop some
small green chilies, and an onion and soak for about fifteen minutes in

fresh lime juice and salt. Chop a tomato and combine with the onion mixture to form a "salsa." Combine with the drained beans, add some olive oil, gently stirring without breaking the beans and let marinate about an hour so the flavors combine and the beans absorb the flavors.

Although actually a species of *P. vulgaris*, a particular bean grown in the Andes, which comes in a wide variety of colors, deserves mention here. In the high altitudes where water boils at a much lower temperature, it is impractical and fuel inefficient to boil beans. Instead they are fried and popped, rather like corn (cancha, or as they are marketed in the US, corn nuts) – not exactly popped dramatically like popcorn, but until they become crunchy. This bean variety has a hard shell, so the moisture inside builds up pressure and they explode when heated. The same can be done with hard-shelled fava beans. In the Andes these are called nuñas in the Quechua language. They too have been identified in the Guitarrero Cave site and thus may be among the earliest domesticated plants on earth.

Like *P. vulgaris*, the lima bean was taken to Europe some time in the sixteenth century, and also to the Philippines with the Manila galleons. It is widely grown throughout Southeast Asia, particularly in Burma. It was also taken to Africa from Brazil, and is now the primary dried bean eaten in the tropics there and in Madagascar. The lima has been so acculturated in these places that synonyms include Rangoon bean (i.e. Yangon in Myanmar), Burma bean and Madagascar bean. It never really caught on as a major food in Europe, probably because the climate is not ideal for its growth. They did attract the attention of botanists though. De L'Obel's *Icones stirpium, seu plantarum exoticarum* of 1591 is a massive set of meticulously rendered images of exotic and native plants. It includes what many consider to be the first depiction of the large white lima, speckled lima and the small sieva. Here it is called *Phaseolus Brasiliani*, and from the picture of the huge swollen pod, it is fairly unmistakable.

Lima beans are grown in Spain though, and the traditional paella Valenciana includes a fat variety called the garrafón. In its original form, a paella was made of rice with rabbit and snails, but today it can include shellfish, as well as both green beans and the lima.

Lima beans thrived, however, in North America, particularly in the South. They were brought there long before colonial times and were grown by Native Americans. Cooked like other beans, they seem to have been the preferred species for delicacy and sweetness in the early Republic. An adventurous and very international cookbook appeared in the early nineteenth century authored by someone who called herself (or himself) Priscilla Homespun, a strange choice for a pseudonym considering the contents. In the second edition of 1818 of *The Universal Receipt Book* we are offered this intriguing recipe. A spider is an iron pan with built-in legs that can be set over hot coals in the hearth and a dredging box is a small perforated container out of which flour is shaken for dredging meat or flouring a work surface.

An Excellent French Fricasee of Beans, So As to Resemble the Taste of Meat

Take Lima or frost beans, and after boiling them sufficiently to eat, brown some butter, taking care to season it well with salt, in an iron bake pan or spider, previously warmed or heated. Put into it your beans, after letting them drain a few moments, and fry them till they begin to turn brown, then mix with them a few onions finely chopped or shredded, and continue the frying for a short time longer, adding some parsley. When the beans appear to be nearly cooked, put to them a very little water, and sprinkle them over well with flour from a dredging box, some salt, and a little black pepper, and let them stew for a few minutes. When done stir into them the yolk of an egg beatup with a spoonful of water, to which add a like quantity of vinegar. A spoonful of mushroom catsup will likewise be found to improve their taste greatly, but it should be added when the flour is put to them.

A lima bean recipe and method of preservation is also included in Mary Randolph's classic *The Virginia Housewife* of 1824.

Lima, or Sugar Beans

Like all other spring and summer vegetables, they must be young and freshly gathered: boil them till tender, drain them, add a little butter, and serve them up. These beans are easily preserved for winter use, and will be nearly as good as fresh ones. Gather them on a dry day, when full grown, but quite young: have a clean and dry keg, sprinkle some salt in the bottom, put in a layer of pods, containing the beans, then a little salt – do this till the keg is full; lay a board on with a weight, to press them down; cover the keg very close, and keep it in a dry, cool place – they should be put up as late in the season, as they can be with convenience. When used, the pods must be washed, and laid in fresh water all night; shell them next day, and keep them in water till you are going to boil them; when tender, serve them up with melted butter in a boat. French beans (snaps) may be preserved in the same manner.

According to Eliza Leslie (*Directions for Cookery*, 1840), the lima bean was the preferred species in the nineteenth century. "These are considered the finest of all the beans, and should be gathered young. Shell them, lay them in a pan of cold water, and then boil them about two hours, or till they are quite soft. Drain them well, and add to them some butter and a little pepper." Catherine E. Beecher and Harriet Beecher Stowe (author of *Uncle Tom's Cabin*) composed an extremely popular guide to household management called *The American Woman's Home*. In a section on cookery, basically a tirade against the dreadful culinary abuse of food in the US, they nonetheless burst forth with enthusiasm when mentioning fresh vegetables in the US, in particular the bounty of lima and other beans. They mention that when travelers return from Europe the first thing that strikes them is "such ripe juicy tomatoes, raw or cooked; cucumbers in brittle slices; rich, yellow sweet potatoes; broad lima beans, and beans of other and various names; tempting ears of sweet corn steaming in enormous piles; great smoking tureens of the savory succotash, an Indian gift to the table for which civilization need not blush." If any passage suggests that Native American foods were wholeheartedly adopted in nineteenth-century America, this is it. Even the sourpuss Mrs. Trollope, who had practically nothing nice to say about Americans, suddenly burst forth with enthusiasm over limas. "They have a variety of beans unknown in England, particularly the lima-bean, the seeds of which is dressed like the French harrico; it furnishes a very abundant crop, and is a most delicious vegetable: could it be naturalized with us it would be a valuable acquisition."

The succotash mentioned above is the classic lima bean dish in the US. It is a word which entered the English language directly from Narraganset (*msikwatash* or *msickquatash*). It was indeed first cooked by Native Americans, sometimes with bear meat, and adapted thereafter to suit Anglo tastes. It is always cooked with fresh green limas out of the pod and corn, but otherwise a variety of vegetables can be added including butter and cream. The canned variety popular in the twentieth century was truly loathsome, and may have given rise to what cartoon fans will recognize as Daffy Duck's favorite expletive: Suffering Succotash! This older recipe is from *Housekeeping in Old Virginia* published in 1878.

> *1 pint shelled Lima beans*
> *1 quart green corn, cut from the cob*
> *1 quart tomatoes, prepared and seasoned as for baking*
>
> *Boil the corn and beans together till done, then drain off the water and pour in a cup of milk, a tablespoon of butter, and salt to the taste. Let it boil up, and then pour in the tomatoes. Let all simmer an hour. Baked or stewed dishes should have cracker or brown biscuit grated on top, before sending to the table.*

One other place lima beans show up is in the classic Kentucky Burgoo. This is a long-cooked soupy stew of mutton or lamb, chickens and a wide variety of vegetables, corn and beans. It is traditionally served at parties during the Kentucky Derby and there is fierce rivalry among those who prepare it.

As with other bean dishes, limas also appeared in the traditional chuck wagon serving cowboys on the seasonal roundup. Recalling times past, the *Chuckwagon Cookbook* recounts the cook of the CY Ranch, one Hi Pockets, "who could make honey of lima beans and could stretch his menu to serve any number of visiting ranchers along with cowpunchers on the roundup." His signature lima beans with steak is something that could only have been invented in this context.

Soak 2 cups lima beans overnight. Simmer beans until nearly done. Use dutch oven or large casserole to cook this in.

2 lbs. round steak   ½ tsp. dry mustard
1 tsp. salt   1 tbsp. brown sugar
few grains pepper

Tenderize steak by pounding, cut into 4 pieces. Roll steak in flour. Put layer of beans, then layer of steak, then layer of beans. Repeat until casserole is nearly full of steak and beans. Mix remaining dry ingredients with 1 cup tomatoe juice and 1 tbs. bacon fat. Pour mixture over beans and meat. Place an onion on top and bake until meat is tender and beans are done. Add a little water from time to time if mixture becomes too dry.

A final word of caution about lima beans: they should not be eaten raw. Although breeders claim modern cultivars are safe, some types, apparently the darker ones, contain glucosides, which break down into hydrocyanic acid when chewed and thus must be cooked in several changes of cooking water. Cooking destroys these poisons, but it is still claimed that a steady diet of lima beans can cause goiter. It is also claimed that cooking raw lima beans releases hydrogen cyanide gas, which disrupts respiration, especially of birds, so keep Polly far from the kitchen if you prepare them fresh.

Scarlet Runners

Phaseolus coccineus or runner beans, best-known of which is the scarlet runner, were first domesticated in the highlands of Mexico around 2000 BCE, remains of which were found at a site in Tehuacan. Archaeological remains of wild forms date back to 7000 BCE. The plant gets its name from the color of its vibrant flowers, reminiscent of cochineal, a scarlet dye and foodstuff obtained from an American insect. Their English name reveals everything about their character, showy and brazen, and always on the move. They are also unusual among bean plants because they are perennial where the ground doesn't freeze, and they twine in a clockwise direction, unlike common beans which go the other way. Also, when emerging from the ground, the cotyledons remain buried and the first leaves one sees are true leaves. They can be eaten immature pod and all, dried as mature beans and even the bright flowers can be eaten in salads. The tuberous root too is eaten in Central America. Runner beans also come in various colors, including a jet-black variety, the so-called painted lady, and the potato bean named for its size and starchy texture. (Though other American species share this name: *Pachyrhizus tuberosus* or yam bean and *Apios americana*, a kind of groundnut.)

Scarlet runners were first planted in Europe as an ornamental, and are still today. They were brought to Spain some time in the sixteenth century, where strangely and almost imperceptibly they took the place of fava beans in many traditional dishes, and even borrowed a form of their name as fabes (rather than habas – in modern Spanish f shifted to h). The most important of these scarlet runner dishes is the celebrated fabada asturiana, made with a huge white variety of runner bean called, appropriately enough, the fabada bean or Judía de la Granja after the place the finest are grown (La Granja de Sans Ildefonso). Legend says that the fabada, again originally made with fava beans, was offered to the Moors as they were making their way north in their conquest of Spain in the eighth century. Being so stuffed they couldn't continue, the region remained in Christian hands. Made with this New World bean, the recipe has hardly changed. The Judía de la Granja itself is said to have been first cultivated in the gardens of the palace at La Granja laid out by King Felipe V in 1721 where they were gradually selectively bred for size and pale color. A 2.2 pound bag of these beans can be bought online for about $20. Along with the other requisite ingredients it is hardly an inexpensive dish, but worth the effort nonetheless.

Fabada Asturiana

Soak the beans overnight. The next morning, put the beans in fresh water in a terracotta cazuela and simmer gently with a piece of salt pork until the beans begin to be tender. You will probably have to keep topping off with more water throughout the cooking process. Next add a chopped onion, some garlic, a spoon of smoked Spanish paprika (pimentón), and a good pinch of saffron threads and then a few links of chorizo (Spanish cured sausage, rather than the fresh Mexican variety), and morcilla (a Spanish blood sausage) both pierced a few times so they don't burst and let everything cook together for about an hour until thick and bright yellow. You can also add chopped tocino, a kind of Spanish bacon (not to be confused with the Filipino variety, which is a distant relative). Also, the cazuela should be shaken, not stirred, to prevent breaking the beans. To serve, spoon out beans in bowl with a few slices of each sausage.

There are many words for New World beans in Spanish – alubia, frijole and the mysterious judíos – which usually refers to *Phaseolus* species including the scarlet runner. The name seems to imply that it has some association with Judios or Judia, meaning Jew, though there is no historical evidence of this, and it is probably a false etymology. The word was used in the Middle Ages, referring to an Old World species, and may be a corruption of the word *habicheula* or *favichuela* – meaning a little fava. Around 1100 the word *judiheula* is found in Mozarab writings (that is, Christians living under Moorish rule) as a variant of *fusihuela* (meaning a little faseol) and from this the word *judía* appears to descend. That is, it meant *Phaseolus* all along.

The scarlet runner did very well among gardeners in the Netherlands, and a synonym is the Dutch case-knife bean. In France it is called the haricot d'Espagne, in German a Feuerbohne or fire bean. But this species thrived best in the cool and wet climate of England. *P. coccineus* was brought there by John Tradescant (father and son of the same name, both gardeners of Charles I). In 1633 these beans were planted in the family garden in Lambeth, known as The Ark, which also housed the first museum in England opened to the public, a cabinet of curiosities collected from around the world. Both Tradescants are buried nearby in St. Mary-at-Lambeth, now a museum of gardening history. The plant caught on particularly well in England, especially as an ornamental. They are said to have been first popularized as food by eighteenth-century agricultural writer and curator of the Chelsea Physic Garden, Philip Miller, who called it the *Phaseolus Indicus, fiore coccineo, seu punico*, yet he notes that already they "are very common in the English gardens, being planted for the Beauty of its scarlet flowers." Furthermore "it will thrive in the City, the Smoke of the Sea-coal being less injurious to this Plant than most others, so that it is often cultivated in Balconies, &c. and, being supported either with Sticks or Strings, grows to a good Height, and produces flowers very well." Scarlet runners are to this day popular as both flowers and food in Britain.

Thomas Jefferson planted scarlet runners in 1812 noting "Arbor beans, white, crimson, scarlet, purple ... on long walk of garden." But this plant never really caught on in the US as food, and is still fairly hard to find as either a green vegetable or dried bean.

One of the most celebrated forms of *P. coccineus* is found in Greece – a large variety called Fasoulia gigantes or Elefantes Kastorias (meaning elephant beans due to their enormous breadth), which since 2003 has been given protected status by the EU. It is grown in the prefecture of Kastoria, way in the north on the banks of the Aliakmonas River and Lake Kastoria where it thrives in the cool summers of this mountainous region. There is an annual fair in nearby Lakkomata, as well as a festival every winter in Florina, honoring a soup made of these beans (though it can be made with others too), which also celebrates St. Nicholas who is revered for having fed the poor with it. The Greek bean soup called fasolátha has become so popular that a common saying runs "*Fasolátha pou trefi tin Ellada*" or All of Greece is raised on bean soup.

Fasolátha

Soak beans overnight, drain, and then put them in a pot covered with water, bring to a boil and drain in a colander once again. Next fry chopped onions, carrots and celery in a soup pot until fragrant and browned. Add a clove or two of garlic, finely chopped, and a good pinch of thyme and oregano. Add soaked beans and cover with water. Bring to a boil and then lower the heat and gently simmer until the beans are tender. Add chopped tomatoes and salt and gently simmer. When ready to serve, put soup in bowls and garnish with chopped parsley, freshly ground pepper and a hearty drizzle of olive oil. The flavor can also be perked up with a squeeze of lemon juice.

The most obscure member of this *Phaseolus* group is *P. polyanthus*, or year bean, only recently recognized as a distinct species. It is not found in archaeological sites at all, and since it is very similar to wild forms, the assumption is that it was domesticated fairly recently. In Mexico it is known as botil (though the same name is also used for scarlet runners), in Guatemala piloya, dzich or piligüe depending on the region. In Colombia it is called petaco, cache or matatropa. In recent decades it has been marginalized because it is considered inferior to kidney beans, which are more expensive, and as coffee plantations and livestock rearing proliferate, fewer people grow this bean.

11

Tepary Beans: Native Americans

The tepary bean (*Phaseolus acutifolius*) is one of the smallest and toughest of beans with remarkable resolve and stamina. It comes in both white and brown cultivated forms, but early in the century there were no fewer than forty-six distinct colors. They require lengthy cooking but are also particularly sweet and nutty tasting. The plant withstands, and even prefers, arid desert conditions rather than regular irrigation and is thus uniquely adapted to the American Southwest. Like its wild progenitors, it is planted only when there is rainfall. Then it positively thrives in blistering heat, quickly sending down long roots and producing seeds which in turn survive until the next desert rains. This also explains its tiny size. In the time that it takes most large beans to grow and mature, they would wither in this heat. The tepary guzzles up water and reproduces as quickly as it can, as is the case with other tiny beans, such as the lentil and east Indian moth bean. Beans selected for size are naturally much more dependent on humans and irrigation to survive; the tepary is a desert bean.

The origins of the bean are debated since wild forms are found stretching from the Southwest through Central America. Archaeological remains in Puebla, Mexico, date back 5,000 years, but it is not known where it was first domesticated. A strong claim is made for domestication, perhaps independently, in the Southwest where wild varieties can still be found. At the very least, the so-called "land races" present there have adapted to survive where few other beans could.

Remarkably, just as the beans have adapted to this climate, so too have the people there in a kind of symbiosis with the bean. That is, their bodies have adapted over millennia to make efficient use of a low-fat and high fiber diet based on teparies. Some scientists contend that they also evolved to store fat efficiently as a kind of insurance against lean seasons. The use of plants such as mesquite, cholla cactus buds, prickly pear cactus (saguaro) and teparies also provides soluble fibers which form gels that slow digestion and prevent swings in blood sugar levels which trigger hunger pangs. That is, the indigenous diet was ideally suited to life in the desert and an unpredictable food supply.

One group in particular depended on this bean, formerly called the Papago, which means "bean people" from the word *papah* (meaning bean) and *ootam* (people). As of 1986 the tribe legally changed its name to Tohono O'odham, which means desert people, considering the older name derogatory. Nonetheless the historic connection of this people with the tepary is of paramount importance; the name itself comes from the Indian word *t'pawi*. There are many stories about the origin of the name, but the nicest one takes place in 1701 when the beans were the principal crop being grown at the Mission Nuestra Señora de los Dolores in New Mexico. When Spanish visitors asked what they were growing, the response was *T pawi* – It's a bean. In fact, for the Desert People it was the staple, not corn. It supplied 49 percent of their protein, as well as iron, niacin and calcium.

As recently as the 1930s the Tohono O'odham grew 1.5 million pounds of teparies a year. Half a century later the bean had almost completely disappeared. So too had this people's original way of life. A modern diet high in fats and sugar combined with an increasingly sedentary lifestyle left them at serious risk of diabetes and heart disease. The population of the Tohono O'odham reservation now has one of the highest rates of type 2 late-onset diabetes on earth. And if the theory of a fat storage gene is true, then a steady and predictable diet would quickly lead to obesity.

How this happened is a familiar story. Old World crops and domesticated animals were introduced by the Spanish, as well as cooking methods such as frying in oil. Then in the twentieth century, in an effort to acculturate Indians, they were sent to English-language schools, encouraged to adopt Anglo lifestyles, and many fought in wars where they learned about mainstream culture. And of course, slowly their traditional diet was largely replaced with non-indigenous foods: white flour, sugar and fats. This modern diet was seen as progressive, affluent and American. Government programs also subsidized these foods under the assumption that they were more nutritious. Modern systems of irrigation were introduced in the name of progress, which benefited neither the tepary nor the Tohono O'odham.

The recovery of tepary beans in recent years has been on the one hand an attempt to curtail rampant health problems, but it has also been a way to recover indigenous culture and cuisine. Rejecting the supposedly traditional Indian foods of past generations such as greasy fry bread, this is a return to the original diet and agricultural complex. The effort to revive traditional Native American culture has been developing for many decades, but it's only very recently that Tohono O'odham have seen the indigenous diet as a way literally to survive as a distinct community. A very interesting group, called Tohono O'odham Community Action (TOCA) has been sponsoring the planting of teparies. This largely follows the work of Gary Nabham in researching vanishing indigenous species in Arizona through Native Seeds/SEARCH as well as the more recent RAFT (Renewing America's Food Traditions), which has a "red list" of 700 endangered traditional foods.

For the Indian, eating teparies is a way to recover health and identity. Terrol Dew Johnson, who leads TOCA group, says, young Indians, as well as older ones, have been alienated from their own culture. These foods reintroduce them to their traditions. They are used in ceremonies and carry the stories of the Desert People. One such story involves Coyote running with a bag of tepary beans; when he tripped they spilled out and flew into the sky creating the Milky Way. Look up at night, there are white teparies scattered across the heavens. Eating tepary beans is thus a way of recovering lost identity.

What is particularly fascinating about this case is not only the way these beans are promoted as an object of tribal pride, but how they're marketed beyond the reservation. Being savvy about economic prospects, these farmers understood that they could capture a segment of a gourmet niche for rare and authentic species that connect to place and *terroir* (something that is part and parcel of the whole Slow Food movement). They also sold the allure of a traditional native food – that just happens to be very high in protein and low in fat and sugars. Heritage Foods USA sells them online for $19 for a 2-pound bag. Compare that to about 89 cents for a bag of pinto beans at the supermarket.

Tepary beans represent not only a recovery of traditional Tohono O'odham culture, but also a way for outsiders to feel good about supporting the community as well as eating something rare, authentic and formerly looked down upon as simple and unsophisticated. This is in a sense a new kind of elitism, one that understandably values local sustainable agricultural systems that don't depend on industrial farming and petrochemicals. But it is also a way of purchasing authenticity – and briefly tasting a way of life that is perceived as having been lost with the homogenization of cuisine in the modern era. Just as attitudes toward Native American culture shifted in the latter twentieth century, so too have attitudes toward beans, so firmly associated with these people.

There are a few other fascinating wild beans native to the Southwest that bear mentioning, primarily because they were once gathered as food, and today are almost completely forgotten. All these are in the genus *Phaseolus*, which is merely an accident of taxonomic history. *P. filiformis* is closely related to teparies and grows in much the same places. It is the undomesticated wild desert bean, which according to Gary Nabham, some people still remember eating years ago. They called it a frijolillo; today it is sometimes called the slimjim bean. Another Southwest native is *P. parvulus* or Pinos Altos Mountain bean, even smaller than the others, but also edible. *P. pedicellatus* is the Sonoran bean, *P. polymorphus* is the oddly named variable bean (which is just a translation of the Latin) native to Texas. *P. polystachios* is the thicket bean and *P. ritensis* the Santa Rita Mountain bean, native to Arizona. There are even more. It is not as if there weren't many beans native to North America, as there were once many native peoples. Both the beans and the people were marginalized by modern agriculture; new people came in and so too did big blustering beans like *P. vulgaris*.

I learned, literally today August 9, 2006, as I write these words, Slow Food and RAFT are holding a cooking competition in San Francisco featuring tepary beans and a few other endangered bean species. Among the finalists' entries are *White Tepary Bean and Vegetable Cassoulet, Brown Tepary Bean Puree with Indian Fry Bread and Tempura Squash Blossom; Velvety White Tepary Beans with Cotija Cheese; Grilled Flank Steak and Tomato-Jalapeño Jam; and Chicken and Tepary Bean Pozole*. As of my writing, the winner was not yet announced.

I offer something a little less fashionable, hopefully approaching traditional cooking methods.

Tepary Bean Stew

Soak the teparies overnight and in the morning change the water. Boil them gently in a covered earthenware pot over a bed of hot coals for about two hours, though it may take longer. Then season with salt and add one cut up rabbit, preferably wild, though domestic works very nicely. Any other wild game would also be appropriate. Add a handful of chicos, which are corn kernels dried in a horno but not nixtamalized like posole. They can be bought on the roadside in New Mexico and have an ethereal smoky flavor. Any dried corn will also work. Also add a soaked and chopped dried red chili pepper if you like and wild green onions. Cook as long and slowly as you can, adding more water if necessary.

12

Soy: China, Japan and the World

Sometimes called the miracle bean or Cinderella bean, the pale waif we know as soy has miraculously emerged as the most widely grown bean on the planet, the darling of the food industries and genetically one of the most extensively modified of all plants. But this transformation did not happen overnight – it has been in process for a few thousand years, stretching back to the time when soybeans were first fermented, processed into milk and curd and made into a variety of condiments bearing little resemblance to the humble bean. Few of us are familiar with soy as a bean, and for very good reason: it is fairly unpalatable as such, with a slightly bitter taste and unpleasantly beany odor. In consequence, soy is almost always processed into something else. The green, lightly boiled and salted edamame from Japan is probably the only form of whole soy one is likely to encounter, and these are made from a very specific cultivar bred for its mild flavor and consumed immature.

Glycine max is the Latin name for the soybean, which was descended from another wild bean, *Glycine soja*. Confusingly the genus is also divided into sub-genera, separating a set of wild Australian cousins. The bean that interests us was first cultivated in the eastern half of Northern China, based on recent DNA evidence, probably around the Yangzte River or to the north about 3,000 years ago, though some make a claim for Mongolia. That makes it a relative latecomer among the ancient beans, but with an extremely long pedigree nonetheless. As in the process of domestication elsewhere, the beans grew in size, the plant grew taller and sturdier and the pod held its seeds rather than shattering. The former is useful for humans, the latter, for the plant to propagate itself in the wild.

Among the Chinese, soybeans are considered one of the five ancient sacred grains, including glutinous and regular millet, wheat, beans and rice. By tradition these crops were introduced by the second celestial emperor Shen Nung, in his book on medicine variously dated between 2800 and 2300 BCE, which pre-dates the actual domestication of soy. Shen Nung is also credited with the invention of agriculture and for having tried thousands of plants to discover their therapeutic virtues, the last of which killed him, a remarkable self-sacrifice. Shen Nung is purely the stuff of myth, but it is significant that later dynasties would attribute the origin of soy to a mythical founder of their civilization, in recognition of its central importance in the Chinese diet. Although archaeological evidence may eventually push back the origin of soy domestication, 1100 BCE is for the moment the earliest certain date.

In any event, soy did become central to Chinese culture and cuisine, whose development, along with the many marvelous transformations of soy, is the result of several fortuitous factors. Unlike the other ancient cultures which domesticated beans, China has had a long and almost uninterrupted historical development, with a stable and centralized empire stretching across many millennia. Since the Zhou dynasty (c. 1000–250 BCE) government functionaries organized irrigation projects, kept tax records, introduced the use of iron implements, and also promoted the cultivation of soybeans. Most importantly, the court and its cookery were not isolated from the general population. There was a degree of social mobility, unlike say in India, through service in the state bureaucracy. Bureaucrats learned about cuisine at court and took these fashions to their outposts. They had enough wealth and enough servants to maintain large kitchens and permanent professional chefs. This assured that culinary techniques would spread beyond the walls of the emperor's palace.

Another important factor, as in the development of any complex cuisine, is the central role of the family, and the reverence toward elders. This assured that recipes would be handed down within households from older generations to the younger, that traditions and kitchen technologies would be maintained intact over centuries. The importance of filial piety, obedience to elders, and ancestor worship may have played some part in the long and stable development of culinary traditions in China. Combined with a wealth of indigenous ingredients and an absence of food taboos that translated into a willingness to eat practically anything, it is no surprise that China developed one of the most complex and sophisticated cuisines on earth.

The spread of Confucian philosophy may also have been a part of this development. Unlike in the West where the individual and autonomy are treasured values, in China the harmony and order of society is maintained through proper behavior and deference to superiors, whether in the household, state or cosmos. Individual rights and desires are subordinated to the good of the whole and to avoid misunderstandings or conflict a complex ritualized code of behavior governs daily interaction as well as table manners. The use of chopsticks emerged as a way to banish the violence of knives from the table. Prescribed ways of eating, the order of meals and a classic repertoire of recipes flourished here centuries before they did in Western Civilization. All these factors may explain how the cultivation of soy and its transformation into so many different products spread throughout the empire and remained intact so long.

One final factor which must not be discounted was the influence of Buddhism and the vegetarian diet dictated by the principle of non-violence. Although it may only have been Buddhist monks who followed this diet strictly, it meant that invention of vegetable alternatives was of prime importance. Nicknames for soy include "meat without bones" and "Cow of China." Tofu thus became a central part of monastic cuisine, and was also a central feature in places where Buddhist vegetarianism was practiced, as in Japan. In China there was also a tradition for Buddha's birthday on April 8, when soy and adzuki beans would be given to temple visitors.

The Han dynasty (202 BCE to CE 220), roughly contemporaneous with ancient Rome, with whom they traded, witnessed the confluence of these many factors: a centralized bureaucracy based on Confucian principles, social mobility and political stability. Most importantly, the state consciously promoted agricultural innovations through the publication of books, government extension agents, irrigation projects and development of new crops. For example, grapes and alfalfa were introduced, as well as new fruits and sugarcane. The agricultural treatise of Fan Sheng-chih of the first century BCE describes multiple cropping of wheat and millet, how to irrigate rice fields and rotate legume crops to serve as green manure, which also of course fixed nitrogen in the soil. Technologically this was also the period that developed gunpowder, the compass, high-fired porcelain, the hammered iron wok and not coincidentally the very first fermented soy products. Storing food by means of fermentation was just as important as growing food and cooking it. Sheng-chih also noted that soybeans were grown as a kind of insurance crop, as it will survive when grains such as millet fail. But in their unprocessed state, soybeans were considered a rather course food appropriate for the rural masses. A history of the Han dynasty (Han Shu) written about CE 90 stated that whenever there is a famine, people subsist on little other than soybeans and other grains.

The importance of soy in this dynasty is also corroborated by archaeological findings, more specifically the recovery of the remarkably preserved body of a particular woman who died in 168 BCE, the wife of Li-ts'ang the Marquis of Tai. Her last meal, the remains of which were in her stomach, included musk melon seeds. She was also buried with a full retinue of foods to enjoy in the afterlife including rice, wheat, glutinous and regular millet and soybeans – the five sacred grains, as well as red lentils. There were also a wide range of fruits, roots, meat, fish and poultry and amazingly instructions on how to cook them and a list of necessary seasonings which included whole fermented soybeans (shih) probably similar to fermented black beans still used today and a kind of fermented soybean paste (jiang or chiang). The word *shih* is also recorded in Han dynasty textbooks, evidence of its popularity.

The importance of fermenting soybeans was not only a matter of preservation. Although they could not have known this, fermentation counteracts the anti-nutritional factors present in soy. Soybeans contain what are called trypsin inhibitors, which prevent the pancreas from producing a digestive enzyme important in breaking down protein. Raw or improperly cooked soybeans can also cause an enlarged pancreas; they inhibit growth and lead to cancerous tumors. Phytic acid present in soy also hinders the absorption of iron and zinc, which are necessary for proper function of the nervous system. The phytates essentially fuse with the metal ions, including calcium, forming compounds that pass directly through the digestive tract unchanged. Fermentation destroys these toxins and the enzymes involved in the process also break down soy making it more digestible, and in a sense pre-cooking them so they require less fuel. In many products there are also microorganisms involved in the fermentation process which provide vitamins. In other words, fermenting soybeans not only made them more interesting and tasty, but also provided a range of more nutritious foods that could support a large population.

The jiang or soybean paste mentioned above is the ancestor of miso and soy sauce. The word was used in the third century BCE and merely meant any salted and fermented product. The *Analects*, compiled by the followers of Confucius, even specify that certain forms of jiang are appropriate to season particular foods so the flavors harmonize. After fermented meat and fish, eventually beans were processed in the same fashion, with molds grown on rice (such as *Aspergillus oryzae*). These are mentioned in the first century BCE by one Shih Yu, but the process of making the bean paste or doujiang is only described in CE 535. Basically steamed soybeans were mixed with powdered starter made from rice wine (containing yeasts) along with yellow mold and salt, all left to ferment together. The resulting paste was then used as a condiment or a flavoring in composite dishes.

The invention of tofu is also traditionally set in this period, being ascribed to one Liu An, grandson of the founder of the Han dynasty through an illegitimate father and prince of Huainan, who lived from 179 to 122 BCE. He is revered as an alchemist, and with a certain logic the first to learn how to curdle soy milk. There is in fact no mention of tofu in his extant writings, and there is no mention of tofu at all until many centuries later in the early Sung dynasty. More likely, the invention was an accident. There are references to soy milk at this time, which is made merely by pulverizing the beans in water. The addition of unrefined sea salt, perhaps first an experiment in preservation, would cause the liquid to coagulate. The solids would then be separated from the liquid, exactly as in cheese making, and then pressed to form a solid block. Gypsum (calcium sulfate) or nigari (in Japanese, which is mostly magnesium chloride with other minerals refined from sea salt) are the preferred coagulants today. Others speculate that tofu making could have been learned from Mongols or even from India, two cultures that already knew how to coagulate milk into various cheese-like products.

Tofu was also over the centuries transformed further into related products. It could be deep fried and a resulting pocket stuffed with other savory ingredients. It could be marinated or fermented, which we will encounter shortly. Yuba or bean curd skins are another by-product made from the upper layer of soy milk that is heated and cooled. The skin is removed from the milk and dried. These brown sheets are then reconstituted and used to wrap other foods, cut into noodles or crumbled into prepared dishes.

Another significant development of the Han and later dynasties was the elaboration of a complex medical system, which as in the West categorized beans and bean products in dietary prescriptions tailor-made for every individual. The foundation of Chinese medicine is ascribed to another celestial emperor of the third millennium BCE, Huang-ti or the Yellow Emperor, whose classic *Nei Ching* forms the basis of one of the longest lived medical traditions on earth. In fact the work was compiled ages after Huang-ti was supposed to have lived. Nonetheless, it profoundly influenced the ideas surrounding beans and their usage in China. In this system the human body is directly affected by external forces such as wind, cold, moisture and so forth. We are a microcosm of the greater cosmos, governed by the same opposing yin and yang forces. Through our bodies also flows a kind of universal energy principle called qi or chi. An abundance of qi is an indication of sound nourishment, strength and emotional balance; a lack of qi makes you weak and susceptible to diseases. Diseases also arise from internal imbalances of heat, cold, moisture and dryness, as well as clogs in the passages through which qi flows. Acupuncture is one way to open these passages. The foods we eat directly influence our inner physiological functions and this is why diet forms the foundation of Chinese medicine. Basically yin foods are used to counteract yang disorders and vice versa, but weather, emotions, exercise, sleep patterns and a whole range of other variables are also taken into account by the Chinese physician.

Soybeans are not all categorized alike in this system. Black soybeans are a yang food, denoting heat, and are thus used extensively for colds and the like. Many medicines were also made from black soybeans. Modern science corroborates some of these uses, and there has been a recent wave of popularity for black foods, including soy.

White or yellow soybeans, on the other hand, were considered cold or yin, or sometimes neutral, and somewhat heavy on the body. How they are processed also influences their somatic effect. T'ang dynasty physicians postulated that stir-roasted beans are excessively heating, while when boiled they are dangerously chilling. Fermented as shih they also cool, but only in the form of jiang are they balanced and appropriate for a healthy body. Thus medical theory itself promoted the use of fermented products over simply cooked ones.

Soy sauce is the other major soy product used in Asia and it too has a fascinating history. Originally it was a liquid drawn from the bean paste jiang and in Chinese the word *jiangyou* means exactly that. Our word soy, for the bean and the sauce, is actually derived from the Japanese word *shoyu* (soy sauce) not from the Japanese name for the bean, daizu, or from the Chinese name dodou. Its first appearance in English is credited to none other than philosopher John Locke, who in 1679 mentioned in his journal that mango and saio are two sorts of sauces brought from the East Indies. Later references simplified the term further, with soy or soya being the most common form, again, referring to the sauce rather than the bean.

The origin of soy sauce may stretch back to the Han dynasty as well, if not earlier, as there are references to jiang liquid, though they may refer to something drawn off any fermented product, perhaps a fish sauce, something like modern nuoc mam, or even Roman garum. Remarkably, the first certain description of soy sauce dates back only to the sixteenth century, not long before Europeans were already importing it, and the word *jiangyou* came into common usage only in the seventeenth century. Its production was similar to the manufacture of bean paste, involving koji mold as well as wheat or barley and cooked soybeans with salt. This was fermented in huge vats outside and periodically stirred. After several months the solids would be pressed down and the liquid decanted as a light and delicate first grade soy sauce. The solids could also be rehydrated and fermented again several more times for darker lesser grades.

Soy products were also very important in Japan from an early date, and although there were probably similar indigenous forms, the range of soy products were introduced from China probably around the same time Buddhism was, in the sixth century. Since four-legged creatures had been banned as food in Japan since the seventh century, vegetable-based sources of protein to supplement fish, as well as soy seasonings became all the more important. Hishio, a kind of soy paste, was already in use at this time. It developed into both miso paste and both forms of soy sauce: tamari, which is merely liquid drained from miso and including no wheat, and then shoyu, which does contain wheat.

Regulations concerning the production and taxation of miso were put in place in 701 by the Emperor Monmu, but the word miso only appeared about a century later and was formed from the characters for flavor and throat. Miso was used as a universal flavoring, and there were dozens of varieties ranging from darker, stronger and more salty pastes to lighter and sweeter varieties. In general most are made by first steaming rice or barley and letting a mold form, *Aspergillus oryzae*. The resulting product is called koji. This is then added to cooked soybeans, water and salt and left to ferment for up to two years. There has developed a certain connoisseurship over miso as sophisticated as that used to judge wines, with specific geographic origins and preferred years of production. The finest miso pastes fetch prices comparable to the finest wines too.

The use we are most familiar with in the West is miso soup containing tofu and vegetables, which emerged in the Kamakura period (1185–1333) specifically as a vegetarian food appropriate for Zen Buddhists. The soup spread from the temples and Shogun courts to become a popular food among the masses, to such an extent that a common saying ran "everything is alright as long as there's miso." Significantly, soy in this form became more than a mere flavoring in Japan, but a staple food eaten at breakfast and to conclude most meals, and one that could be preserved indefinitely without refrigeration. In a sense the soup is also instant, as it need not be made with fresh ingredients. There are hundreds of different misos available in the West today; shiro miso is a reddish mild form appropriate for this soup, quite different from aka miso, which is darker and saltier.

> *Begin by making a dashi stock, this can be purchased as an instant powder but its flavor is a little brash. More subtle is the homemade version, only slightly less instant, which is made from dried bonito flakes and kombu, a dried seaweed. Begin with a large piece of seaweed and bring to the boil in a pot of water, skimming off foam. Just before the water boils remove the seaweed and throw in a few handfuls of bonito flakes. Bring to a boil again, then remove from the heat. Allow the flakes to settle and drain. Into the clear soup you can add slivers of green onion, cubes of tofu, perhaps radish or carrot cut into elegant shapes, and a few strands of wakame, a more delicate seaweed. These should be considered a garnish, and no more than a few pieces should grace each bowl. Cook gently until these are tender. Lastly, take some of this stock and add it to a bowl with some miso paste to thin it out and then return to the pot. Do not boil after this point. Serve immediately.*

Japanese soy sauce or shoyu can also be traced back to this period. By tradition it was developed from a form of miso named Kinjanzi, after the temple in China where the Zen Buddhist priest Kakushin learned to make it in the thirteenth century. He is said to have discovered that the liquid drawn from this miso made an excellent condiment, then called tamari or murasaki, meaning deep purple. Shoyu doesn't appear in the written record until 1559 in the diary of Yamashina Kototsugu, but was probably in use long before this time. Shoyu is also frequently mentioned in the *Ogusa Ryori-sho* cookbook written about the same time by a leading cooking school family of Kyoto, and used as a seasoning in a wide variety of dishes. From this time it was also produced in great volume commercially. Its use truly proliferated in the Edo period (1600–1867) and came to be associated with that quintessentially Japanese food – sushi.

Why this happened is largely the result of the intentional isolation and unique development of Japanese culture without outside influence. In Edo, the major city, as well as Osaka and Kyoto, it was largely the urban sophisticated elites who patronized the classical Japanese arts – music, theater, painting, as well as cuisine. In what might be considered the very first restaurant culture, chefs and restaurant owners vied for attention with innovative dishes, beautiful tableware and tranquil gardens. What they invented was classical Japanese haute cuisine, with its emphasis on simplicity and purity of flavor, minimalist design of the plate and a reverence for unaffected natural beauty. Food was elegantly arranged rather than slopped onto the plate, and even the serving vessels, ceramic and lacquerware bowls, became aesthetic statements in their own right. This was the period in which the tea ceremony and kaiseki ryori (the elaborate meal that can go with the tea ceremony) was perfected, as well as the famous raku tea bowls. It is in this context that shoyu became the ideal condiment, something which heightens the flavor of food without disguising it, adding a subtle complexity when used judiciously. In recent years this flavor-enhancing principle, the fifth flavor or umami, has received a great deal of attention. Essentially the natural glutamates found in mushrooms, kombu seaweed and fermented soy have been shown to enhance and intensify the flavor of other foods.

The soy sauce companies of Higeta and Yamasa, still in business today, trace their origins to this period, being founded in 1616 and 1645 respectively in the

Choshi to the east of Edo (today Tokyo). It was also at this time that roasted wheat made its way into the recipe, providing a deeper flavor and color. In 1661 the earliest family that would later become the Kikkoman company began producing shoyu in Noda. At the same time it began to be carried by Dutch merchants to Europe, which is how John Locke came across it and made the first mention of soy sauce in English.

Although its origins are widely disputed, another significant soy product became popular in Japan at this time – natto. Today it is made of whole tiny soybeans, but in the past was often chopped, cracked or mixed into miso soup. For the uninitiated, it is without doubt one of the most perplexing foods to be found on this planet. Imagine tiny brown beans in a kind of caramel-colored mucus, exuding an earthy odor of ammonia and rotting compost. Then plunge in the chopsticks and lift a few beans to your mouth. From the beans stretches a web of sticky strings that if you are even slightly uncoordinated attach themselves to your face and clothes. The longer the strings, the more highly prized the natto. To test this, presumably you have to step back several paces from the table and hope the strings don't permanently adhere to the floor. The flavor is surprisingly mild though and not salty, which is probably why the beans are normally seasoned with soy sauce and mustard. They are a little more manageable served on a bed of rice, and for die-hard bean lovers they can be a very appealing novelty.

Unique among fermented beans, natto is made with the bacterium *Bacillus natto* rather than with mold. It is thus distinguished from hamanatto, fermented with regular koji mold. In natto enzymes actually pre-digest the whole soybeans, so they require no cooking. For a country with a scarcity of cooking fuel this is obviously a boon. The fermentation of natto also makes nutrients more available, for instance, there is more riboflavin than in cooked soybeans.

A few other notorious fermented bean products deserve recognition. In sixteenth-century China, or perhaps earlier, something vaguely like actual dairy-based cheese was invented. Popularly called sufu outside of China or appropriately enough "stinky tofu," it is essentially tofu that has been inoculated with mold spores and allowed to ferment. There are dozens of different types, pickled or brined and flavored. All are comparable in texture and aroma to a good ripe Camembert and are eaten in a comparable fashion, as a savory morsel on its own or as an appetizer. It can also be incorporated into recipes or served over rice porridge. It was allegedly Chairman Mao's favorite food. Interestingly, sufu might be considered the ancestor of the dairy free cheeses sold today for vegans and those allergic to milk products.

Tempeh is another form of fermented soy, but quite distinct from those discussed above. First, it originated in Indonesia, probably Java. The soybean was introduced about a thousand years ago and tempeh may be nearly as old, though written references date only to a few centuries ago. It is made by taking quickly boiled and hulled soybeans and inoculating them with *Rhizopus oligosporus* mold. This breaks down the beans, which are wrapped in banana leaves for about two days resulting in a solid cake, which is then sliced and used in mixed dishes, fried or steamed. Unlike tofu, tempeh is very dense, slightly lumpy and in flavor very meaty, and with about 20 percent protein, it compares nutritionally with meat. It is also one of the few vegetable sources of vitamin B12. Other kinds of tempeh are also made with other beans such as winged beans and jack beans, as well as grains. The popularity of tempeh is partly explained by its appealing texture and flavor, but it also makes sense as a source of protein for the most densely populated place on earth, where raising animals large scale for food is impractical. The fermentation, as with related products, also decreases the trypsin inhibitors as well as the oligosaccharides that cause flatulence. That is, if any bean product holds promise as the meat substitute of the future, it is like to be tempeh.

Tempe Goreng

Take slices of tempe and marinate them in a combination of salt water, crushed garlic and crushed coriander. Drain and then deep fry in coconut oil. These can be eaten as a snack or served over rice.

Soy in the West

The first Europeans to discuss the soybean and soy products were early visitors to Asia, usually arriving with the Portuguese, who by this time had built a string of maritime trading posts stretching from India to Indonesia, China and Japan. These commentators rarely recognized the connection between the bean and foods made from it. The Florentine merchant Francesco Carletti visited Nagasaki, Japan, in 1597 and wrote in his *Ragionamenti del mio viaggio intorno al mondo* (Memoirs of my trip around the world):

> They prepare various sorts of dishes from fish, which they flavor with a certain sauce of theirs which they call *misol*. It is made of a sort of bean that abounds in various localities, and which – cooked and mashed and mixed with a little of that rice from which they make the wine already mentioned, and then left to stand as packed into a tub – turns sour and all but decays, taking on a very sharp, piquant flavor. Using this a little at a time, they give flavor to their foods, and they call *shiro* what we would call a potage or gravy. They make this as I have said, of vegetables and fruit and fish all mixed together, and even some game, and then eat it with rice, which serves them as bread...

Similarly in 1665, the Dominican missionary Friar Domingo Fernández Navarrete in his *Tratados historicos* gives the first description of tofu. "I will here briefly mention the most usual, common and cheap sort of food all China abounds in, and which all Men in that Empire eat, from the Emperor to the meanest Chinese; the Emperor and great Men as a Dainty, the common sort as necessary sustenance. It is call'd Teu Fu, that is Paste of Kidney Beans." Of course, he was wrong about the bean, but he goes on to describe how it is made, though he apparently did not see it.

> They drew the Milk out of the Kidney-Beans, and turning it, make great Cakes of it like Cheeses, as big as a large Sive, and five or six fingers thick. All the Mass is as white as the very Snow, to look to nothing can be finer, It is eaten raw, but generally boil'd and dress'd with Herbs,

Fish, and other things. Alone it is insipid, but very good dress'd as I say and excellent fry'd in Butter. They have it also dry'd and smok'd, and mix'd with Caraway-seeds, which is best of all. It is incredible what vast quantities of it are consum'd in China, and very hard to conceive there should be such abundance of Kidney-Beans. That Chinese who has Teu Fu, Herbs and Rice, needs no other Sustenance to work.

Of the latter observation, he is absolutely correct and even comments that many Chinese people prefer it to chicken, but alas no European visitor would touch it.

Missionaries like Navarrete were not always welcome though and after their experience with the Portuguese, the Japanese decided to kick them out and close their ports to the West. Only the Dutch were allowed to trade on a small artificial island in the harbor at Nagasaki called Deshima as of 1641. This was a conscious policy of isolation, and no Westerners were allowed to set foot on Japanese soil. It was here in 1690 that the German botanist Engelbert Kaempfer showed up after a long series of travels to Persia, Indonesia (the Dutch colony of Batavia) and then finally Japan. Here he lived for the next couple of years as medical officer of the Dutch East India Company and was able to make friends with a young man named Imamura Gen'emon, who was appointed to him as a servant and companion. Ostensibly the Japanese wanted to learn something of Western medicines. Kaempfer learned the language and was allowed to travel to the capital of Edo to the Imperial palace and in his years there learned all he could of native customs and flora, including the use of soybeans. *Amoenitatum exoticarum* (On Exotic Pleasantries) published in 1712 is his account, and is the first explanation in the West of how soybeans were processed and used as food. He explains that *Phaseolus daidsu* (remember nearly all exotic beans were called phaseolus) is similar to other phaseolus, but the pods are a little hairy and contain only two or sometimes three beans, which are similar to peas. His description of their use in Japanese cuisine merits a full quotation. This is my translation from his Latin, with his punctuation and sentence structure left more or less intact for flavor:

The place of legume in Japanese cooking could fill the page; Indeed from it is made: a porridge called Miso, which is added to dishes for consistency in the place of butter, for butter is an unknown thing to these skies; then Sooju which the celebrated sauce is called, which is poured on, if not all dishes, then certainly fried and roasted ones. The way of making both I will describe:

For preparing Miso, they take one measure of Máme or Daidsu beans which are thoroughly cooked until soft in water for a long time, which they pound into a smooth paste. To the paste, while continually pounding, is mixed common Salt, four measures in summer, in winter three; for less salt added makes the process quicker, but less durable. Then in quantity equal to the beans is added, while repeatedly pounding, Koos, i.e. hulled rice which has been partially steamed with pure water and then cooled, in a warm storeroom, one or two days and nights, and left to rest until it contracts. This mixture (which is the consistency of porridge or a poultice) is placed into a wooden vessel which had once contained the beer popularly called Sacki, and before use, one or two months it remains undisturbed. Koos gives the paste a pleasant taste, and preparing it, like porridge of the Germans, requires the expert hand of a master; On account of which those who work in making it are in a unique position and sell it prepared.

To make Sooju they take the same beans cooked to the same softness; Muggi, i.e. grain, either barley or wheat (with wheat the product is darker) coarsely ground; and common Salt in equal parts, or a single measure of each. The beans are mixed with the crushed grain and in a hot place the mixture is left for a day and night so that it ferments. Then in a clay pot salt is added to the mass and stirred while pouring water, commonly two and a half measures: which being done, the mass is well covered and the next day and following days stirred at least once (better twice or thrice) with a shovel. This work continues two or three months, the mass is pressed and drained, and the liquid is kept in wooden vessels; the older it is, the clearer and better. Water is again added to the drained mass to moisten, it is stirred a few days and pressed.

Soybean plant specimens also had a brush with fame in the early eighteenth century. In the 1730s the young Carolus Linnaeus was employed at Hartekamp (near Haarlem in the Netherlands) by George Clifford to catalogue the contents of his herbarium. Clifford was director of the Dutch East India Company and received plant specimens from around the world, which were carefully dried and mounted on paper, including soy. In 1737 Linnaeus produced his *Hortus Cliffortianus*, in which he began to develop the binomial system of nomenclature which we still use to this day. It was here, for example, that he decided to give the banana the name *Musa paradisiaca*, under the assumption that it was the forbidden fruit in the Garden of Eden. Soy was also among the first plants newly named, after the most familiar soy product known in Europe, which was soy sauce. The name he eventually settled on was *Dolichos soja*, which stuck until the twentieth century.

Despite the interest of botanists, soy and soy products did not gain much appreciation in the West, which remained by in large addicted to the meat-based diet. But by the nineteenth century this would begin to change under the influence of the vegetarian movement, formally organized in Britain and the US about mid-century. Before then the common term was Pythagorean – and actually there are some very interesting nutritional studies of vegetarian diets in eighteenth-century France and Italy. But the idea of avoiding meat, stemming from ethical concerns, really only caught on in the mid-nineteenth century. One path of the vegetarian movement started with a woman in New York, Ellen G. White, who began to have religious visions in 1844 at the age of seventeen. These visions would continue throughout her life and eventually lead to the founding of the Seventh Day Adventist Church. Among the various tenets the church adopted, based on a vision White had in 1863, was the abstention from tobacco, alcohol and flesh and the idea that only natural remedies should be used to cure illness. Within a few years this led to the founding of a sanitarium in Battle Creek Michigan, and naturally an effort to find non-meat-based alternatives for the diet. The sanitarium and others like it flourished into the twentieth century, especially under the direction of John Harvey Kellogg (whom we all know as the inventor of various breakfast cereals marketed by his brother William Keith – the W.K. on the box.)

It was John Harvey who first became interested in soy and soy products, as early as 1917, as an ideal food for diabetics. (Even before that in 1893 his wife Ella Eaton's cookbook *Science in the Kitchen*, mentions vegetable casein – and that the Chinese manufacture cheese from peas and beans.) In his 1921 book *The New Dietetics*, after reading a few contemporary works about the role of soybeans in the Asian diet, he began to promote tofu, soy milk, soy sauce and sprouts as high protein meat alternatives. He also came out with various publications promoting soy right through the 1930s. Up to this point soybeans were largely used for animal fodder and as a way to fix nitrogen in the soil. But for most people in the early twentieth century, soybeans were considered animal food (one of Kellogg's articles was entitled "Soy as Human Food"), or more interestingly, food of Asians, whose culinary habits few people had any interest in imitating.

Regardless, experts increasingly argued that soy products are ideal for vegetarians, providing necessary proteins, fats and vitamins (whose role in nutrition scientists were just beginning to understand). In fact Kellogg kept up a correspondence with William Morse, the most important soy promoter of this era, who had direct knowledge of Asian diets. But for some reason most soy products were never widely accepted, even among the vegetarians (with the exception of soy sauce, which had been around since the seventeenth century).

The reason for this appears to be the obsession in American culture at this point with hygiene and food technology. Strangely, for a group so interested in natural and wholesome foods, this did not yet mean unprocessed or whole foods. Processing was seen as something efficient, hygienic and scientifically proven to be more nutritious. This is why when soy products were eventually mass marketed to the public, they were not sold as simple traditional tofu, miso and so forth (something we are more familiar with in recent decades) but rather it was products with modern sounding names like Kumyzoon – something no one seems to have understood, and this was changed to Lac Vegetal, and in the end a soy milk treated with *Lactobacillus acidophilus* (one of Kellogg's pet obsessions stemming from his ideas of colonic hygiene – something that is still a concern among health food advocates and even mainstream nutritionists).

Later down the road there were soy gluten wafers, soy flour, soy kee (a coffee substitute) and a canned soy "meat" called Protose. (It's also about this time that he got Henry Ford interested in soy; Ford began to make soy plastics to go in his cars, and he even wore a suit made entirely of soy fiber.) The industrial uses of soy and soybean oil are all direct descendents of these experiments – today soybean is the number two crop in the US – which is the largest producer in the world. A book of this early health food era which uses protose, nuttolene and savita (a meat-like extract) is *The Life Abundant Cook Book* by Helen Pack Bell and Ethel M. Campbell. The temptation to offer one of their dreadful recipes cannot be resisted, so here is a bean loaf; do use soy here.

Two cups beans, 1 cup brown rice, 1 tablespoon butter, 1 tablespoon whole wheat flour, 1 teaspoon salt, 1 tablespoon onion juice, 1 tablespoon parsley, dash paprika. Wash and boil the beans as usual, drain. Wash, boil and drain the rice as usual; put the hot beans and rice through the chopper. Rub the soft butter and flour until smooth; add to the hot beans and rice; add the onion juice, parsley, salt; mix well. Put the mixture in a baking pan, smooth top, bake in hot oven 30 minutes, or until brown. If this is too dry, add a little milk.

But back to Kellogg, the best part of the story is that Kellogg was most interested in marketing new technologically enhanced, highly nutritious products, something he couldn't really do if promoting traditional and still, in most people's minds, Asian foods like soy. Part of this stems, again, from the obsession with novelty and technology and the need to turn a profit. But it also seems to be unwillingness on the part of the public to adopt foods associated with Asian peoples. For example, among the very few Asian cookbooks published in the early twentieth century there is the *Chinese-Japanese Cookbook* by Sara Bosse and Onoto Watanna (pseudonyms apparently) published in 1914. It does include tofu in a few recipes, some that might appeal to the Western palate, such as a

Satsuma Soup which includes fried tofu (aburage) and miso paste (described as soybean and rice cheese) with chicken and vegetables. One wonders where one could have found such ingredients in 1914.

In any case, the comments in the preface suggest that the authors were battling an ingrained prejudice. They say

> there is no reason why these same dishes should not be cooked and served in any American home. When it is known how simple and clean are the ingredients used to make up these Oriental dishes, the Westerner will cease to feel that natural repugnance which assails one when about to taste a strange dish of a new and strange land.

It may not be coincidental that traditionally processed soy-based foods really only sold in the West after there was greater understanding of Chinese and Japanese cuisines, after negative attitudes toward Asian peoples themselves changed, and when the definition of natural came to mean minimal adulteration.

The United States in the mid-twentieth century witnessed two ideologically unrelated if not completely divergent promoters of soy. On the one hand, there was the counter-culture movement, to a great extent vegetarian, which sought unprocessed "natural" foods as a remedy to what they saw as the insidious control of the modern food industry with its highly processed, unhealthy foods and environmentally destructive practices. The apprehension over processed foods, preservatives and pesticides was first brought to widespread public attention in books like Rachel Carson's *Silent Spring*. Vegetarian diets provided part of the solution to contemporary fears about overpopulation and famine, and were popularized in books like Frances Moore Lappé's *Diet for a Small Planet* as well as other popular vegetarian cookbooks. Because of its high protein content and perceived health benefits, soy was one of the prime foods promoted by such works. Part of the mystique was also a fascination for Eastern philosophy and religion, and a desire to eat ancient soy foods such as tofu and tempeh.

At the very same time, American agribusiness promoted soy for industrial uses. Using modern technology, a high grade cooking oil could be pressed from soy and the residual cakes used as cattle fodder. This oil also became the low-cholesterol choice of fat in the form of margarine and shortening. Soy flour could be used as a high protein extender in baked products. The refined protein or TVP (textured vegetable protein) could be used as a meat substitute or filler as in "Hamburger Helper." Among the more important industrial uses was soy lecithin, a stabilizer used in ice cream and dozens of other foods, as well as in cosmetics, pharmaceuticals, paint, plastic, soap and so forth.

Despite their ideological differences, these two groups for all practical purposes worked in tandem to make soy not only one of the most profitable crops in the country, but also one that supplied much of the world with soy, as well as domestic manufacturers of industrially processed soy "health foods." That is, as Warren Belasco points out in his *Appetite for Change*, the health food movement sold out, losing its original back-to-the-earth, locally grown and cooperative origins as soy products went mainstream and small local producers were bought out by huge multinational companies. Though one might see this as the industry's move to capitalize on anything that makes money, the two opposed groups, in the end, served each other's purposes, as well as soy's. In any grocery store in the country, there is not only the traditional tofu but also soy burgers, tofutti ice cream, soy nuts, etc. etc. Belasco calls the soybean the "icon of the countercuisine." It would also become a major icon of the food industry.

Soy Today

In recent years there has been a great deal of concern about the negative health consequences of consuming trans fats found in hydrogenated vegetable oils, primarily soy. Since the USDA began requiring the labeling of products containing trans fats in 2006, the industry has been forced to act. That is, people could consciously choose not to buy products containing shortening. To counter this fear the food industries, most notably Cargill, have been developing soybeans which contain a lower level of lineolic acid, which causes rancidity, thus obviating the need for hydrogenation. Much of this research was conducted at Iowa State University. When Kellogg announced that it would use the new oil to make crackers, naturally the producers responded enthusiastically. Asoyia is one company that produces this oil and they claim that the oil can be used longer to fry (which may not be a good thing for the consumer, although fried foods are purported to stay crisp longer too) and most interestingly that this oil is not made from a genetically modified plant. It appears that as with most food products the industries are eventually forced to cater to popular demand, especially as the public becomes better informed about what they eat. Other companies are also producing the new oil, Monsanto with its trademarked Vistive line and Pioneer with Nutrium. Although thus far the new beans have not been genetically modified, it is likely that new varieties will be. After all, unless they can be patented, there is little hope of cornering the market.

These new oils are merely a tiny indication of the myriad ways soybeans are likely to change in the future, more rapidly than ever before in history. Despite the current backlash against genetically modified foods, particularly in Europe, food manufacturers in the US are not allowed to disclose the use or absence of genetically modified organisms. Only by buying foods labeled organic can one buy non-GM soy. Most GM soy, however, finds its way into the food supply through various routes, either fed to cattle which are then consumed by people, in the form of processed ingredients which are used in making other foods, or in foods which are said to promote health, like tofu and soy milk. Since they were first planted in 1996, the growth of GM crops has also increased dramatically, with the US accounting for more than half the acreage, a large proportion of which is soy grown principally in the Midwest. GM crops also account for about a quarter of all crops grown in the world. Following the US, Argentina grows about a third of the GM crops, mostly soy, followed by Canada, Brazil and China. In the US, as of 2004, 85 percent of all soybeans grown were genetically modified.

Thus far the main benefit of GM soy has been herbicide tolerance; the plants survive when sprayed with Roundup and other herbicides made by the very same companies that patent the new soy seed. Resistance to insects has been another direct benefit. It makes sense that farmers enthusiastically planted the new beans, hoping to save on chemical pesticides and increasing their yields in a market that demands enormous output and with a government that subsidizes such operations. Consumers have seen few tangible benefits though and concerns over possible unknown side effects (on the environment and health) of the so-called frankenfoods, let alone the moral issues of "tampering with nature" have far outweighed any other possible good, including improved nutrition. The fact that no long-term studies of the effects of GM crops have been carried out is equally unsettling. That is, most wonder why genetic modification is necessary when conventional breeding practices have proved so worthwhile in the past. Even the GM giants are now being forced to consider the same question; Monsanto's Vistive bean was developed through traditional breeding, though using computer technology to find the exact gene markers and get exactly the traits they were looking for. The company even hopes that a third line of Vistive oil will soon be marketed directly to consumers.

The latest buzz about genetically modified soy concerns the findings of a Russian scientist named Irina Ermakova, delivered at a conference in October 2005. In a feeding experiment with three separate groups of pregnant rats conducted before conception through the offspring's infancy, one group was fed a regular diet, another fed Monsanto's Roundup Ready soy, and the last regular soy. Ermakova found that the offspring of the first group had a mortality rate of 6.8 percent, the second 55.6 percent and the last 9 percent. That is, it wasn't a soy diet per se that killed the baby rats, but only the GM soy, and those that survived were scrawny and malnourished. Russian scientists concluded that GM foods can affect "the posterity of humans and animals." Whether human health should be implicated here is a matter for debate, but it is interesting that it is only far from US funding agencies that such research is even being attempted. What this means for pregnant women who eat GM soy, let alone babies who drink soy formula, one can only guess, but the US public has perhaps rightfully learned to distrust what industry experts say is safe. Some scientists now counter these findings, saying the article wasn't peer reviewed and the methodology faulty. Strangely many of them are at institutions in prime soy growing areas, where state funding and lobbying money are closely tied.

On the other hand, the vast majority of soybeans grown in the US are fed to livestock, nearly half to poultry and the rest to pigs and cows. Wouldn't someone have noticed if there was such a stark mortality rate among their offspring? In many cases soy farmers are exactly the same people feeding these animals; would they accept such a cut into their profits? The breeders in the highly integrated livestock industries would never accept a 50 percent reduction in productivity. Another possibility is that since the genetic make up of soybeans is fairly unstable, the Russian scientists may have gotten a batch of "bad" soy for use in their experiments. This fact alone should be enough to cause some concern, especially if this soy makes its way along the food chain into our bodies.

In fact soy, genetically modified or otherwise, has received exactly the opposite kind of attention in the last decade. Medical research has been stressing the need to cut down on saturated fat in a largely meat-based diet for some time, hence replacing meat with other sources of protein, but recently particular phyto-nutrients in soy have been found to lower the incidence of breast cancer, uterine and prostate cancer. These are the isoflavones: glycitein, genistein and the very appropriately named diadzein (from Chinese *daidzu*). These are phytoestrogens, substances that are very close to estrogen in the human body, and which have been used in therapy for hormone-related cancers and especially for menopausal women. They also seem to slow the rate of growth of cancer cells and many other health claims have been made.

Whether these developments are the result of the perennial American obsession with quick fixes and fad remedies is not yet clear. Nor is it surprising that medical research that catalyzes these trends is conducted in places that grow a lot of soy and are always looking for new uses, or that research funds directly or indirectly support soy-related projects. It was the same with wine and antioxidants, and oats for lowering cholesterol. This is not the place to contest medical research, but only to point out the ways this research is immediately and dramatically translated into new products on grocery shelves and new ways for consumers to ingest soy. Humans pay a lot more for food than cattle, and if manufacturers can frighten people into eating more soy, they will do it. Even if it means promoting a genetically modified, highly processed product in which the nutrients have been degraded, the amino acid lysine in particular. Can soy oil processed with extraordinarily complex chemical processes really be good for us? Are our bodies really equipped to process such things as textured vegetable protein, or the newest Soy7 developed by Archer Daniels Midland, which makes its way into pasta? Can the phytoestrogens in soy really be good for everyone? And what of all the anti-nutritional factors, the trypsin inhibitors and phytic acid which steals iron and zinc from the body, not to mention calcium, which is supposed to be one of the nutrients soy supplies?

As these words are being written numerous scientific studies are beginning to temper the wild enthusiasm for soy products that was launched about a decade ago, particularly regarding the ability of soy to lower cholesterol. This is how science works, and it's a good thing. The business of food, however, and in particular the burgeoning market for nutraceuticals, will ensure that new soy foods appear for a long time to come. Some of these products fail; take for example the recent attempt to put algae genes into soy to boost levels of omega-3 fatty acids, which are good for the heart. It turns out the oil tastes fishy and consumers would never buy it. There are probably dozens of other examples that never leave the laboratory. But some surely will and if current trends are any indication, like the animals we consume, in coming years we too will be made up of greater and greater proportions of soy.

Postscript – The Future of Beans

With the certain exception of the wonderchild soy, which shows no signs of losing industrial support, it is difficult to say exactly what will become of beans in the future. There is every indication of the trend mentioned at the start of this book – that as nations "develop" and become more Westernized (i.e. wealthy), they do tend to eat more meat and less beans. I entertain no notion that we will in our lifetimes see beans eradicated or banished from places where they have traditionally been indispensable, as in India and Mexico. But the statistics do suggest that people around the world eat beans less than they used to. As long as Western values predominate, beans will slowly continue to be marginalized, or they will be sold as elite heirloom varieties, a trend as we have seen, that is well underway. Maybe this is the only hope for beans, a good conceptual makeover and good marketing. But I do worry about the ugly ducklings, the plain brown or white beans that aren't stupendously huge or dazzlingly diminutive, and those that have no historical associations or ethnic allure – but that can always be invented.

The greater change, and one that is starkly apparent in any grocery store, is that dried beans may very well become a thing of the past – just as using bones to make stock has practically vanished. Who has the time? And who will have the time to cook dried beans if we continue at this phrenetic pace? The immediate future of beans lies in a can. This means that like most food products we eat, they will be controlled by fewer and larger companies, conglomerates that control everything from the ground the beans grow in to the processing, distribution networks, marketing and retail. Admittedly, unlike most vegetables, beans from a can are not really that awful either.

The other, almost inevitable, trend is that whereas soy has enjoyed most of the scientific research, other beans will attract attention, especially when industries realize that there are other species with high oil and protein content. Soy may very well lose the limelight when other species can be grown on a massive scale in tropical countries. Eventually these too will be genetically modified, but only when some other use for them is discovered – maybe as a new fuel source or synthetic building material. This is anyone's guess; they will certainly be used to feed animals as long as people want meat. In fact, the direction of most bean research today is to find a better fodder crop.

For humans, and for the table, the future of beans is simple enough. They will be objects of nostalgia for those with the leisure to evoke the good old "slow" days, or to recall the ethnic homeland. They will be revered in traditional dishes, even if without the ham hock, or marveled at for their strangeness and novelty. (I predict winged beans will show up any day now in supermarkets.) Beans will continue to be touted as the best source of vegetable protein, as the means of feeding the world without destroying the planet. If our current meat-eating regime somehow collapses or we witness sudden unprecedented population growth, I do hope we remember beans. And I hope in some small way, whatever happens, that I have contributed to their survival.

Bibliography

Modern Bean Cookbooks

Barrett, Judith. *Fagioli*. New York: Rodale, 2004.

The Bean Book. Guildford, CT: The Globe Pequot Press, 2001.

Beans, Beans, Beans: California's Finest Recipes. Dinuba, CA: California Dry Bean Advisory Board. n.d.

Bingham, Rita. *Country Beans*. Edmonton, OK: Natural Meals in Minutes, 1994.

Blomfield, Barb. *Fabulous Beans*. Summertown, TN: The Book Publishing Co., 1994.

Chesman, Andrea. *366 Delicious Ways to Cook Rice, Beans, and Grains*. New York: Plume, 1998.

Currie, Violet and Kay Spicer. *Full of Beans*. Campbellville, Ontario: Mighton House, 1993.

Dojny, Brooke. *Full of Beans*. New York: Harper, 1996.

Elliot, Rose. *The Bean Book*. London: Thorsons, 2000. 1st ed. 1979.

Fischer, Shayne K. *Bean Lover's Cookbook*. Phoenix, AZ: Golden West Publishers, 2005.

Geil, Patti Bazel. *Magic Beans*. New York: John Wiley, 1996.

Green, Eliza. *Beans*. Philadelphia: Running Press, 2004.

Gregory, Patricia. *Bean Banquets from Boston to Bombay*. Santa Barbara, CA: Woodbridge Press, 1992.

Guste, Roy F. *The Bean Book*. New York: W.W. Norton, 2001.

Hughes, Meredith Sayles. *Spill the Beans and Pass the Peanuts*. Minneapolis: Lerner, 1999.

Jenner, Alice. *The Amazing Legume*. The Saskatchewan Pulse Development Board, Regina, Saskatchewan: Centax Books, 1984.

Karn, Mavis. *Beans, Beans: The Musical Fruit*. St. Louis, MO: MRTC, 1990.

Kerr, W. Park. *Beans*. New York: William Morrow, 1996.

Keys, Margaret and Ancel Keys. *The Benevolent Bean*. Garden City, NY: Doubleday, 1967.

Leblang, Bonnie Tandy and Joanne Lamb Hayes. *Beans*. New York: Harmony Books, 1994.

Longnecker, Nancy. *Passion for Pulses*. Nedlands: University of Western Australia Press and Tuart House, 1992.

Midgeley, John. *The Goodness of Beans, Peas and Lentils*. New York: Random House, 1992.

Miller, Ashley. *The Bean Harvest Cookbook*. Newtown, CT: Taunton Press, 1998.

Olney, Richard, consultant. *Dried Beans & Grains*. Alexandria, VA: Time Life Books, 1982.

Pitzer, Sara. *Cooking With Dried Beans*. Pownal, VT: Storey Communications, 1982.

Ross, Trish. *Easy Beans*. Vancouver, British Columbia: Big Bean Publishing, 2003.

Saltzman, Joanne. *Romancing the Bean*. Tiburon, CA: H.J. Kramer, 1993.

Stapley, Patricia. *The Little Bean Cookbook*. New York: Crown, 1990.

Stone, Sally and Martin Stone. *The Brilliant Bean*. New York: Bantam, 1988.

Turvey, Valerie. *Bean Feast*. San Francisco, CA: 101 Productions, 1979.

Upson, Norma S. *The Bean Cookbook*. Seattle, WA: Pacific Search Press, 1982.

White, Joyce. *Soul Food*. New York: Harper Collins, 1998.

Scientific Reference Works

Ackroyd, W.R. and Joyce Doughty. *Legumes in Human Nutrition*. Rome: FAO, 1982.

Duke, James A. *Handbook of Legumes of World Economic Importance*. New York: Plenum Press, 1981.

Dupont, Jacquiline and Elizabeth Osman, eds. *Cereals and Legumes in the Food Supply*. Ames, IA: Iowa State University Press, 1987.

Gepts, P. "*Phaseolus vulgaris*" in Sydney Brenner and Jeffrey H. Miller eds *Encyclopedia of Genetics*, pp. 144–5. San Diego, CA: Academic Press, 2001.

Matthews, Ruth H. *Legumes: Chemistry, Technology and Human Nutrition*. New York: Marcel Dekker, 1989.

Salunkhe, D.K. and S.S. Kadam. *Handbook of World Food Legumes*. Boca Raton, FL: CRC Press, 1989.

Smartt, J. *Grain Legumes: Evolution and Genetic Resources*. Cambridge: Cambridge University Press, 1990.

Zohary, Daniel and Maria Hopf. *Domestication of Plants in the Old World*. Oxford: Clarendon Press, 1988.

Primary Sources

Abel, Mary Hinman. US Department of Agriculture Farmer's Bulletin No. 121. *Beans, Peas and other Legumes as Food.* Washington, DC: Government Printing Office, 1906.

Acosta, José de. *Natural and Moral History of the Indies.* Tr. Frances M. López-Morillas. Durham, NC: Duke University Press, 2002.

Alamanni, Luigi. *La coltivazione.* Milan: Istituto Editoriale Cisalpino-La Goliardica, 1981.

Alcott, William A. *Vegetable Diet.* New York: Fowlers and Wells, 1853.

Alcott, William A. *The Young House-Keeper, Or, Thoughts on Food and Cookery.* Boston: George W. Light, 1838.

Altamiras, Juan. *Nuevo Arte de Cocina.* Barcelona: Juan de Bezàres, 1758.

Anonimo Toscano. *Libro della cocina.* Online at staff-www.uni-marburg.de/~gloning/an-tosc.htm.

Anonimo Veneziano. *Libro di cucina del secolo XIV,* ed. Ludovico Frati. Bologna: Arnaldo Forni, 1986.

Anthimus. *De observatione ciborum,* tr. Mark Grant. Totnes, Devon: Prospect Books, 1996.

Apicius, tr. Christopher Grocock and Sally Grainger. Totnes, Devon: Prospect Books, 2006.

Appert, Nicholas. *The Art of Preserving.* New York: D. Longworth, 1812.

Artusi, Pellegrino. *La scienza in cucina e l'arte di mangier bene.* Facsimile, Florence: Giunti, 1991.

Athenaeus. *The Deipnosophists,* tr. Charles Burton Gulick. New York: G.P. Putnam's Sons, 1927.

Audot, Louis-Ustache. *French Domestic Cookery, Combining economy with Elegance and adapted to the Use of Families of Moderate Fortune.* London: Thomas Boys, 1825.

Battam, Anne. *The Lady's Assistant.* London: R. and J. Dodsley, 1759.

Batuta, Ibn. *The Travels of Ibn Batutah,* ed. Tim Mackintosh-Smith. London: Picador, 2002.

Beans: Grown in Michigan. Lansing, MI: Michigan Bean Commission, *c.* 1965.

Beecher, Catharine E. and Harriet Beecher Stowe. *The American Woman's Home.* New Brunswick, NJ: Rutgers University Press, 2004.

Beeton, Mrs. *Mrs. Beeton's Book of Household Management.* Oxford: Oxford University Press, 2000.

Bell, Helen Peck and Ethel M. Campbell. *The Life Abundant Cook Book.* Denver, CO: The World Press, 1930.

Benedictus de Nursia. *Opus ad sanitatis conservationem.* Rome: Lignamine, 1475.

Benzi, Ugo and Ludovico Bertaldi. *Regola della sanita et natura dei cibi*. Turin: Heirs of Gio. Domenico Tarino, 1618.

Berkeley Co-op Food Book: Eat Better and Spend Less. Palo Alto, CA: Bull Publishing Co., 1980.

Bockenheim, Jean de. In Bruno Laurioux. *Une Histoire culinare du Moyen Âge*. Paris: Honoré Champion, 2005.

Bonnefons, Nicholas de. *The French Gardener*, tr. John Evelyn. London: SS. For Benjamin Tooke, 1672.

Bosse, Sara and Onoto Watanna. *Chinese-Japanese Cookbook*. Chicago: Rand McNally, 1914.

Bridgman, Edward P. *Early Recollections and Army Expressions*. Typed Manuscript, 1894–5. James B. Pond Papers, Clements Library, University of Michigan.

Brillat-Savarin, Jean-Anthelme. *The Philosopher in the Kitchen*, tr. Anne Drayton. Harmondsworth: Penguin, 1970.

Bruyerin Champier, Jean. *De re cibaria*. Lyon: Sebast. Honoratum, 1560.

Buc'hoz, Pierre-Joseph. *Dictionnaire des plantes alimentaires*. Paris: Samson, 1803.

Calanius, Prosper. *Tracité pour l'entretenement de santé*, tr. Jean Goeurot. Lyon: Jean Temporal, 1533.

Cardano, Girolamo. *Opera omnia*. Lyon: Huguetan et Ravaud, 1663.

Cardenas, Juan de. *Problemas y secretos maravillosos de Las Indias*. Mexico City: Academica Nacional de Medicina, 1980.

Carletti, Francesco. *My Voyage Around the World*, tr. Herbert Weinstock. New York: Pantheon, 1964.

Carqué, Otto. *Natural Foods: The Safe Way to Health*. Los Angeles: Carqué Pure Food Co., 1926.

Carter, Susannah, *The Frugal Colonial Housewife*. Garden City, NY: Dolphin, 1976.

Castelvetro, Giacomo. *The Fruit, Herbs and Vegetables of Italy*, tr. Gillian Riley. London: Viking, 1989.

Cato. *On Farming*, tr. Andrew Dalby. Totnes, Devon: Prospect Books, 1998.

Champlain, Samuel. *Les Voyages de Sieur de Champlain*. See Quinn below.

Child, Lydia Maria. *The American Frugal Housewife*. Mineola, NY: Dover, 1999.

Chiquart's "On Cookery": A Fifteenth century Savoyard Culinary Treatise, tr. Terence Scully. New York: Peter Lang, 1986.

Chomel, Noel. *Dictionaire oeconomique*. Lyon: Pierre Thenel, 1709.

Clinton, Bill. *My Life*. New York: Knopf, 2005.

Cogan, Thomas. *The Haven of Health*. London: Thomas Orwin, 1589.

Collingwood, Francis. *The Universal Cook*. London: R. Noble, 1792.

Columbus, Christopher. *The Log of Christopher Columbus*. Camden, ME: International Marine Publishing Company, 1987.

Cook, Anne, Mrs. *Professed Cookery*. London: 1760.

The Cook Not Mad. Watertown, NY: Knowlton & Rice, 1830.

Corrado, Vincenzo. *Del cibo pittagorico*. Naples: Fratelli Raimondi, 1781. Facsimile, Bologna: Arnaldo Forni, 1991.

Corrado, Vincenzo. *Il cuoco galante*. Naples: Stamperia Raimondiana. Facsimile, Bologna: Arnaldo Forni, 1990.

Crescenzi, Pietro de'. *Opus ruralium commodorum*. Augsburg: Johann Schüssler, 1471.

Curye on Inglysch: English Culinary Manuscripts of the Fourteenth Century (Including the Forme of Cury), eds Constance B. Heiatt and Sharon Butler. Published for the Early English Text Society. London: Oxford University Press, 1985.

Dallas, E.S. *Kettner's Book of the Table*. Reprint, London: Centaur Press, 1968.

Dawson, Thomas. *The Good Housewife's Jewel*. Introduction by Maggie Black. Lewes, East Sussex: Southover Press, 1996.

De Lune, Pierre. *Le cuisinier*. In *L'art de la cuisine française au XVIIe siècle*. Paris: Payot et Rivages, 1995.

De Serres, Olivier. *Le théâtre d'agriculture et mesnage des champs*. Reprint, Arles: Actes Sud, 2001.

Dodoens, Rembert. *Frumentorum, leguminum, palustrium*... Antwerp: Plantin, 1566.

Douglas, William. *A Summary ... of British Settlements in North America*. Boston: Rogers and Fowle, 1749.

Dumas, Alexandre. *Grande dictionnaire de cuisine*. Paris: Alphonse Lemerre, 1873.

Durante, Castor. *Il tesoro della sanita*. 3rd ed., Venice: Domenico Imberti, 1643.

Estienne, Charles and Jean Liebault. *Maison Rustique or The Country Farme*, tr. Richard Surflet. London: Arnold Hatfield, 1606.

Evelyn, John. *Acetaria*. Reprint, Totnes, Devon: Prospect Books, 1996. 1st ed. 1699.

Felici, Costanzo. *Scritti naturalistici I. Del'insalata*. Urbino: Quattro Venti, 1986.

Fisher, Mrs. *The Prudent Housewife*. London: T. Sabine, 1750.

Francatelli, Charles Elmé. *A Plain Cookery Book for the Working Classes*. London: Bosworth and Harrison, 1861.

Frazer, Mrs. *The Practice of Cookery*. Dublin: R. Cross, 1791.

Frederick, Mrs. *Hints to Housewives*. London: MacMillan, 1880.

Fuchs, Leonhart. *De historia stirpium commentarii insignes*. Basel, 1542. CD-ROM ed. Karen Reeds. Berkeley: Octavo, 2003.

Galen. *On the Properties of Foodstuffs*, tr. Owen Powell. Cambridge: Cambridge University Press, 2003.

Garlin, Gustave. *La bonne cuisine*. Paris: Garnier Frères, 1898.

Gaudenzio, Francesco. *Il panunto Toscano*. Bologna: Arnaldo Forni, 1990.

Gazius, Antonius. *Corona florida medicinae*. Venice: Ioannes and Gregorius de Gregoriis, 1491.

Gerarde, John. *The Herball or General Historie of Plantes*. London: John Norton, 1597.

Gissing, George. *The Private Papers of Henry Ryecroft*. London: Archibald Constable & Co, 1903.

Glasse, Hannah. *The Art of Cookery*. Bedford, MA: Applewood Books, 1997.

Good Huswifes Handmaide for the Kitchen. Bristol: Stuart Press, 1992.

Gourmet's Book of Food and Drink. New York: Macmillan Co., 1935.

Granado, Diego. *Libro del arte de cocina*. Madrid: Sociedad de Bibliófilos Españoles, 1971. 1st ed. 1599.

Hale, Sarah Josepha. *Early American Cookery*. The Good Housekeeper, 1841. Mineola, NY: Dover, 1996. (Original title *The Good Housekeeper*.)

Hale, Thomas. *A Compleat Body of Husbandry*. London: T. Osborne, 1758–9.

Hammond, Elizabeth. *Modern Domestic Cookery and Useful Receipt Book adapted for Families in the Middling & Genteel Rank of Life*. London: Dean & Munday, 1820.

Harder, Jules Arthur Harder. *Harder's Book of Practical American Cookery*. San Francisco, n.p., 1885.

Hariot, Thomas. *A Brief and True Report of the New Founde Land of Virginia*. London, 1588. Reprint, New York: Dover, 1972.

Harrison, Sarah. *The House-Keeper's Pocket-Book*. London: R. Ware, 1755.

Haskins, C.W. *The Argonauts of California*. New York: Fords, Howard & Hulbert, 1890.

Henderson, William Augustus. *The Housekeeper's Instructor*. London: J. Stratford, 1790.

Hernández, Francisco. *The Mexican Treasury: The Writings of Dr. Francisco Hernández*, ed. Simon Varey. Palo Alto, CA: Stanford University Press, 2000.

Herrera, Gabriel Alonso. *Libro de agricultura*. Valladolid: San Francisco Fernandez de Cordova, 1563.

Hessus, Eobanus. *De tuenda bona valetudine*. Frankfort: Christian Egenolffs, 1571.

Hippocrates, tr. W.H.S. Jones. Cambridge, MA: Harvard University Press, 1967.

Homer. *The Iliad*, tr. Robert Fitzgerald. Garden City, NY: Anchor, 1975.

Homespun, Priscilla. *The Universal Receipt Book*. Philadelphia: Isaac Riley, 1818.

Hughson, D. *The New Family Receipt Book*. London: W. Pritchard, 1817.

Hunter, Alexander. *Culina Famulatrix Medicinae or Receipts in Modern Cookery*. York: Wilson and Son, 1810.

Jefferson, Thomas. *Thomas Jefferson's Garden Book*, ed. Edwin Morris Betts. Chapel Hill, NC: University of North Carolina Press, 2001.

Jones, Evan, ed. *A Food Lover's Companion*. New York: Harper and Row, 1979.

Joubert, Laurent. *Erreurs populaires*. Bordeaux: S. Milanges, 1587.

Kaempfer, Engelbert. *Amoenitatum exoticarum*. Lemgo: Heinrich Wilhelm Meyer, 1712.

Kellogg, Mrs. E.E. *Science in the Kitchen*. Chicago: Modern Medicine Publishing Co., 1893.

Kettilby, Mary. *A Collection of Above Three Hundred Receipts*. London: Printed for Mary Kettilby, 1728.

Kitab Wasf al-At'ima al-Mu'tada (the Book of the Description of Familiar Food), tr. Charles Perry. In *Medieval Arab Cookery*. Totnes, Devon: Prospect Books, 2001.

Kitchen Directory and American Housewife. New York: Mark H. Newman, 1846.

Kitchiner, William. *Apicius Redivivus or the Cook's Oracle*. London: S. Bagster, 1817.

L'Art de la cuisine française au XVIIe siècle. Paris: Payot et Rivages, 1995. (L.S.R., *L'art de bien traiter* 1674, Pierre de Lune, *Le cuisinier* 1656, Audiger, *La maison réglée* 1692).

La Chapelle, Vincent. *The Modern Cook*. London: Thomas Osborne, 1736.

La Varenne, François Pierre. *Le cuisinier François*. Paris: Montalba, 1983.

Lancelot de Casteau. *Overture de cuisine*. Anvers/Bruxelles: De Schutter, 1983.

Lappé, Frances Moore. *Diet for a Small Planet*. Tenth Anniversary ed. New York: Ballantine, 1982.

Lemery, Louis. *A Treatise of All Sorts of Foods*. London: T. Osborne, 1745.

Leslie, Eliza. *Directions for Cookery*. Philadelphia: E.L. Carey, 1840.

Libellus de arte coquinaria, eds Rudolph Grewe and Constance B. Heiatt. Tempe, AZ: Arizona Center for Medieval and Renaissance Studies, 2001.

Liber de coquina. Online at staff-www.uni-marburg.de/~gloning/mul2-lib.htm.

Libre de sent sovi, ed. Rudolph Grewe. Barcelona: Editorial Barcino, 1979.

Liger, Louis. *Le Menage des champs et de la ville*. A. Luxembourg: n.p., 1747.

Livre fort excellent de cuisine. Lyon: Olivier Arnoulet, 1555.

L'Obel, Matthias de. *Icones stirpium seu plantarum exoticarum*. Antwerp: Officina Plantiniana, 1591.

Lobera de Avila, Luis. *El vanquete de nobles cavalleros*, ed. José M. López Piñero. Madrid: Ministerio de Sanidad y Consumo, 1991.

Loesser, Frank. *The Complete Lyrics of Frank Loesser*, ed. Robert Kimball. Westminster, MD: David McKay, 2003.

Lucian, tr. A.M. Harmon. New York: Macmillan, 1913.

Maceras, Domingo Hernàndez de. *Libro del arte de Cozina*. Salamanca: Ediciones Universidad de Salamanca, 1999.

Marin, François. *Les dons de comus*. Paris: Chez la veuve Pissot, 1750.

Markham, Gervase. *A Way to Get Wealth.* London: E.H. for George Sawbridge, 1676.

Martino, Maestro [of Como]. *Libro de arte coquinaria*, eds Luigi Ballerini and Jeremy Parzen. Milan: Guido Tommasi, 2001. Tr. Jeremy Parzen as *The Art of Cooking.* Berkeley, CA: University of California Press, 2005.

Mason, Charlotte, Mrs. *The Lady's Assistant.* London: J. Walter, 1755.

Massialot, François. *Le nouveau cuisinier royal et bourgeois.* Paris: Claude Prudhomme, 1716.

Massonio, Salvatore. *Archidipno overo dell'insalata.* Venice: Marc'antonio Brogiollo, 1627.

Matthioli, M. Pietro. *I discorsi.* Venice: Felice Valgrisio, 1597.

May, Robert. *The Accomplisht Cook.* London: Obadiah Blagrave, 1685. 1st ed. 1660. Reprint: Totnes, Devon: Prospect Books, 2000.

McElfresh, Beth. *Chuckwagon Cookbook.* Denver: Sage Books, 1960.

Ménagier de Paris. The Goodman of Paris, tr. Eileen Power. London: The Folio Society, 1992.

Messisbugo, Christoforo di. *Banchetti.* Ferrara: Giovanni de Buglhat and Antonio Hucher, 1549.

Miller, Philip. *The Gardener's Dictionary.* London: John and James Rivington, 1747.

Milton, John. *The Poetical Works.* New York: Edward Kearney, 1843.

Moffett, Thomas. *Health's Improvement.* London: Thomas Newcomb, 1655.

Montagné, Prosper and Prosper Salles. *Le grand livre de cuisine.* Paris: Flammarion, 1929.

Montiño, Francisco Martínez. *Arte de cocina.* Barcelona: Maria Angela Marti, 1763. Online at http://www.bib.ub.es/grewe/showbook.pl?gw57. 1st ed. 1611.

Moxon, Elizabeth. *English Housewifry.* Leeds: George Copperthwaite, 1758.

Muhammad, Elijah. *How to Eat to Live.* Online at http://www.muhammadspeaks.com/HTETL8-13-1971.html.

Navarrete, Domingo. *The Travels and Controversies of Friar Domingo Navarrete*, ed. J.S. Cummins. Cambridge: The Hakluyt Society, 1962.

Nonnius, Ludovicus. *Diaeteticon.* Antwerp: Petri Belleri, 1645.

Noonan, Bode. *Red Beans and Rice: Recipes for Lesbian Health & Wisdom.* Trumansburg, NY: The Crossing Press, 1986.

Nuñez de Oria, Francisco. *Regimento y aviso de sanidad.* Medina del Campo: Francisco del Canto, 1586. 1st ed. *Vergel de sanidad* 1569.

Parmentier, Antoine August. *Recherches sur les végétaux nourissans.* Paris: Imprimerie Royale, 1781.

Pasquin, Anthony. *Shrove Tuesday, a satiric rhapsody.* London: J. Ridgway, 1791.

Petronio, Alessandro. *De victu romanorum*. Rome: In Aedibus Populi Romani, 1581.

Pisanelli, Baldassare. *Trattato della natura de' cibi et del bere*. Venice: Domenico Imberti, 1611. Facsimile, Bologna: Arnaldo Forni, 1980.

Plato. *Plato's Republic*, tr. G.M.A. Grube. Indianapolis, IN: Hackett, 1974.

Platina (Bartolomeo Sacchi). *On Right Pleasure and Good Health*, ed. Mary Ella Milham, Tempe, AZ: Medieval and Renaissance Texts and Studies, 1998.

Plumptre, Bell. *Domestic Management*. London: B. Crosby, 1810.

Proper Newe Booke of Cokerye, A, ed. Anne Ahmed. Cambridge: Corpus Christi College, 2002.

Proper Newe Booke of Cokerye, A. ed. Jane Hugget. Bristol, Stuart Press, 1995.

Quinn, David B., ed. *New American World: A Documentary History of North America to 1612*. 5 vols. New York: Arno, 1979.

Rabisha, William. *The Whole Body of Cookery Dissected*. Facsimile of 1682 ed. Totnes, Devon: Prospect Books, 2003.

Raffald, Elizabeth. *The Experienced English Housekeeper*. London: A. Millar, 1787.

Romoli, Domenico. *La singolare dottrina*. Venice: Gio. Battista Bonfadino, 1593. 1st ed. 1560.

Rousseau, Jean-Jacques. *Emile*, tr. Allan Bloom. New York: Basic Books, 1979.

Rupert of Nola. *Liber de doctrina per a ben server*. Online at www.cervantesvirtual.com.

Rutter, John. *Modern Eden*. London: J. Cooke, 1767.

Sahagún, Bernardino de. *Historia general de las cosas de Nueva España*. México: Porrúa, 1956.

Sampson, Emma Speed. *Miss Minerva's Cook Book: De Way To A Man's Heart*. Chicago: Reilly & Lee Co., 1931.

Scappi, Bartolomeo. *Opera*. Venice, 1570. Facsimile, Bologna: Arnaldo Forni, 2002.

Sebizius, Melchior. *De alimentorum facultatibus*. Strasbourg: Joannis Philippi Mülbii and Josiae Stedelii, 1650.

The Sensible Cook, tr. Peter Rose. Syracuse, NY: Syracuse University Press, 1989.

Sharpe. M.R.L. *The Golden Rule Cookbook*. Boston: Little Brown, 1919.

Sherson, Erroll. *The Book of Vegetable Cookery*. London & New York: Frederick Warne, 1931.

Shore, W. Teignmouth. *Dinner Building*. London: B.T. Batsford, 1929.

Simmons, Amelia. *American Cookery*. New York: William Beastall, 1822.

Simmons, Amelia. *American Cookery*. Bedford, MA: Applewood Books, 1996. Facsimile of 1796 ed.

Smith, E. *The Compleat Housewife*. London: Studio Editions, 1994. 1st ed. 1758.

Soyer, Alexis. *The Pantropheon*. Reprint, London: Paddington Press, 1977.

Soyer, Alexis. *Soyer's Shilling Cookery for the People*. London: Routledge, 1860.

Spencer, Edward. *Cakes and Ale*. London: Grant Richards, 1897.

Strachey, William. *Historie of Travaile into Virginia Britannia*. See Quinn above.

Thoreau, Henry David. *Walden*. New York: Signet Classic, 1980.

Tractatus de modo preparandi et condiendi omnia cibaria. Online at www.staff.uni-marburg.de/~gloning/mull-tra.htm.

Treasured Armenian Recipes. Detroit Women's Chapter of the Armenian General Benevolent Union, 1949.

Trollope, Mrs. *Domestic Manners of the Americans*. London: Whitaker, Treacher & Co., 1832.

Two Fifteenth Century Cookbooks, ed. Thomas Austin. Early English Text Society. Reprint, Rochester, NY: Boydell and Brewer, 2000.

Tyree, Marion Fontaine Cabell. *Housekeeping in Old Virginia*. Richmond: J.W. Randolph & English, 1878.

The Viandier of Taillevent, ed. Terence Scully. Ottowa, Canada: University of Ottowa Press, 1988.

Venner, Tobias. *Via recta ad vitam longam*. London: Edward Griffen, 1620.

Virgil. *The Georgics*, tr. L.P. Wilkinson. Harmondsworth: Penguin, 1982.

Webster, A.L. *The Improved Housewife, or Book of Receipts; With Engravings for Marketing and Carving*. Creative Cookbooks, 2001.

White, John. *Art's Treasury of Rarities*. London: G. Conyers, 169?.

White, Suzanne Caciola. *The Daily Bean*. Washington, DC: Lifeline Press, 2004.

Williams, Lindsay. *Neo Soul*. New York: Avery/Penguin Group, 2006.

Wilson, J.M. *The Rural Encyclopedia*. Edinburgh, 1852.

Worlidge, John. *A Compleat System of Husbandry and Gardening*. London: J. Pickard, 1716.

Wyatt, Sir Thomas. *Collected Poems*, ed. Joost Daalder. London: Oxford University Press, 1975.

Secondary Sources

Achaya, K.T. *A Historical Dictionary of Indian Food*. New Delhi: Oxford University Press, 1998.

Achaya, K.T. *The Story of Our Food*. Hyderguda, India: Universities Press, 2000.

Anderson, E.N. *The Food of China*. New Haven: Yale University Press, 1988.

Andrews, A.C. "The Bean and European Totemism." *American Anthropologist*, 51 (1949): 274–92.

Arber, Agnes. *Herbals*. Cambridge: Cambridge University Press, 1986.

Benoussan, Maurice. *Les particules alimentaires*. Paris: Maisonneuve & Larose, 2002.

Belasco, Warren. *Appetite for Change*. New York: Pantheon, 1989.

Berzok, Linda Murray. *American Indian Food*. Westport, CT: Greenwood, 2005.

Birri, Flavio and Carla Coco. *Cade a fagiolo*. Venice: Marsilio, 2000.

Branham, R. Bracht. *The Cynics*. Berkeley, CA: University of California Press, 1997.

Brennan, Jennifer. *Curries and Bugles*. London: Penguin, 1992.

Brumbaugh, Robert S. and Jessica Schwartz. "Pythagoras and Beans: A Medical Explanation." *Classical World*, 73(7) (1980): 421–2.

Burnett, John. *Plenty and Want: A Social History of Diet in England from 1815 to the Present Day*. London: Scolar Press, 1979.

Carney, Judith. *Black Rice: The African Origin of Rice Cultivation in the Americas*. Cambridge, MA: Harvard University Press, 2001.

Chang, K.C., ed. *Food in Chinese Culture*. New Haven: Yale University Press, 1977.

Coe, Sophie D. *America's First Cuisines*. Austin, TX: University of Texas Press, 1994.

Colbert, David, ed. *Eyewitness to America*. Westminster, MD: Vintage Books, 1998.

Conlin, Joseph R. *Bacon, Beans, and Galantines*. Reno, NV: University of Nevada Press, 1986.

Dalby, Andrew. *Food in the Ancient World From A–Z*. London: Routledge, 2003.

Darby, William J., Paul Ghalioungui and Louis Grivetti. *Food: The Gift of Osiris*. London: Academic Press, 1977.

Dary, David. *Oregon Trail*. New York: Knopf, 2004.

Eco, Umberto. "Best Invention; How the Bean Saved Civilization." *New York Times*, p. 136. April 18, 1999.

Enneking, D. "A bibliographic database for the genus *Lathyrus*." Cooperative Research Centre for Legumes in Mediterranean Agriculture Occasional publication No. 18: 1998.

Fery, F.L. "New opportunities in *Vigna*." In J. Janick and A. Whipkey eds *Trends in New Crops and Uses*. Alexandria, VA: ASHS Press, 2002.

Flandrin, Jean-Louis and Massimo Montanari, eds. *Food: A Culinary History*. New York: Columbia University Press, 1999.

Foster, Nelson and Linda S. Cordell, eds. *Chilies to Chocolate*. Tucson, AZ: The University of Arizona Press, 1996.

Garnsey, Peter. *Cities, Peasants and Food in Classical Antiquity*. Cambridge: Cambridge University Press, 1998.

Garnsey, Peter. *Food and Society in Classical Antiquity*. Cambridge: Cambridge University Press, 1999.

Gitlitz, David M. and Linda Kay Davidson. *A Drizzle of Honey*. New York: St. Martin's Press, 1999.

Gouste, Jérôme. *Le haricot*. Arles: Actes Sud, 1998.

Gunderson, Mary. *The Food Journal of Lewis and Clark*. Yankton, SD: History Cooks, 2002.

Harris, Marvin. *Cannibals and Kings*. New York: Vintage Books, 1978.

Heiser, Charles B. *Seed to Civilization*. Cambridge, MA: Harvard University Press, 1990.

Helstosky, Carol. *Garlic and Oil*. Oxford: Berg, 2004.

Kelly, Ian. *Cooking for Kings: The Life of Antonin Carême*. New York: Walker, 2004.

Krokar, James P. "European Explorer's Images of North American Cultivation." The Newberry Library, 1990. Online at www.newberry.org.

Lev-Yadun, Simcha, Avi Gopher and Shahal Abbo. "The Cradle of Agriculture." *Science*, June 2, 2000, pp. 1,602–3.

Levenstein, Harvey. *Paradox of Plenty*. Berkeley, CA: University of California Press, 2003.

Levenstein, Harvey. *Revolution at the Table*. Berkeley, CA: University of California Press, 2003.

Levine, David. *At the Dawn of Modernity: Biology, Culture and Material Life in Europe After the Year 1000*. Berkeley, CA: University of California Press, 2001.

MacDonald, Janet. *Feeding Nelson's Navy*. London: Chatham, 2004.

McWilliams, James E. *A Revolution in Eating*. New York: Columbia University Press, 2005.

Magnavita, Carlos, Stephanie Kahlberger and Barbara Eichhorn. "The Rise of Organisational Complexity in Mid-first Millennium BC Chad Basin." *Antiquity*, 78 (301) (September 2004).

Maynard, W. Barksdale. *Walden Pond: A History*. Oxford: Oxford University Press, 2004.

Montanari, Massimo. *Alimentazione e cultura nel Medioevo*. Rome: Laterza, 1992.

Montanari, Massimo. *The Culture of Food*. Oxford: Blackwell, 1994.

Nabham, Gary Paul. *Gathering the Desert*. Tucson, AZ: University of Arizona Press, 1985.

Obeysekere, Gannath. *Imagining Karma*. Berkeley, CA: University of California Press, 2002.

Oddy, Derek J. *From Plain Fare to Fusion Food: British Diet from the 1890s to the 1990s*. Woodbridge, Suffolk: Boydell Press, 2003.

Pérez-Maillaína, Pablo E. *Spain's Men of the Sea*. Baltimore: Johns Hopkins University Press, 1998.

Pillsbury, Richard. *No Foreign Food*. Boulder, CO: Westview Press, 1998.

Popenoe, Hugh, *et al. Lost Crops of the Incas*. Washington, DC: National Academy Press, 1989. Online at www.nap.edu.

Proceedings of the Symposium on "Origins of Agriculture and domestication of Crop Plants in the Near East" ICARDA, 1977. Online at www.ipgri.cgiar.org.

Richards, John F. *Unending Frontier: An Environmental History of the Early Modern World*. Berkeley, CA: University of California Press, 2003.

Rotzetter, Anton. "Mysticism and Literal Observance of the Gospel in Francis Assisi." In Christian Duquoc and Casiano Floristan (eds) *Francis of Assisi Today*. New York: Seabury Press, 1981.

Salt, Henry Stephens. *Life of Henry David Thoreau*. London: W. Scott, Ltd., 1896.

Scarborough, John. "Beans, Pythagoras, Taboos, and Ancient Dietetics." *Classical World*, *75*(6) (1982): 355–8.

Shurtleff, William and Akiko Aoyagi. "History of Soybeans and Soyfoods: 1100 B.C. to the 1980's." Unpublished manuscript. Online at www.thesoydailyclub.com.

Sudhalter, Richard M. *Stardust Melody: The Life and Music of Hoagy Carmichael*. Oxford: Oxford University Press, 2003.

Tate, M.E. "Vetches: Feed or Food?" *Chemistry in Australia*, *63* (1996): 549–50.

Thompson, Paul B. and Thomas C. Hilde, eds. *The Agrarian Roots of Pragmatism*. Nashville, TN: Vanderbilt University Press, 2000.

United States Department of Agriculture, Economic Research Service. *Dry Beans*. Online at www.ers.usda.gov/Briefing/DryBeans/

"U.S. Capitol Bean Soup" at www.soupsong.com/rsenate.html.

Witt, Doris. *Black Hunger: Soul Food and America*. Minneapolis, MS: University of Minnesota Press, 2004.

Wright, Clifford. *A Mediterranean Feast*. New York: William Morrow, 1999.

Index